国家出版基金项目
NATIONAL PUBLICATION FOUNDATION

THE CHINESE PATH

DEVELOPMENT PATH OF INFORMATIZATION WITH CHINESE CHARACTERISTICS

ZHU YAN

Translated by
LI WEIBIN

Proofread by
ZHANG JIE

中国财经出版传媒集团

经济科学出版社
Economic Science Press

·北 京·

图书在版编目（CIP）数据

中国特色信息化发展道路 = Development Path of Informationization with Chinese Characteristics：
英文 / 朱燕著；李伟彬译. -- 北京：经济科学出版社，2025.5

（《中国道路》丛书）

ISBN 978-7-5218-5892-1

Ⅰ.①中… Ⅱ.①朱…②李… Ⅲ.①中国经济-研究-中国-英文 Ⅳ.①G203

中国版本图书馆 CIP 数据核字（2024）第 098989 号

责任编辑：孙怡虹　魏　岚
责任校对：徐　昕
责任印制：张佳裕

中国特色信息化发展道路
ZHONGGUO TESE XINXIHUA FAZHAN DAOLU
Development Path of Informatization with Chinese Characteristics
朱　燕　著
李伟彬　译
经济科学出版社出版、发行　新华书店经销
社址：北京市海淀区阜成路甲 28 号　邮编：100142
总编部电话：010-88191217　发行部电话：010-88191522
网址：www.esp.com.cn
电子邮箱：esp@esp.com.cn
天猫网店：经济科学出版社旗舰店
网址：http://jjkxcbs.tmall.com
固安华明印业有限公司印装
787×1092　16 开　18.5 印张　512000 字
2025 年 5 月第 1 版　2025 年 5 月第 1 次印刷
ISBN 978-7-5218-5892-1　定价：85.00 元
（图书出现印装问题，本社负责调换。电话：010-88191510）
（版权所有　侵权必究　打击盗版　举报热线：010-88191661
QQ：2242791300　营销中心电话：010-88191537
电子邮箱：dbts@esp.com.cn）

Preface

The Chinese path refers to the path of socialism with distinctive Chinese characteristics. As Chinese President Xi Jinping points out, it is not an easy path. We are able to embark on this path thanks to the great endeavors of the reform and opening up over the past 30 years and more, and the continuous quest made in the 60-plus years since the founding of the People's Republic of China (PRC). It is based on a thorough review of the evolution of the Chinese nation over more than 170 years since modern times and carrying forward the 5,000-year-long Chinese civilization. This path is deeply rooted in history and broadly based on China's present realities.

A right path leads to a bright future. The Chinese path is not only access to China's development and prosperity, but also a path of hope and promise to the rejuvenation of the Chinese nation. Only by forging the confidence in the path, theory, institution and culture can we advance along this path of socialism with Chinese characteristics. With this focus, *The Chinese Path Series* presents to readers an overview in practice, achievements and experiences as well as the past, present and future of the Chinese path.

The Chinese Path Series is divided into ten volumes with one hundred books on different topics. The main topics of the volumes are as follows: economic development, political advancement, cultural progress, social development, ecological conservation, national defense and armed forces building, diplomacy and international policies, the Party's leadership and building, localization of Marxism in China and views from other countries on the Chinese path. Each volume on a particular topic consists of several books which respectively throw light on exploration in practice, reform process, achievements, experiences and theoretical innovations of the Chinese path. Focusing on the practice in the reform and opening up with the continuous exploration since the founding of the PRC, these books summarize on the development and inheritance of China's glorious civilization, which not only display a strong sense of the times, but also have profound historical appeal and future-oriented impact.

The series is conceived in its entirety and assigned to different authors. In terms of the writing, special attention has been paid to the combination of history and reality, as well as theory and practice at home and abroad. It gives a realistic and innovative interpretation of the practice, experience, process and theory of the Chinese path. Efforts are made on the distinctive and convincing expression in a global context. It helps to cast light on the "Chinese wisdom" and the "Chinese approach" that the Chinese path has contributed to the modernization of developing countries and solutions to human problems.

On the basis of the great achievements in China's development since the founding of the PRC, particularly since the reform and opening up, the Chinese nation, which had endured so much and for so long since the modern times, has achieved tremendous growth—it has stood up, become prosperous and grown in strength. The socialism with distinctive Chinese characteristics has shown great vitality and entered a new stage. This path has been expanded and is now at a new historical starting point. At this vital stage of development, the Economic Science Press of China Finance & Economy Media Group has designed and organized the compilation of *The Chinese Path Series*, which is of great significance in theory and practice.

The program of *The Chinese Path Series* was launched in 2015, and the first publications came out in 2017. The series was listed in a couple of national key publication programs, the "90 kinds of selected publications in celebration of the 19th CPC National Congress", and National Publication Foundation.

Editorial Board of *The Chinese Path Series*

Contents

Chapter 1
Introduction: Basic Theory of
Informatization

1.1　Fundamental concepts of informatization

From the perspective of the evolution of human civilization, human society has roughly experienced three social development stages of agriculturalization, industrialization, and informatization. Informatization is the current trend of economic and social development in the world, the latest stage of the development of human civilization, and the inevitable choice for China to build a moderately prosperous society in all respects and realize socialist modernization. This section mainly elaborates and summarizes the related concepts of informatization.

1.1.1　Informatization

1.1.1.1　Classic definition of informatization

Japan was the first country to adopt the concept of informatization. In 1963, Japanese sociologist Tadao Umesao first mentioned "informatization" in his book *Information Industry Theory*, while in 1964, Japanese scholar Jiro Kamishima first used the concept of "information society" in his book *On the Sociology of Information Society*. In 1967, the Japanese Research Group on Science, Technology and Economics elaborated on informatization, which is a dynamic development process of evolution from industrial society to information society. After Japanese scholars proposed the concepts of informatization and information society, these concepts were widely used and appeared in the documents of the United Nations in 1998. *Knowledge Societies*, published by the United Nations, defined and discussed informatization that, "Informatization is both a technological and social process. It requires changes in management processes, organizational structures, production skills, and production tools in the production of products or services."[1]

In 1997, at the first National Informatization Work Conference held in China, informatization was defined as "the historical process of cultivating and developing new productive forces represented by intelligent tools and making them benefit the society".[2] In October 2002, the National Informatization Leading Group of China approved the promulgation of the Key Special Plan of Informatization in the 10th Five-Year Plan of National Economic and Social Development, which defined the connotation of information technology as that, "Informatization is a comprehensive system with the wide application of information technology as the leading, information resources as the core, information network as the foundation, information industry as the support, information talent as the basis, and regulations, policies and standards as the guarantee."[3] In May 2006, General Office of the Central Committee of the Communist Party of China (CPC) and General Office of the State Council issued the 2006-2020 National Information Development Strategy, which pointed out that "Informatization is the historical process of making full use of information technology and developing and utilizing information resources to encourage information exchange and knowledge sharing, improve the quality of economic growth, and promote the transformation of economic and social development."[4]

Chinese scholar Zhou Hongren argues in his book *On Informatization* that "Informatization is a process of socio-economic change caused by the information revolution." He defines informatization as "a process of using modern information technology to fully transform the production of information and knowledge in human society and thus lead to a complete change in the organizational and economic structure of the production system of human society, and a process of promoting the social transformation of human society from an industrial society to an information society".[5]

---

[1] Robin Mansell, Uta Wehn, et al., *Knowledge Societies: Information Technology for Sustainable Development*, Oxford: Oxford University Press, 1998.

[2] Zhou Xiaohu, Chen Fen, *Information Management Case: Chinese Enterprise Study*, Beijing: Economy& Management Publishing House, 2014, p. 4.

[3] National Informatization Leading Group, "Key Special Plan of Informatization in the 10th Five-Year Plan of National Economic and Social Development", *China Information Almanac* 2002, http://www.cia.org.cn/information/information-01-xxhgh-3.htm.

[4] General Office of the CPC Central Committee and General Office of the State Council, "2006-2020 National Information Development Strategy", Chinese Central Government Official Website, Mar. 19, 2006, http://www.gov.cn/gongbao/content/2006/content_315999.htm.

[5] Zhou Hongren, *On Informatization*, Beijing: People's Publishing House, 2008, p. 97.

According to the above typical definitions, informatization is a historical process of economic and social transformation in all aspects, and such transformation is driven by the innovation of information technology. Information technology is the driving force and source of informatization. Without the innovation and development of information technology, informatization will be unsustainable and the economic and social transformation will be interrupted. Informatization is the process of applying information technology to the economy first, and then expanding its application to political, social, cultural, military and other fields to finally achieve the overall transformation and development of society. As long as the innovation of information technology is sustainable, informatization is an everlasting dynamic development process.

Therefore, we can decompose informatization into three consecutive processes of innovation of information technology, application of information technology, transformation of economy and society. The information technology (hereinafter referred to as IT) innovation is the source and starting point of informatization, the wide application of IT is its process, and the comprehensive change and transformation of economic society, i.e., the transition from industrial society to information society, is its ultimate purpose. The information technology that promotes the IT application should be widely used and highly permeable information technology, and the technology that cannot be transformed into scientific and technological achievements cannot contribute to the improvement of productivity and the transformation of economy and society. A well-developed information resource sharing network and information dissemination media can promote information exchange and resource sharing, so that information technology can be transformed into real productivity, improve the level of productivity development, and enhance the quality of economic growth. The IT application can not only improve productivity, but also change the way enterprises produce and organize, the way products are exchanged, and the way they are consumed, which eventually leads to changes in the production relations of the whole society. The process of informatization achieves economic and social transformation, why is informatization also known as the information revolution. Informatization has facilitated the transition from industrial society to information one, and the information society has become the latest stage of human civilization after the information revolution.

1.1.1.2 Elements and classification of informatization

A sustainable informatization process must consist with six basic elements: information technology, information resources, information infrastructure, information application platforms, information talents, and information-related policies. Information technology is the driving force and source of informatization. Information, along with energy and materials, are listed as the three major resources in the world today. Information resources here refer to the information content and the processed data useful for decision-making and they are regarded as the basic elements of the IT application. Information infrastructure mainly refers to the collection of various information transmission media and network systems. Information infrastructure is part of the national infrastructure, so it is mostly constructed by state investment because of its wide coverage and high construction costs. Information application platform is the application process of transforming information technology and information resources into actual productivity. Through integration with specific industries and enterprises, it promotes economic growth and social transformation. Information talents and information policy provide a support for the IT application. Without information talents with highly sophisticated knowledge, the innovation of information technology and the management of the informatization process will not be sustainable. Furthermore, without a sound information technology policy supported by the state, information technology will also fall into chaos. Therefore, these six elements are indispensable elements in the process of informatization, and together they provide the impetus and support for the sustainable development of information technology.

Informatization can be divided into various types from different perspectives. From the perspective of the main participants in informatization, it can be divided into macro national informatization, meso industrial informatization, and micro enterprise informatization; from the perspective of the three major industrial levels, informatization can be classified into agricultural informatization, industrial informatization and service informatization; from the perspective of industrial chain, informatization can be categorized into research and development (hereinafter referred to as R&D) and design informatization, production process informatization, marketing management informatization, etc.; from the perspective of the type of human activities, informatization can be subdivided into economic informatization, political informatization, social informatization, military informatization, etc.; from the perspective of the majority of consumers directly involved in the field of information, informatization can be categorized into e-commerce, e-government, digital city (including medicine, education, employment, social security), etc.

1.1.2 Information technology

Information technology (IT), also known as information and communications technology (ICT), is a technology that extends human information functions, including the acquisition, storage, transmission and processing of information. Information transmission media such as telegraph, telephone, and television are known as traditional information technology. Since the 1970s, due to the emergence of microelectronics technology, the two pillars of computer technology and communication technology have been continuously integrated and developed, and modern information technology based on microelectronics technology featuring digitization has emerged. Modern information technology mainly includes computer technology, communications technology, microelectronic technology, software technology, sensor technology, integrated circuit technology, display technology and control technology.

1.1.2.1   Information technology revolution

So far, there have been three technological innovations with universal application that have affected the economic and social development methods of all mankind in the history of human civilization, including steam technology, electric power technology, and information technology. In the 1760s, the invention and utilization of the steam engine started the first industrial revolution. In the 1870s, electricity became a new energy and put into application, and mankind entered the age of electricity. In the 1940s (1946), John W. Mauchly and J. Presper Eckert developed ENIAC, the world's first electronic digital computer, in the United States, which opened the era of human information technology. After the computer was invented and put into use, the innovation process of information technology was accelerated, with its application expanding, and the information revolution developed deeply. In 1947, Bell Labs invented the world's first transistor; in 1951, the first business computer system UNIVAC-1, was born; in 1956, the second generation of computers made with transistors was created; in 1965, the world's first commercial satellite communication system was put into operation; in 1971 the world's first microprocessor Intel 4004 was designed; and in 1976, the world's first supercomputer Cray-1, was created, with a computing speed of 250 million per second. All of them are landmark innovative developments in information technology. In the 21st century, information technology has achieved breakthroughs through continuous innovation, and entered the stage of large-scale application in various fields, significantly promoting economic development and social transformation.

1.1.2.2   New generation of information technology

The internet has shown strong vitality after its global popularity, and various information technologies based on the internet carry on innovating and developing. New generation of information technology, such as communication networks, the

Internet of Things, network convergence (including telecommunication network, computer network, and cable television network), new flat-panel displays, high-performance integrated circuits, cloud computing, and high-end industrial software, have been making breakthroughs. Cloud computing and the Internet of Things are representatives of the new generation of information technology.

(1) *Big data and cloud computing*

Big data is a collection of data that cannot be captured and processed by conventional software tools within a certain period of time, while cloud computing is a new model for distributed processing and mining of massive data. The concept of "cloud computing" was first introduced by Eric Schmidt, then CEO of Google, in 2006. The National Institute of Standards and Technology (NIST), US Department of Commerce, considers cloud computing to be a model in which a shared pool of configurable computing resources (e.g., networks, servers, storage, applications, and services) can be accessed conveniently and on-demand over a network at any time and from anywhere.[1] In the Report on the Work of the Government (2012) issued by the State Council of the People's Republic of China, cloud computing appears as an accompanying form of note and is defined as "a model for the addition, utilization, and delivery of internet-based services, typically involving the provision of dynamically scalable and often virtualized resources over the internet. It is a product of the development and convergence of traditional computer and network technology, which means that computing power can also be circulated as a commodity through the internet."[2]

Cloud computing is a new way of computing based on the internet, and a product of the convergence of computer and network technology. It is a virtual computing resources pool that provides users with various computing resources in the pool through the internet. Since the ordinary internet services cannot meet the increasing size of users and the growing complexity of service content, cloud computing centralizes massive data and quickly provides users with various computing resources in the resource pool through the internet, which can process tens of millions or even billions of pieces of information within seconds, improving data processing capabilities and information

---

[1] Mell P., Grance T, *The NIST Definition of Cloud Computing*, National Institute of Standard and Technology, 2011.

[2] Wen Jiabao, Report on the Work of the Government, delivered at the Fifth Session of the Eleventh National People's Congress on March 5, 2012, The State Council of the People's Republic of China, Mar. 15, 2012, http: // www. gov. cn/test/2012-03/15/content_2067314.htm.

dissemination speed. With the help of high-tech means of distributed computing, network storage and virtualization, cloud computing analyzes and processes big data to realize flexible deployment of resources, featuring incomparable superiority of reliability, high scalability, versatility, ultra-large scale, and on-demand services. It is certainly true that cloud computing has gone through four stages of power plant model, utility computing, grid computing and cloud computing before developing to the present level. With the development of economy and the need of big data processing, cloud computing plays an increasingly significant role in the intelligent production and management of enterprises.

(2) *Radio Frequency Identification and the Internet of Things*

Radio frequency identification (RFID) technology is a kind of non-contact automatic identification technology realized through radio frequency communication, and carries out non-contact two-way data transmission between the reader and the radio frequency card to achieve the purpose of identification and data exchange of the target. The Internet of Things (IoT) is a kind of network developed based on the RFID, which is considered to be the third wave of information revolution after computer and internet.

As early as 1995, Bill Gates mentioned the "Internet of Things", and in 1999, Professor Kevin Ashton of MIT formally introduced this concept. In 2005, the International Telecommunication Union (ITU) released the ITU Internet Reports 2005: The Internet of Things. The report proposed the interconnection among any objects at any time and any place, as well as the ubiquitous network, omnipresent computing and other related contents of the IoT, and defined the IoT as "a network that connects any objects to the internet by means of information sensing devices such as QR code reading devices, radio frequency identification devices, infrared sensors, global positioning system and laser scanners according to the agreed protocol, and carries out information exchange and communication, so as to achieve intelligent identification, positioning, tracking, monitoring and management".[1] In 2006, the ITU held a workshop on RFID in Geneva to conduct in-depth analysis and discussion on issues related to the IoT. In Report on the Work of Government (2012), the IoT was introduced as a supplementary note. China defines the IoT as "a network that connects any object to the internet for information exchange and communication through information sensing devices in accordance with the agreed protocols to achieve intelligent identification, positioning, tracking, monitoring and management. It is a network that extends and

---

[1] ITU, *ITU Internet Reports 2005: The Internet of Things*, WSIS in Tunis, Tunisia on Nov. 17, 2005.

expands on the internet."[1] The four key technologies of IoT are article identification technology (RFID), article sensing technology (sensor technology), article thinking technology (intelligent technology), and article information embedding technology (nanotechnology). Articles are ubiquitously computed and interconnected by a series of intelligent conduction and identification methods of information embedding, sensing, recognizing, and thinking.

The IoT is an extension and application based on the internet, and its user side extends from human to human to object to object, which is the exchange and identification of information between objects. By means of the information media such as radio frequency technology, intelligent sensor technology and global positioning system, things and things, people and things, people and people can be interconnected, and a "ubiquitous" social network can be formed through ubiquitous network computing. The interoperability and intelligent features of IoT enable it to play an increasingly important role in social life such as product manufacturing, industrial monitoring, government work, environmental protection and intelligent transportation. The innovation and development of a new generation of information technology characterized by digitalization and intelligence is increasingly becoming a key element of economic growth and social transformation.

After the 1970s, the development of modern information technology has gone through the following four stages: computer mainframe stage, local area network stage, internet stage, IoT and cloud computing stage. With the continuous innovation and development of information technology, the level of information technology has gradually increased. However, the increase in the level of information technology is not only marked by innovations in information technology, but more importantly the penetration and application of information technology in the economic, political, social, and military spheres. Information technology has to be transformed into real productivity and make an important contribution to economic growth as well as to social transformation.

1.1.3 Information industry

In 1963, the Japanese sociologist Tadao Umesao mentioned some ideas related to information industry in his work *Information Industry Theory*. In 1977, the concept of

---

[1] Wen Jiabao, Report on the Work of the Government, delivered at the Fifth Session of the Eleventh National People's Congress on Mar. 5, 2012, The State Council of the People's Republic of China, Mar. 15, 2012, http: // www.gov.cn/test/2012-03/15/content_2067314.htm.

"information industry" appeared in American economist Marc Porat's paper Information Economy: Definition and Measurement, in which he divided the social economy into four categories: agriculture, industry, service industry and information industry, and divided the information industry into primary information sector and secondary information sector.

In 1997, the North American Industry Classification System (NAICS) first introduced the information industry as a separate and complete industry sector. Information industry includes information technology products manufacturing and information service.

In 1998, the Organization for Economic Co-operation and Development (OECD) established a complete classification system for the information industry based on the United Nations' International Standard Industrial Classification (ISIC) of All Economic Activities, and divided the information industry into two parts: information technology manufacturing and information technology services. In 2007, the OECD redefined the information industry and added the information technology trade industry to the information technology manufacturing and information technology service industries.

The information industry in a broad sense refers to all fields based on electronic computers and directly related to the processing of information content, involving the production, processing, storage, circulation and distribution of information, including the information product manufacturing industry, information service industry, and even the R&D industry of information technology, various telecommunication network operation industry, and education of information technology personnel. The information industry can also be summarized as an industry that transforms information into commodities. With the advancement of information technology, the scope of the information industry has been expanding.

In the current study of information industry, information industry is regarded as the quaternary industry which is different from agriculture, industry and service industry, belonging to knowledge, technology and information-intensive industrial sector. The development of the quaternary industry is closely integrated with the primary industry, secondary industry and tertiary industry. The quaternary industry is a booster for the development of the other three industries and is an important strategic industry for the country, playing an important role in promoting national economic growth and development.

1.1.4   Information economy

Information economy is a new type of economy based on information, knowledge and intelligence. It is a form of economy based on modern information technology, information resources and supported and led by information industry. Information economy is the penetration and performance of information technology in the economic field. The information economy is a modernized economic form after the agricultural and industrial economies, with higher production efficiency compared with the first two economic forms, and is an economic form dominated by knowledge-intensive, technology-intensive and information-intensive industries.

The concept of "information economy" was first proposed by American scholar Fritz Machlup in his book *The Production and Distribution of Knowledge in the United States* published in 1962, in which he believed that the information economy includes five aspects: education, scientific research and development, communication media, information facilities, and information activities. In 1977, Marc Porat carried on and developed Machlup's research in the Information Economy: Definition and Measurement. Using specific data for economic analysis, he argues that capitalist countries such as the United States have transitioned to an information economy with more than half of their economic activity related to information activities from the mid to late 1960s to the 1970s.[1]

The information economy has become the dominant force of economic growth because of its low energy consumption, high efficiency, digitalization, and individualized needs. The 2016 China Information Economy Development Report released by China info 100 shows that in 2015, the share of the information economy in the GDP of developed countries worldwide was around 50%, becoming an important driving force for economic growth. From 2008 to 2015, the growth rate of information economy in major countries such as China, the United States, Japan, and the United Kingdom was 1.57-4.05 times faster than the growth rate of GDP, and the share of information economy in GDP increased by 12.3-21.2 percentage points. From 2002 to 2015, China's information economy grew from 10.0% to 27.5% of GDP, contributing 31.4% to GDP growth, and has become an important engine of China's economic development.[2]

1.1.5 Information society

The information society is the inevitable result of the development of information

---

[1] Xu Wenping, Chen Tong, "New Theory of Information Economy Based on Comparison of Information Economy and Commodity Economy", *Journal of Northwest A&F University* (*Social Science Edition*), 2011(5), pp. 100-106.

[2] ChinaInfo100, 2016 China Information Economy Development Report, ChinaInfo 100 Website, Jan. 14, 2017, http: //www.chinainfo100.com.

science and technology, and is the response of information technology in all fields of production and life in the whole society. The concept of "information society" was first used by Japanese scholar Jiro Kamishima in 1964 in his book *On the Sociology of Information Society*, in which he argued that Japan was rapidly entering the information society. In 2003, the Declaration of Principles issued by the World Summit on the Information Society (WSIS) in Geneva stated, "Our common desire and commitment to build a people-centered, inclusive and development-oriented Information Society, where everyone can create, access, utilize and share information and knowledge, enabling individuals, communities and peoples to achieve their full potential in promoting their sustainable development and improving their quality of life." [1] Therefore, the information society is a people-oriented and inclusively developed society with the goal of using information resources to achieve sustainable social development.

The stages of human civilization development can be summarized as agricultural society, industrial society and information society according to the characteristics of production forces, especially the means of production. The mechanization and electrification of production tools bring human civilization from agricultural society to industrial society; the intellectualization and digitalization of production tools lead human civilization from industrial society to information society. The comprehensive application of information technology in the economic, political, cultural and military fields has promoted the development of people's production and lifestyle towards informatization, intellectualization and digitalization. The information society is a unified union of information-based production forces and production modes, information-based social organization and management structures, information-based transaction methods, digital lifestyle, information-based governmental forms, and intelligent military systems.

The information society includes the following main characteristics: first, information industry and knowledge industry are in the dominant position, and the output value created by information economy is absolutely in the lead; second, the main body of labor force is information producers and disseminators, and intelligent robots have become the main force of production instead of traditional labor force; third, globalization is further enhanced, and the way of trade and settlement is intelligent;

---

[1] The State Information Center (Administration Center of China E-government Network), China Information Society Development Report 2016, The State Information Center Official Website, May 15, 2016, http: //www.sic. gov.cn/index.htm.

fourth, smart earth and digital city have changed people's way of life and interaction, and healthcare, education, insurance, transportation, etc. are increasingly dependent on intelligent devices.

To build a moderately prosperous society in all aspects, China must achieve simultaneous development of industrialization, informatization, urbanization and agricultural modernization, among which informatization is the accelerator of the other three. Informatization is not the ultimate goal, but an indispensable production force factor to achieve the other three. The achievements of informatization are reflected in the application to economic, political, cultural, social and military fields and in the transformational development of society. The application and impact of information technology in the economy is mainly manifested in the penetration and integrated development of information technology to agriculture, industry and service industries. Informatization brings the modernization of agriculture to a higher level, moving towards intelligence and networking; informatization enables the new type of industry to a higher level, gradually realizing smart manufacturing and personalized production; informatization enhances the information-intensity and knowledge-intensity of the service industry, increasingly approaching modern service industry.

1.2 Influence of the information revolution

The dramatic development of modern information technology has led to tremendous changes in the economic and social structure and triggered a global information revolution, thus exerting a wide impact on all aspects of the world's economic, political, military, cultural, social and other productive life.

1.2.1 Influence on the economy

1.2.1.1 Influence on agriculture

The informatization of agriculture is an inevitable requirement for changing agricultural production methods and realizing agricultural modernization. The impact and infiltration of informatization on agriculture involves all specific aspects of technology development, production, management, market and consumption in the agricultural field. The widespread application of modern information technology in agriculture can promote the restructuring of the agricultural economy, improve the level of informatization in all aspects of production, distribution, exchange and consumption, so as to enhance market competitiveness, realize the intelligence, digitalization and networking of agriculture, and finally accelerate the process of agricultural modernization.

Modern information technology applied in agriculture mainly consists of computer technology, communication system, internet, artificial intelligence, global positioning system, geographic information system, remote sensing technology, etc. The widespread application of informatization in agricultural production, represented by computer technology, contributes to the informatization of agricultural production and management, the convenience of agricultural information access, the networking of agricultural support systems, and the intelligence of agricultural expert systems, thus improving agricultural production efficiency and market flow. The specific content is as follows:

Firstly, the informatization of the agricultural production process can increase the level of automation, enhance production modes and boost the efficiency of labor production. Information technology has upgraded agricultural infrastructure equipment and increased its level of intelligence to achieve full automation of production. Automatic transmission of information, automatic computer control and remote sensing control greatly conserve human and material resources, help reduce production costs and increase profit levels.

Secondly, the informatization of the circulation process of agricultural products can promote the development of information networks, e-commerce and modern logistics, substantially reducing the cost of circulation. Information technology can integrate agriculture and geographically dispersed farmers into the global economic platform, bringing agricultural products and markets together seamlessly. Farmers can obtain timely market information through the network system and produce according to the market demand so as to reduce the risk of production. The development of agricultural e-commerce can realize the networking of agricultural trade as well as the networking of financial, logistics and other trade services, expanding markets and reducing costs.

Thirdly, the informatization of the agricultural management process is conducive to improving the efficiency of agricultural management. By developing and building a web-based office system and establishing an open database for agricultural government management, the government is able to realize the networking of administrative approval and market supervision, while improving the speed of release and dissemination of relevant policies.

The application of information technology and information networks in agriculture is instrumental in realizing the integration of technology research and development departments, agricultural production departments, agricultural business departments, service departments such as finance and logistics, government management departments and consumers, thus improving agricultural production efficiency, reducing production and transaction costs, and ultimately realizing comprehensive modernization of agriculture. At present, the level of agricultural informatization in developed countries is already very high. Numerous farms and agricultural companies in the US are already using network technology universally. In Japan, more than 400 agricultural networks were developed as early as the end of 1994, and computer popularity in the agricultural production sector reached 93%.

1.2.1.2 Influence on manufacturing industry

The influence of information technology on manufacturing industry is reflected in every link of manufacturing industry chain, including informatization of manufacturing technology, informatization of production process, informatization of management, etc. The integration and penetration of information technology in the whole industry chain of manufacturing industry will facilitate the economic restructuring of manufacturing industry, the conversion of production mode, the change of organization mode and the development of service-oriented manufacturing, which will in turn improve the operational efficiency and enhance the competitiveness of enterprises.

Firstly, information technology gives birth to the development of the emerging industries; in the meantime, it also promotes the optimization and upgrading of industrial structure. The development of information technology spurs the development of new industries with information technology as its core, and can drive the differentiation and reorganization of traditional industries to realize the optimal allocation of resources, improve the informatization level of traditional industries and the added value of products, and finally to promote the optimization and upgrading of industrial structure.

Secondly, information technology promotes the change of enterprise production modes. The application of information technology helps to improve the technology level of production equipment and automation and intelligence, promote the transformation of enterprises from extensive production to intensive production so as to increase resource utilization, reduce resource consumption to achieve sustainable development of enterprises.

Thirdly, information technology promotes the change of enterprise organization methods. IT and information networks enhance internal information flow, enabling companies to transition from traditional vertical, multi-layered management structures to flatter management models and divisional systems. A networked platform will facilitate the free flow of enterprise information resources between management group and executors, improving management and execution efficiency to reduce costs.

Fourthly, information technology facilitates the development of service-oriented manufacturing industry. Along with the application of information technology and the development of information networks, enterprises can quickly and easily obtain information about consumers' needs, so the manufacturing of enterprises will shift from product-centered manufacturing to consumer demand-centered manufacturing. Enterprises no longer focus only on the manufacturing aspect of the product, but more on service-oriented aspects such as product development and design, marketing management, technical consulting, and after-sales service.

1.2.1.3   Influence on service industry

Based on modern information technology and advanced management concepts, the traditional service industry is gradually transforming into a modern service industry characterized by information-intensity and knowledge-intensity. The modern service industry is grounded on an intelligent information infrastructure, and information resources and information networks are pushing the development of services towards customization and precision. The integration of all aspects of information technology services will greatly improve the economic efficiency and international competitiveness of the service industry.

Firstly, information technology enables the optimization and upgrading of traditional service industries. The extensive infiltration of information technology into the traditional service industry is conducive to improving the level of informatization of the service industry, contributing to its transformation into a modern service. Information technology has changed the service mode of traditional service industries such as retail, logistics, finance and public life services, rendering them networked, intelligent and digital so as to keep improving service quality and service efficiency.

Secondly, information technology promotes the emergence and development of emerging services. Information technology has promoted the emergence and development of new industries such as communication services, information technology services and information content services with information technology as the core. Telecommunications services, internet services, and information consulting services are gaining momentum with the development of information technology.

Thirdly, information technology facilitates the development of productive services industry. Productive services are services that arise along with the development of information technology and knowledge economy and are oriented to productive enterprises rather than directly to individual consumers. Modern enterprises, apart from the production chain, gradually extend the industrial chain and develop high value-added links of the industrial chain such as technology research and development, marketing management, logistics, consulting services and customer service. In order to meet the constantly externalized functions of enterprises, producer services have gradually flourished. The scope of the producer service industry specifically comprises R&D design and other technical services for production activities, cargo transportation, warehousing and postal courier services, information services, financial services, energy conservation and environmental protection services, production leasing services, business services, human resource management and training services, wholesale brokerage agency services, production support services, etc.

1.2.2 Influence on politics

Information technology not only has caused major changes in the economy, but also has changed the way government administration and public services are delivered. The level of informatization in the economic field is increasing, and the government, as the macro-controller of the economy, is bound to undergo corresponding changes in its means and ways of governance. The application of information technology to the political sphere is mainly reflected in the development of e-government.

E-government refers to the use of information technology, especially internet technology, by government departments to establish a networked public service platform for government affairs, such as information dissemination, public services, economic management, social management, comprehensive supervision, macro-control and other official government activities. The development of e-government has improved government public service capability and government office efficiency. The impact of the information revolution on the government's comprehensive governing capacity is mainly reflected in the following aspects.

Firstly, the networked public service platform has improved the speed and transparency of information dissemination. Through the information technology network public service platform, the government, on the one hand, timely releases various policies and regulations and information, which improves the speed of information dissemination. On the other hand, the government uses this platform to publish all kinds of administrative approval and supervision information in a timely manner, which increases the transparency of government work.

Secondly, the social management and comprehensive monitoring information network has enhanced the comprehensive social management and supervision ability. With the superiority of the internet, the government can establish a comprehensive social management system to effectively respond to various emergencies, thus improving the government's emergency response capability. The government has improved its ability to regulate the market and society and to make macro decisions through information systems such as approval, taxation, banking, customs, and security.

Thirdly, the government has used information technology to improve government processes and has established a public and community-centered e-government system. Through the information network, the government is able to understand the needs of the public; and through interaction and communication with the public, it is able to better grasp public needs and realize the transformation from a management-oriented government to a service-oriented government, thus contributing to the harmonious development of society.

Fourthly, the establishment and improvement of the government's internal information system is useful for the communication between the upper and lower levels of the government as well as between related departments at the same level to improve the speed and efficiency of the office.

E-government is the development trend of the new service-oriented government. E-government is an essential means for the government to use information technology to achieve the functions of economic management and market surveillance, social management, public services and internal collaboration. According to the different objects, e-government can be categorized into government-to-government (G2G), government-to-business (G2B), government-to-customer (G2C), and government-to-employee (G2E).

1.2.3   Influence on society and culture

The development and widespread use of information technology will first have an impact on the economic and political spheres, and will then bring about changes in the structure of social organization and people's way of life. Specifically, people's education, social security, healthcare, way of life, employment, interaction, and thinking pattern will be changing with the advancement of information technology.

Information technology promotes the development of educational infrastructure and teaching information resources in the direction of digitalization and networking, and teaching, and research and other educational methods are subsequently changed. With the application of computer and network communication technology in education, new models such as multimedia computer-assisted instruction (MCAI), network teaching, and virtual reality simulation teaching are commonly adopted. The new teaching mode has changed the teacher-centered education in the past, and the digital and networked teaching methods have enabled students to participate extensively, with the majority of students becoming active learners and explorers, and their learning enthusiasm and learning efficiency have been greatly improved. In addition, educational resources such as distance learning, digital libraries, and online exams broaden the educational coverage, which provides the foundation for universal education.

As a form of national income redistribution, social security is conducive to achieving social equity, maintaining social harmony, and increasing the level of public welfare. Generally speaking, social security comprises social insurance, social assistance, social welfare, veteran services, etc. The combination of information technology and social security and the establishment of social security information network can implement the unified management of social security recipients' information, establish mobile electronic archives, monitor the protectors dynamically, and improve the service and management of social security.

E-health has become an international development trend with its great superiority. E-health reflects not only in medical equipment and means, but also in medical process and management. The improvement of information technology has promoted the intellectualization and digitization of medical equipment, enhancing the accuracy of instruments and the efficiency of treatment. The hospital has optimized and simplified the consultation process by establishing a management information system and a unified information platform for all aspects of consultation; it has improved the efficiency of medical services and reduced patient waiting and consultation time by collecting and registering patient information through intelligent means, establishing a patient database and building electronic archives. Doctors use medical network platforms to realize telemedicine with the help of electronic patient files, expanding the scope of treatment and reducing the cost of treatment. At the same time, information technology helps promote the development and improvement of the national public health system and improve the country's comprehensive service capacity in disease prevention and control, health supervision, and public health emergencies.

The information revolution has had a significant impact on the cultural sphere in various countries, in which the values and people's ways of life are showing a trend of diversification. With the development and extensive application of the internet, people have access to a wide variety of cultural knowledge, local customs, world views and values, and the trend toward the integration of world cultures is becoming more and more apparent. The development of information technology has promoted the networking of cultural communication means, and information media such as internet radio and online media have increased the speed of dissemination of intellectual and cultural contents, which enhances the world influence of different cultures.

Information technology has transformed the way people live and commute. Shopping, education, and entertainment can all be done through the internet. Digital cities and digital communities are gradually being established, and basic living services such as water, electricity and gas can be accessed through network information platforms. Intelligent appliances such as floor cleaning robots and electric rice cookers with reservation function provide convenience for family daily life and improve people's quality of life. Information technology has also brought convenience to transportation and tourism, job hunting and employment, and the digital earth has changed from an ideal to a reality.

1.3 General trends of world information technology

Information technology (IT) is the engine of transformation and upgrading of economic production modes and way of social life. Countries around the world are striving to seize the opportunities brought by the information revolution, formulate and implement various policies, and vigorously develop national IT application to facilitate the production forces transformation of information technology and realize a successful transformation from industrial society to information society. On November 18, 2016, the *Evaluation Report on National Informatization Development* (2016) released by China Internet Network Information Center (CNNIC) pointed out that "Globally, large economies represented by the United States, the United Kingdom, Japan, China and Russia possess a strong information industry foundation and a huge user market scale, so their advantages in informatization is obvious. Sweden, Finland as the representative of the Nordic countries, their IT application is at high and stable level. Asian countries are not balanced in the development of information technology, countries such as Japan, Republic of Korea and Singapore have been among the world's leading ranks, while West Asia, South Asia countries still have more space to improve."[1] Countries with high informatization levels are mainly concentrated in North America and Western Europe. Among those western countries, the United States' informatization level improves faster, rising from the sixth in the world in 2012 to the first in the world in 2016; and in Asia, the informatization level of Japan, Republic of Korea and Singapore also is higher. The top ten countries in terms of information technology level in 2016 are shown in Table 1–1.

Table 1–1　　List of the top ten countries in terms of the level of Information technology application

Country	Total index in 2016	Ranking in 2016	Ranking in 2015	Ranking in 2014	Ranking in 2013	Ranking in 2012
The United States	84.1	1	6	6	6	6
The United Kingdom	82.7	2	2	3	4	8
Japan	81.5	3	10	16	14	3
Sweden	81.4	4	7	1	1	1
Republic of Korea	81.0	5	3	8	8	4
Finland	80.4	6	1	2	2	2
Netherlands	80.3	7	11	4	3	7
Singapore	80.1	8	8	15	13	14
Israel	78.6	9	5	7	7	5
Germany	78.5	10	9	10	12	12

Source: China Internet Network Information Center, *Evaluation Report on National Informatization Development* (2016).

1.3.1　Countries around the world are making development plans to accelerate informatization

The development of informatization attributes to the collaborative innovation and promotion of government, enterprises and society. By formulating policies conducive to the development of information technology to promote information technology innovation and production forces transformation of scientific and technological achievements, governments create a favorable environment for the accelerated development of information technology, and strive to seize the high ground in the information field.

---

[1] China Internet Network Information Center, *Evaluation Report on National Informatization Development* (2016), China Internet Network Information Center Network, 2016, http: //www.cnnic.net.cn/hlwfzyj/hlwxzbg/hlwtjbg/201611/t20161118-56109.htm.

The developed countries and regions of the United States, the European Union, Japan, and Republic of Korea have treated informatization development strategies as an important part of their national (regional) strategies and formulated national (regional) strategies and plans that meet their national realities and conditions to promote the development of informatization. Since the 1990s, the US government has formulated a number of national development plans: in 1993, the Clinton administration formally proposed the "National Information Infrastructure (NII)," plan to congress then in 1994 it launched the "Global Information Infrastructure (GII)", and in 1996 it introduced the "Next-Generation Internet (NGI)". The EU's information planning basically started at the same time as that of the United States, with the formulation of a social action plan "Europe's way to the Information Society" in 1994 and a ten-year development strategy in 1999. The government of Republic of Korea also made an early start on information technology application, establishing the "Basic Plan for Promoting Informatization" in 1996, the "Cyber Republic of Korea 21 Initiative" in 1999, and the "u-Republic of Korea" national IT application in 2004. The Japanese government formulated a five-year informatization development plan "e-Japan Strategy" in 2001 and "u-Japan Strategy" in 2004, focusing on the construction of high-speed networks, e-commerce, e-government, human resource development, and network security. In 2008, the Russian government formulated the "Information Society Development Strategy in the Russian Federation" and later introduced the Strategy for Developing the Information Technology Sector in the Russian Federation in 2014-2020 and until 2025 in an effort to achieve catch-up development.

In the 21st century, India, Brazil and other developing countries and emerging economies have also formulated various development plans and policy measures in the world trend of informatization application, striving to seize the opportunities of informatization application development and facilitate economic and social transformation and development by using information technology.

1.3.2　Internet popularity is gradually increasing as a driving force of world economic growth

In the world, network broadband has entered a period of popularization and speed-up, modern information technology based on computers and the internet is developing at a high speed, and a new generation of information technology such as the Internet of Things, cloud computing and mobile internet is constantly innovating. The US government has released the Federal Cloud Computing Strategy, Technologies and

Policies to Support Data-Driven Innovation, and the Strategy of Cybersecurity; the German government has issued the Digital Agenda 2014-2017; the UK government has launched the Digital Economy Strategy 2015-2018; and the Mexican government has introduced the National Digital Strategy 2013. With internet technology as the basic starting point, these governments are aiming to drive socio-economic development and improve national competitiveness through digital innovation.

Driven by the policies of governments, internet popularity and growth rates are increasing year by year worldwide. In 2014, the global internet growth rate was 6.6%, and 44% of households worldwide had internet access at the end of 2014. The 2016 Digital Report, released by *We Are Social*, the world's largest social media specialist communications company, shows that the number of internet users worldwide reached 3.42 billion in 2016, equivalent to 46% of the global population, with an annual increase of 10%, in which Iceland became the country with the highest internet popularity rate of 98%. From 2012 to 2014, the number of countries using email increased from 126 to 132, and the usage rate rose from 65% to 68.4%. On the basis of the development of the internet, the value added of the economy based on the internet has been increasing. From 2006 to 2014, the value created by the internet accounted for 21% of the value of GDP growth in 13 economically leading countries: the United States, China, the United Kingdom, Brazil, Canada, France, Germany, India, Italy, Japan, Republic of Korea, Russia, and Sweden. From 2011 to 2014, the global IT industry grew at an average annual rate of 2.6%, which is higher than the global GDP growth rate.[1]

1.3.3 Innovation of IT application through society makes breakthrough

Countries around the world have been using information technology to innovate teaching methods, and the knowledge dissemination function of online education has been enhanced, such as 3D printing courses in the US and teachers and students communicating in a 3D virtual world in the UK. Massive open online courses (MOOC), which emerged in the United States as a new type of online course, has revolutionized online education by providing more students with free, high-quality college courses. In the field of healthcare, new models of medical services such as online appointments and telemedicine have emerged, and developed countries such as the United Kingdom and the United States have established universal digital health records, which have improved the ability of hospitals to assess patients and the

---

[1] The Compilation Committee of China Informatization Almanac, *China Informatization Almanac* 2015, Beijing: Publishing House of Electronics Industry, 2016, p. 386.

accuracy of medical treatment. The American Diagnostic Consultation & Services has achieved networked sharing of all medical resources across the United States and facilitated the development of telemedicine. Telemedicine has been implemented in 14 of Mexico's 32 states. The creation of a patient database made it possible to provide personalized, patient-centered care. Canada has established an electronic healthcare record that can be operated interactively, and has developed a unified standard for sharing and exchanging medical information. Digital employment and social security platforms provide for cross-regional information sharing and off-site services, such as the US social security information platform that makes social security benefits available to its citizens in many countries around the world.

1.3.4   E-government serves as a common form of government public service

All governments are actively using information networks and cyberspace to conduct governmental activities and establish online governments. E-government has begun to change from a static website for releasing information to a stage of two-way interaction between government and enterprises, and government and the public. The United States has formed different types of e-government at the federal, state and city and county levels of government, which all work together to form an online government. Singapore's "integrated government" provides services through a networked platform by consolidating various government functions and has established an e-Citizen Center. The EU's E-Government Action Plan provides a "one-stop" service to the public. "Smart Government Implementation Plan" of Republic of Korea has contributed to the country's rapid adaptation to the smart age. Countries and regions such as the US, Europe and Japan have enacted a series of regulations, formulated development plans and established standardized portals to improve government public service capabilities. Web-based office platforms that integrate government functions and improve administrative efficiency are rapidly developing worldwide.

Around the world, European countries and the United States have a higher level of e-government. The United Nations E-Government Survey 2016 shows that Europe has the highest E-Government Development Index (EGDI) (reaching 0.7241), followed by the Americas (0.5245), Asia (0.5132), Oceania (0.4154), and Africa (0.2882).[1] According to the EGDI, the global e-government development level is unbalanced. The development of e-government in the African region is still lagging behind, and there is

---

[1]   United Nations Department of Economic and Social Affairs, United Nations E-Government Survey 2016, 2016.

a big gap with developed Europe, and the digital divide is obviously still there.

1.4 Development of the world internet

Xi Jinping pointed out, "In today's world, network information technology is changing rapidly, fully integrated into social production and life, profoundly changing the global economic landscape, the pattern of interests, the security structure. Major countries around the world have made the internet the focus of economic development and technological innovation, taking it as a strategic direction to seek new competitive advantages."[1] In the new period of rapid development of the global information revolution, the internet is commonly used worldwide and is being deeply integrated with various fields, which will certainly have a strategic and global impact on the economic and social development of countries around the world.

1.4.1 Creation and development of the internet

With the convergent development of modern information technology, the internet was born and became an important public information infrastructure for human beings. The internet was born in 1969, when the Defense Advanced Research Projects Agency (DARPA) first produced ARPAnet. In 1971, Ray Tomlinson, an American, developed Email. In 1983, ARPAnet became open to the public, but only to the scientific and military fields. In 1990, the National Science Foundation (NSF) established the NSFnet to replace the ARPAnet, and made it available to the entire community. In 1990, Tim Berners-Lee of the European Organization for Nuclear Research created the World Wide Web, and since then the internet has been accessible to society in the form of web pages, becoming a medium for information transmission and communication.

The popularity and application of the internet has brought mankind into the age of internet. The internet is open, global and sharing, and with the development of the times, it is increasingly becoming an essential information medium and platform for economic development and social life. The commercialization of the internet has made commercial organizations, governments, customers and other subjects involved in economic exchanges and social interactions into a node of the internet. Modern information technology and the internet have become important driving forces of today's information revolution.

---

[1] "Xi Jinping Presided over the Central Political Bureau Group Study Session to Emphasize the six 'Acceleration' to Build a Cyberpower", *People's Daily* (*Overseas Edition*), Oct. 10, 2016.

1.4.2   World internet development status

1.4.2.1   Internet has become a strategic infrastructure

From a worldwide perspective, the internet is actively promoting a new wave of informatization development, and many countries have made the development of broadband networks the focus of strategic deployment to seize the commanding ground of economic competition. There are already 145 countries and regions in the world to promote broadband from the perspective of national strategies, where national broadband strategies have been introduced to speed up the construction of ultra-high-speed fiber optic broadband, to promote the renewal of information infrastructure. Information infrastructure is entering a new period of broadband popularity and acceleration. The United States has developed the National Broadband Plan (US), which proposes to achieve download rates of at least 100 Mbps and uplink speeds of 50 Mbps; Canada has formulated the "Broadband Canada: Connecting Rural Canadians"; the EU has made the "EU Digital Agenda", which proposes that by 2020 at least 50% of European households will have access to the internet at a rate of 100 Mbps; the UK has launched the "Digital Britain" initiative; Sweden has formulated the "Swedish Broadband Strategy", which seeks to enable 90% of Swedish households and enterprises to have access to 100 Mbps high-speed networks by 2020.[1]

1.4.2.2   Rapid development of the global internet

In a global context, the information infrastructure is entering a new period of broadband popularity and acceleration, with the rapid growth of information networks, the steady increase in broadband access, and the gradual increase in the number of internet users. Mankind has entered the era of globally interconnected information networks. The internet has covered 224 countries and regions worldwide, and some developed countries have achieved full internet coverage. Data from the Measuring the Information Society Report 2014 shows that the global internet has been maintaining strong momentum, and as of 2014, there were 3 billion internet users worldwide, with Europe's internet popularity rate having reached 75%, ranking first in the world, and 2/3 of the people in the Americas already using the internet. The global fixed broadband popularity rate has reached 10%, the number of mobile cellular subscribers has approached 7 billion, and 44% of households worldwide have internet access, of which 78% of households in developed countries have access to the internet. Data from the Measuring the Information Society Report 2015 shows that the internet continued to

---

[1] Compiled by CCID Think Tank, 2014 (12).

grow rapidly in 2015, with the number of people online reaching 3.2 billion, accounting for 43.4% of the global population, and global cellular mobile users approaches 7.1 billion, with cellular mobile signals covering more than 95% of the world's population. By the end of 2015, about 46% of households worldwide will have internet access at home, up from 30% in 2010. Data from the Measuring the Information Society Report 2016 shows that the total number of internet users was about 3.9 billion by the end of 2016, accounting for 47% of the global total because of the continuous improvement in the popularity of the internet infrastructure. Mobile internet is growing rapidly, and mobile broadband has covered 84% of countries and regions worldwide.

The global popularity of fixed broadband and mobile broadband has increased year by year, and broadband download rates have made leaps and bounds. According to data released by the International Telecommunication Union, internet popularity rates in countries such as Iceland, Luxembourg, Norway and Denmark have exceeded 95%, and large economies such as Japan, the United Kingdom and Germany have reached about 90%; fixed broadband popularity rates in Switzerland, the Netherlands, Republic of Korea and Denmark have surpassed 40%; mobile broadband popularity rates in Singapore, Finland, Kuwait and Japan is over 120%.[1] Ultra-high-speed broadband and mobile broadband worldwide have also entered the fast lane of development. According to data released by the United Nations Broadband Commission, in terms of ultra-high-speed broadband development, as of early 2014, Morocco's popularity rate of ultra-high-speed broadband was 44.7%, ranking first in the world, and Switzerland, Denmark, the Netherlands, France and Republic of Korea all had popularity rates of more than 38%. In terms of ultra-high-speed mobile broadband popularity, Singapore ranks first in the world with a high rate of 135.1%, while the popularity rates of Finland, Japan, Australia, Bahrain, Sweden, Denmark are all above 107%.

1.4.2.3 Developing countries have become the growth pole of internet development

The internet construction in developing countries, represented by Africa and the Asia-Pacific region, started late but developed rapidly, and has become an important growth pole for global internet development. The Measuring the Information Society Report released by the ITU shows that developing countries' share of total global international bandwidth rose from 9% in 2004 to more than 30% in 2014. The number

---

[1] China Internet Network Information Center, Evaluation Report on National Informatization Development (2016), China Internet Network Information Center Network, 2016, http://www.cnnic.net.cn/hlwfzyj/hlwxzbg/hlwtjbg/201611/t20161118-56109.htm.

of internet users in developing countries already accounts for 2/3 of the total number of internet users worldwide, and the number of internet users has doubled between 2009 and 2014, with the internet popularity rate reaching 32%. The number of mobile cellular subscribers in developing countries already accounts for 78% of the global total, with the most rapid growth in Asia-Pacific and African countries, where popularity rates have reached 89% and 69% in African countries. The number of internet users in Africa increased by 10%, between 2010 and 2014. Data from the Digital Report 2016 released by We Are Social shows that Asia Pacific is the region with the largest absolute number of new internet users, with the number of internet users growing by 200 million in 2016 alone.

Despite the increasing level of internet development in developing countries, internet development is uneven worldwide and the digital divide is noticeable. In 2014, for example, there was a significant gap between developing countries and developed countries in terms of internet access, with 4.3 billion people worldwide still not using the internet, of which developing countries accounted for 90%. By the end of 2015, the proportion of households with residential internet access reached 81.3% in developed countries, compared to 34.1% in developing countries. The Measuring the Information Society Report 2016 states that the average number of people using the internet in developed countries is about 80%, compared to 40% in developing countries, and in less developed countries, the number of internet users is even below 15%. Internet development is also extremely uneven between urban and rural areas, with rural internet popularity far lower than urban, and the urban-rural gap is much higher in developing countries than in developed countries, where the urban-rural gap in internet access rates is only 4% in developed countries, but 35% in developing countries.

The internet is an important information infrastructure for information development and a key information resource for economic growth and social transformation. In the course of the development of the information revolution, the internet is integrating with all areas of the economy and society, releasing tremendous energy resources, constantly enhancing the innovation and forces of production of the real economy, and giving birth to new forms of social development.

Chapter 2
Evolution of Informatization in China

The contemporary information revolution began in 1946, marked by the birth of ENIAC, the first generic electronic digital computer. After the 1970s, the process of the information revolution accelerated. After the founding of the People's Republic of China in 1949 (hereinafter referred to as New China), under the leadership of the Communist Party of China (CPC) and Chinese government, the Chinese people have worked hard to seize the opportunity and take the initiative to meet the challenges of the information revolution. In 1956, Zhou Enlai presided over the formulation of the Long-term Plan for Development of Science and Technology (1956-1967), which clearly put forward the development of electronic digital computers as a national strategy. Since then, China was first to begin its informatization process. Since 1956, the informatization in China has gone through over 60 years. In the past six decades, the informatization path was not smooth, but China has finally embarked on a path of national informatization development with Chinese characteristics in the process of convergence and development of informatization, industrialization and agricultural modernization.

2.1 Preparation stage (1949–1978)

2.1.1 Era of independent innovation launched by electronic communication industry in China

In May 1950, the Government Administration Council of the Central People's Government approved the establishment of National Administration of Telecommunication Industry under the Ministry of Heavy Industry, which was under the administration of the Communication Department of the Central Military Commission. The National Administration of Telecommunication Industry was responsible for the management of the telecommunications industry and enterprises around the country, and the electronics industry of the New China was thus born.

The communications industry adheres to the policy of "self-reliance, supplemented by foreign aid". During the War to Resist US Aggression and Aid Korea, the Chinese government announced that all the communication equipment to meet the requirements of the Chinese People's Volunteers (CPV) should be made in China, which marked the beginning of the path of large-scale independent innovation in China. By 1952, communications equipment such as shortwave and mediumwave radios, shortwave telegraphs, small radio stations could be made in the communications industry on its own in China. In April 1953, the the Government Administration Council approved the transfer of the former National Administration of Telecommunication Industry of the First Ministry of Machinery Industry to the Second Ministry of Machinery Industry, and renamed it the 10th Office of the Second Ministry of Machinery Industry, which mainly produced equipment of communication, navigation and broadcasting. In February 1963, the Central Committee of CPC and the State Council made a decision to separate the 10th General Administration of the Third Ministry of Industry and set up the Ministry of Radio Industry (the Fourth Ministry of Machinery Industry), with four production technology divisions, including the second production technology division in charge of the production technology management of products such as communication enterprises, navigation, computers, radio and television. In September 1963 and June 1964, a specialized conference on small- and medium-sized communication machines and a conference on the serialization of large transmitters were successively held by the Fourth Ministry of Machinery Industry in Beijing.

In 1970, China embarked on researching satellite communication technology and successfully launched the first man-made satellite designed and manufactured by itself. In December 1975, the first analog 10-meter cable satellite communication earth station was successfully developed, and in December 1976, the first digital 15-meter cable satellite communication earth station was successfully invented. The achievements above have laid the foundation for the development of satellite communications in China.

China attached great importance to infrastructural construction of the communications industry before the reform and opening up during 1949-1978. According to partial statistics, there were more than 170 enterprises of the communications industry and nearly 180,000 employers in China, including over 23,000 engineers and other technical personnel. The communications industry in China has built a complete industrial system combining independent R&D with large-scale production, providing a large number of communications equipment and navigation facilities for national economic construction.

2.1.2 Marching towards science in New China, with the development of the computer industry as the symbol

On January 3, 1953, the first Chinese electronic computer research group was established in the Institute of Mathematics of the Chinese Academy of Sciences. The initiative of "marching towards the mastery of science and technology" was proposed by Zhou Enlai at the National Working Conference on Intellectuals in January 1956. Mao Zedong called upon at the Supreme State Conference that "Chinese people should have an ambitious plan to strive to change the economic and cultural backwardness of our country and rapidly reach the advanced level in the world within a few decades."[1] From then on, planning for the development of science in the New China was put on the agenda.

In late August 1956, Zhou Enlai presided over the formulation of the Long-Term Plan for Development of Science and Technology (1956-1967) accompanied by four annexes (Descriptions of Important National Scientific Missions and Central Issues, Description of Planning for Basic Science Disciplines, Emergency Measures in 1956 and Research Highlights in 1957, Name List of Missions and Central Issues), which was the first scientific and technological plan since the founding of the People's Republic of China. Under the guideline of "focusing on development in key areas and working hard to catch up in weak areas", the plan drew six priorities of atomic energy, jet technology, computers, semiconductors, electronics, and automation, and took the R&D of information technology represented by computers as a strategic task. From 1958 to 1959, China invented the first small electron tube computer 103 and large electron tube computer 104 (i.e., the first generation of Chinese computers), and major scientific achievements in the field of science and technology came out one after another.

In January 1973, the Fourth Ministry of Machinery Industry held the First Professional Conference on Electronic Computers in Beijing, deciding to abandon the technical policy of simply pursuing higher computing speed, but to conduct user-oriented R&D. Since then, the R&D stage of electronic computer began to change to the promotion and application stage. In August 1974, the computer DSJ130 passed the appraisal, announcing the successful development of China's serial computer products and marking the beginning of serial mass production in China's computer industry. By the 1970s, the development of computers in China had gradually shifted from R&D to industrialized development stage.

---

[1] Shi Zhongquan, "Mao Zedong and the eighth National Congress of the CPC (I)", *Hunan Tides*, 2016(9), pp. 50-55.

During the period from 1949 to 1978, the electronic communication industry and the computer industry started to develop under the support and guidance of the national government. Since 1949, the Central Committee of CPC and the State Council had seized the opportunity of the development of information technology to take the initiative to meet the challenge, adhered to the policy of "self-reliance", and taken a path of independent development. In the development process, China focused on the adjustment of the policy, and transformed from simple R&D and design to promotion and application and to the stage of large-scale production, so as to continuously meet the needs of users. The incipient exploration before the reform and opening up laid an important foundation for the development of informatization in China.

2.2   Accumulation stage (1978–1992)

In 1978, the Third Plenary Session of the 11th Central Committee of the CPC put forward the slogan of "taking economic development as the central task" , thus shifting the focus of the Party's work to economic development in 1978. Deng Xiaoping made the famous statement that "science and technology are part of the productive forces" at the National Science Conference on March 18, 1978. From the late 1970s to the early 1980s, the Chinese government gradually recognized the urgency of developing IT and began to vigorously promote the application of electronic IT in various aspects of the economy, society, and national defense. During the period from the Third Plenary Session of the 11th Central Committee to the 14th CPC National Congress, the electronic IT in China continued to innovate and develop, accumulating significant power for information technology development in China.

2.2.1   Electronic computer technology as an important link in the development of national science and technology

From December 1977 to January 1978, the heads of relevant parties from various ministries and commissions of the State Council, provinces, municipalities, autonomous regions and Military Commissions held a National Science Conference in Beijing and approved the Outline of National Science and Technology Development Plan (1978-1985) (Draft). The conference highlighted the prominence of eight comprehensive science and technology fields, major new technology areas and leading disciplines that affect the overall situation, including agriculture, energy, materials, electronic computers, lasers, space, high-energy physics, and genetic engineering.[1]

In March 1979, the State Council decided to establish the State Administration of Electronic Computer Industry, which symbolized of the development of computer industry in China. In September 1979, the State Administration of Electronic Computer Industry held the first professional conference on microcomputers, which established the development strategy of fully adopting the international advanced technologies suitable for the needs according to China's national conditions and put forward the policy of focusing on micro and mini computers in the industry.

In October 1982, the State Council decided to set up a "leading group of electronic computers and large-scale integrated circuits", and held the National Expert Validation Meeting on Computer Series Spectrum in December of the same year to establish the selection basis for the development of large- and medium-sized computers as well as miniaturized series of computers. In May 1983, the National Planning Conference on Computer and Large-Scale Integrated Circuit proposed a number of measures to promote the development of computer technology. Electronic computer technology then became an important link in the development of national science and technology.

2.2.2   Policy of vigorously developing the information industry, exploiting information resources, and serving the construction of the Modernization of agriculture, industry, national defense and science and technology

Seizing up the situation, the CPC Central Committee and the State Council fully recognized the importance of developing the information industry. The State Council proposed that the information industry was the core factor to meet the new technological revolution in the world and accelerated the construction of the Four Modernizations (the modernization of agriculture, industry, national defense and science and technology) in China. In February 1984, Jiang Zemin, then Minister of Electronics Industry, argued that China must seize the opportunity and accelerate the development of the electronics industry to narrow the gap with the developed countries, and losing the opportunity will undermine the process of the Four Modernizations. In the same year, Deng Xiaoping wrote the following inscription for *Economic Information Daily*, "Developing Information Resources to Serve the Four Modernizations (modernization of agriculture, industry, national defense, and science and technology)." In 1991, Jiang Zemin stressed that IT application was indispensable to each of the Four Modernizations. It became an

---

[1] Hu Angang, "China's Featured Independent Innovation", *Bulletin of Chinese Academy of Sciences*, 2014(2), pp. 141-157.

important task at that time to vigorously develop electronic information industry and exploit information resources.

In November 1984, the leading group of electronic revitalization unveiled a Report on the Development Strategy of China's Electronics and Information Industry, pointing out that China's electronics and information industry to transfer their tasks as follows. First, the focus on development of the national economy, the Four Modernizations and the entire social life of the track. Second, the basic development of microelectronics and the major development of computer and communication equipment.[1]

In January1987, the National Economic Information Center was established, mainly responsible for national information construction and development research, technical support, monitoring and forecasting and management. In March 1986, the state invested RMB10 billion to launch a high-tech research and development program ("863" program), of which 2/3 invested in information technology projects. In 1989, Jiang Zemin pointed out that electronic information technology is an effective drive to accelerate the revitalization of China's economy and a new technology with its most influential and strongest pervasion.[2] The tremendous development of the electronic information industry and the wide application of electronic information technology are pushing the world into an era of the so-called information economy.[3] In 1992, the 14th CPC National Congress put forward the electronics industry as a new growth point of the national economy, which had greatly promoted the development of China's communications equipment manufacturing industry.

After the reform and opening up of more than a decade, the CPC Central Committee and the State Council attach great importance to the development of information technology, fully understand that computer technology, electronic information technology has become the first productive force to promote economic development, timely launch of the National High Technology Research and Development Program, the electronic computer technology as an important link in the development of national science and technology, vigorously develop the electronics and information industry, the development of information resources, information technology and China's Four Modernization

---

[1] Chen Yundi, "The Development Process of China's Informatization", *Digital Space*, 2003(2), pp. 52-53.

[2] Jiang Zemin, "New Characteristics in the Development in Worldwide Electronic & Information Industry and Strategic Considerations of the Development in Electronic & Information Industry in China", *Journal of Shanghai Jiaotong University*, 1989(6), pp. 1-8.

[3] Jiang Zemin, "New Characteristics in the Development in Worldwide Electronic & Information Industry and the Development Strategic Issues of China", *China Science and Technology Forum*, 1991(1), pp. 2-7.

construction combined. The state adhered to the market-oriented, accelerated the reconstruction of the transfer of military technology to civilian use and the combination of civilian and military production with emphasis on the civilian role, and improved the promotion and application of information technology.

2.3 Start–up stage (1993–1999)

China's information technology construction officially started in 1993. In 1993, the CPC and state leaders put forward the task of accelerating the construction of China's information technology. The launch of three key information-based projects (electronic money, information expressway, and digital customs service) and other major information security programs became a curtain-raiser to China's information technology construction successively.

2.3.1 Three key information-based projects symbolizing of the start of China's information technology construction

While presiding over a meeting of the State Council on March 12 1993, Vice Premier Zhu Rongji proposed the three key information-based projects in electronic money, information expressway, and digital customs service.

The Information Expressway Project marked the launch of the three key information-based projects in order to promote the transformation of scientific and technological achievements and take good use of science and technology to promote economic development. In August 1996, information expressway was officially approved as one of the 107 national key projects. The first stage of information expressway was fully operating in October 1998.

The Digital Customs Service Project aims at promoting the electronic customs declaration business. The electronic customs with digitalization of internal system and external electronic law enforcement were the key parts of the Golden Customs Project. The Golden Customs Project is a special network for the foreign trade sector and was applied for electronic networking for the General Administration of Customs, the Ministry of Foreign Trade and Economic Cooperation, the State Administration of Foreign Exchange, the State Administration of Taxation, General Administration of Quality Supervision, Inspection and Quarantine of the People's Republic of China, the Bank of China, the National Bureau of Statistics, ocean-going transport companies and import and export companies.

The Electronic Money Project, or Digital Money Project, aims to promote credit cards and the application of the credit cards. It is based on computer and communication technology and uses bank cards as a medium to realize currency circulation through electronic information transfer.

2.3.2   Track of organized and well-planned development of China's information technology construction

In 1994, the National Informatization Expert Group was established to provide consultation for the national informatization construction. In 1996, the State Council Leading Group on Informatization was established, with then Vice Premier Zou Jiahua as its leader, to unify the organization and coordination of the nation's informatization work. In March 1998, the Ministry of Electronics Industry and the Ministry of Posts and Telecommunications merged to form the Ministry of Information Industry, which takes charge of promoting informatization of the national economy and social services.

At the National Science and Technology Conference in May 1995, then Premier Li Peng put forward that computer technology should be widely used in finance, taxation, commerce, trade, traffic, transportation and other social services to accelerate the process of informatization of the national economy so as to promote national informatization. At the first national informatization work conference in Shenzhen in April 1997, the State Council Leading Group on Informatization which comprehensively deployed the key work of national informatization construction, pointing out that the country should unify the organization of informatization construction and promote the wide application of information technology in various fields. It marked an important milestone in the construction of information technology in China to promote China's information technology construction gradually transferring to the track of organized and well-planned development.

At this stage, the national informatization project took off with information technology pervading all fields of society, as well as the transformation rate of scientific and technological achievements increasing. The Central Committee of the CPC and the State Council have initially formed the idea of information technology construction in line with China's national conditions, the national unified organization, integrated planning, national power to become an important force in promoting China's information technology construction.

2.4 All–round development stage (2000–2012)

2.4.1 Strategic policy of industrialization driven by informatization

In October 2000, the Fifth Plenary Session of the 15th CPC Central Committee delivered and approved the Proposal of the CPC Central Committee for the Formulation of the 10th Five-Year Plan for National Economic and Social Development, pointing out that "China shall strive to promote the national economy and social informatization as a strategic initiative to fulfil the overall layout of modernization. Moreover, industrialization driven by informatization with the advantages of the later contributed to the leapfrog development of productive forces."[1] This is the first time the country clarified the strategic policy of information technology driven industrialization. The CPC central committee and the State Council envisioned to combine informatization and industrialization from the perspective of strategic development, promote industrial optimization and upgrading with informatization, and accelerate the process of industrialization and modernization in order to achieve leapfrog and catch-up development of China's backward productivity. In order to promote the development of information technology, the state has made the following specific requirements on information technology, information infrastructure, and the development of information industry.

First, promote the innovation and development of information technology and improve the ability of independent innovation. China has taken information technology as a strategic high-tech research and concentrated on making breakthroughs in key areas such as information technology, biotechnology, new material technology, advanced manufacturing technology, and aerospace technology.

Second, strengthen the development and utilization of information resources, promote the application of information technology in the fields of finance, finance and taxation, trade, etc., and accelerate the development of e-commerce, online education, etc.

Third, strengthen the construction of modern information infrastructure, develop and improve the national high-speed broadband transmission network, expand the use of the internet, and increase the popularity of computer and network applications.

Fourth, advance the progress of the information industry through the industrialization of core information technology such as ultra-large-scale integrated circuits, high-performance computers, large-scale system software, ultra-high-speed network systems,

---

[1] "The Proposal of the CPC Central Committee for the Formulation of the 10th Five-Year Plan for National Economic and Social Development", *People's Daily (Overseas)*, Oct. 19, 2000.

a new generation of mobile communication equipment and digital television systems as key fields.[1]

At this stage, the state suggested that multi-faceted information products and network services should be market-oriented and consumers-based to promote the all-round application of information technology in business, education, culture, society and other fields. It's a leap in the process of informatization in China, providing the ideological basis and strategic guidance for the comprehensive development of China's national economy and social informatization. Hu Jintao and other state leaders reiterated to accelerate the innovative development of information technology and industrialization driven by informatization, optimize the industrial structure, and accelerate the informatization of national economy and society in many speeches.

2.4.2 A new trail to industrialization to promote the integration of information technology and industrialization

At the 16th CPC National Congress on November 8, 2002, Jiang Zemin made a report and pointed out that "information technology is an inevitable trend to speed up the realization of industrialization and modernization in China. China should stick to the principles to establish the complementary relationship of informatization and industrialization and start a new path of industrialization where it features high scientific and technological content, effective economic returns, low resources consumption, friendly environment and comprehensive human resource."[2] The state explicitly mentioned a new trail to industrialization to achieve mutual complement and coordination of industrialization and informatization.

In the 17th CPC National Congress on October 15, 2007, Hu Jintao made a report and proposed the development of modern industrial systems promoting the integration of information technology and industrialization vigorously, fostering powerful industry based on the large-scale one, revitalizing the equipment manufacturing industry, as well as eliminating backward industries.[3] The report pointed out a series of vital tasks of

---

[1] The Proposal of the CPC Central Committee for the Formulation of the 10th Five-Year Plan for National Economic and Social Development, *People's Daily (Overseas)*, Oct. 19, 2000.

[2] Jiang Zemin, Build a Well-off Society in an All-Round Way and Create a New Situation in Building Socialism with Chinese Characteristics, Database of the National Congresses of the Communist Party of China, Nov. 8, 2002, http://cpc.people.com.cn/GB/64162/64168/64569/65444/4429125.html.

[3] Hu Jintao, "Hold High the Great Banner of Socialism with Chinese Characteristics and Strive for New Victories in Building a Moderately Prosperous Society in All Aespects", *People's Daily*, Oct. 25, 2007.

informatization, industrialization, urbanization, marketization, internationalization, the full integration of informatization and industrialization to build an industrial power.

2.4.3 Plans of national information development planning to provide strategic deployment for the construction of information technology

In August 2001, the National Informatization Leading Group, with Zhu Rongji as the leader, was reconstituted to further strengthen the leadership of informatization construction and national information security. At the first meeting held the group in December of the same year, Zhu Rongji pointed out that the government should attach great importance to strengthening coordination, insisting on market orientation, preventing duplication of construction, and promoting the construction of informatization in China in a solid manner.[1] The meeting presented that national information technology must follow five guidelines as follows. First, the adherence to be market-oriented and demand-based. Second, the government-led information technology. Third, the combination of information technology and industrial reconstruction. Fourth, the development of competition mechanism and coordination as a whole in order to strive to create a good environment for the development of information technology, to put an end to the duplication of various networks and systems, and to prevent a flurry of construction in accordance with the principle of interconnection and sharing of resources. Fifth, the focus on both external opening up, cooperation and independent research and development.[2]

In October 2002, the National Informatization Leading Group approved the promulgation of the Key Special Plan of Informatization in the 10th Five-Year Plan of National Economic and Social Development, which is the first national informatization plan and a comprehensive document to regulate and guide the construction of national information technology. The plan is designed for the application of information technology, modern information infrastructure and the advancement of electronic information industry as the 10th Five-year of information development of the three major tasks.

In February 2006, the State Council formulated the Outline of the National Program for Long-and Medium-Term Scientific and Technological Development

---

[1] He Jinsong, "The First Meeting of the National Informatization Leading Group Held in Beijing", *Engineering Geology Computer Application*, 2002 (25), p. 31.

[2] Liu Guoguang, "The CPC and Chinese Government's Effort to Promote China's Informatization", *Information China*, 2004 (21), pp. 6-7.

(2006-2020) to add seven aspects of information industry and modern service industry into the outline as a key development area, including modern service industry information support technologies and large-scale application software, key technologies and services of next-generation network, high-performance trusted computers, sensor networks and intelligent information processing, digital media content platform, flat panel display with high-definition large-screen, core application-oriented information security. Moreover, the outline laid a key envision of the development of the intelligent perception technology, self-organizing network technology, virtual reality technology and other information technology as the frontier technology.

In May 2006, the State Council issued the 2006-2020 National Informatization Development Strategy, which is another programmatic document for the development of information technology in China. The strategic priorities of national deployment include promoting IT application in national economy, implementing e-government, promoting IT application through society, improving comprehensive information infrastructure, strengthening the development and utilization of information resources, improving the competitiveness of the information industry, building a national information security assurance system, improving the national information technology application capability, and creating an informatization talent pool. Six strategic action plans were implemented to identify priorities in light of their national conditions, including national information technology application education and training, e-commerce action, e-government action, network media information resources development and utilization, the bridge of the digital divide, and key information technology independent innovation. The state implemented the policy of focusing on development and made full use of the selected units to promote work in the entire area to gradually promote the construction of information technology.

2.4.4 Promoting the construction of information infrastructure to advance triple-network convergence (telecom, radio and TV, and Internet networks)

The Ministry of Industry and Information Technology was established to take charge of the work of national IT application due to super-ministry reform implemented by the State Council in March 2008.

Telecommunications, radio and television, and internet services over a single broadband connection were unrevealed in the Report on the Work of the Government in 2009. In January 2010, the State Council promulgated the Triple-Network Convergence in China which included two stages, namely, trial phase (2010-2012) and popularization phase (2013-2015). The both services of radio and television, and telecommunications were given key priorities to carry out in certain areas where conditions permitted to carry out pilot. Experience should be summarized to promote the overall integration of telecommunications, radio and television, and internet services over a single broadband connection. In March 2010, then Vice Premier Zhang Dejiang emphasized to strengthen independent innovation and try to establish a model of a single broadband connection in telecommunications, radio and television, and internet services in the light of China's conditions during his visit of 2010 China Content Broadcasting Network. The General Office of the State Council unveiled the list of the first the Triple-Network convergence pilot cities, and this work was officially launched on July 1, 2010. The list of of pilot cities to launch the Triple-Network convergence plan at the second stage was released in December 2011.

The General Office of the State Council released the Plan for Promoting Tri-Networks Integration on August 25, 2015 to accelerate the plan implemented across the country. The interconnection of information network infrastructure and resource sharing was driven by the development of the Tri-Networks Integration plan.

At the same stage, the country made a plan to accelerate the development of China's next-generation internet industry in order to build a broadband-based, converged, secure and wide next-generation national information infrastructure, promote the upgrading of website systems, and facilitate the commercialization of the next-generation internet. During the stage, the state accelerated the process of intelligent transformation of key infrastructures, and promoted the R&D and application of new-generation mobile communications, next-generation internet core equipment and smart terminals through building broadband, wide, converged and secure information network infrastructure.

2.4.5 Improvement of information technology in all aspects

Improve information technology in all aspects was pointed out in the 12th Five-Year Plan for National Economic and Social Development of the People's Republic of China. The specific ways were involved in restructuring of key industries, strengthening the technological transformation of enterprises, deepening the application of information technology in R&D, design, manufacturing, marketing management, recycling and other aspects of the product life cycle in three aspects including the acceleration of the informatization of the economy and society, strong network and secure information, and the construction of next-generation information infrastructure so as to improve overall information technology in all aspects. A focus on strategic emerging industries was promoted in the field of new generation of information technology industries such as the new generation of mobile communications, next-generation internet, the Triple-Network convergence, Internet of Things, cloud computing, integrated circuits, OLED, high-end software, high-end servers and information services in order to drive economic restructuring and transformation and upgrading.

Besides, the state actively adopts policies to develop informatization in agriculture, service industry and government to improve informatization in all respects.

2.4.5.1   Development of modern agriculture driven by information technology

The State Council released the National Modern Agriculture Development Plan (2011-2015) in January 2012. The plan added the project of agricultural information construction into one of the key tasks to develop modern agriculture, such as the proposal of building a number of agricultural production and operation information demonstration base and comprehensive agricultural information service platform, the establishment of shared agricultural information comprehensive database, networked information service support system, and agricultural Internet of Things application demonstration. The implementation of agricultural information technology project is the catalyst to guarantee agricultural modernization.

2.4.5.2   Acceleration of logistics service industry information application

In March 2009, the State Council released the Adjustment and Revitalization Plan of the Logistics Industry, pointing out the improvement of informatization of enterprise logistics management and logistics in order to develop modern logistics industry and other industries driven by logistics services, with the support of advanced technology and the focus on logistics integration and informatization. In August 2011, General Office of the State Council unveiled the Opinions on the Policies and Measures for Promoting the Sound Development of the Logistics Industry, which pointed out to promote the innovation and application of logistics technology and strengthen independent R&D of new logistics technologies, with a focus on supporting key technologies such as cargo tracking and positioning, radio frequency identification, logistics information platform, smart transportation, logistics management software, and mobile logistics information services. Meanwhile, the demonstration and application of the Internet of Things should be timely piloted in the field of logistics to improve the efficiency of logistics services and business management.

2.4.5.3 Vigorous development of e–government and improvement of the level of IT application of government services

At this stage, the internet was applied to government management and services to improve the e-government steadily. On January 1, 2006, the Chinese Central Government's official Web Portal (www.gov.cn) was launched. The 165th executive meeting of the State Council on January 17, 2007 adopted the Open Government Information Regulation of the People's Republic of China, which came into effect on May 1, 2008. The main website of central-level transmission network and national e-government network was officially launched to formulate the framework of the unified national e-government network on September 30, 2007.[1]

In order to strengthen the management of government information public, the State Council released the Notice on Further Strengthening the Management of Government Websites, which required a sound mechanism to give full play to the information public and interactive communication role of government websites, as well as standardized management and security to further promote the development of e-government. The subsequent release of the Opinions on Further Promoting Open Government and Enhancing Government Services clarified to promote the application of telecommunications networks, broadband networks, the internet and other modern technological means in government services, with focus on strengthening the construction of government websites and improving portal functions as well as the level of information technology in government services.

2.5　New era of accelerated development (2012 to present)

Facing with the complex world economic environment and the new normal of domestic economic development since the 18th CPC National Congress in November 2012, the CPC Central Committee, with Xi Jinping at its core, risen to the challenge and created new progress to comprehensively deepen reform, contrive new conceptions on the path of IT development with Chinese characteristics, and bear the fruit of historic achievements in China's socialist modernization with its guidance. At the 19th CPC National Congress in 2017, Xi Jinping pointed out, "With decades of hard work, socialism with Chinese characteristics has crossed the threshold into a new era. This is a

---

[1] China Internet Network Information Center (CNNIC), The Internet Timeline of China Over the Years.

new historic juncture in China's development."[1] Socialism with Chinese characteristics has entered a new era, and the construction of information technology has also entered a new period of development. Xi Jinping proposed to actively build an innovative country, boost China's strength in manufacturing, cyberspace, digital, and implementing the strategy of developing the country through science and education, the innovation-driven strategy, the big data strategy and the talent strategy for powerful nation. Xi Jinping's new thoughts on information technology construction were sticked to the people-centered development ideology and actively promote the reform of the internet global governance system under the framework of a community with a shared future for mankind so as to achieve the coordinated development of information technology construction and information security.

Under the leadership of Xi Jinping's important discourses on information technology, China's information technology has entered a new era of the acceleration of development with the ability to innovate and apply information technology enhancing information resources integrating, information infrastructure evolving, upgrading and developing in a coordinated manner between urban and rural areas, e-commerce and e-government upgrading comprehensively, and a series of significant achievements being made in information technology construction.

2.5.1 Introduction and development of the new strategy of the four integrations (industrialization, IT application, urbanization and agricultural modernization)

The strategy of a new road of industrialization—taking the IT industry to promote industrialization and letting industrialization support the development of the IT industry, was put forward at the 16th CPC National Congress. To promote the integration of information technology application and industrialization vigorously was raised at the 17th CPC National Congress. The promotion of IT application was required to be in tandem with coordinated development and positive interaction between new industrialization, urbanization and agricultural modernization at the18th CPC National Congress. Hu Jintao made a report and proposed integrating the development of industrialization, IT application, urbanization and agricultural modernization at the 18th CPC National Congress on November 8, 2012, "We should keep to the Chinese-style

---

[1] Xi Jinping, *Secure a Decisive Victory in Building a Moderately Prosperous Society in All Respects and Strive for the Great Success of Socialism with Chinese Characteristics for a New Era*, Beijing: People's Publishing House, 2017, p. 10.

path of carrying out industrialization in a new way and advancing IT application, urbanization and agricultural modernization. We should promote integration of IT application and industrialization, interaction between industrialization and urbanization, and coordination between urbanization and agricultural modernization, thus promoting harmonized development of industrialization, IT application, urbanization and agricultural modernization."[1]

On December 31, 2012, the CPC Central Committee and the State Council adopted the Several Opinions on Accelerating the Development of Modern Agriculture and Further Strengthening the Vigorous Development of Rural Areas, emphasizing to make overall plans for coordinating development of industrialization, informatization, urbanization and agricultural modernization.

Xi Jinping made a further report to the 19th CPC National Congress on October 18, 2017, that "we must see that the market plays the decisive role in resource allocation, the government plays its role better, and new industrialization, IT application, urbanization, and agricultural modernization go hand in hand".[2]

The overall integration became an important part for national strategic layout since the 18th CPC National Congress. The integration of information technology and industrialization, urbanization and agricultural modernization, drove and catalyzed the development of the latter three to become a new one.

2.5.2　Focus of R&D and application in the new generation of information technology

The focus of R&D and application at this stage put an emphasis on IoT and cloud computing as the representative of the new generation of information technology. The state proactively encouraged technological innovation and boosted the application and promotion of modern information technology such as mobile internet, big data, IoT, cloud computing, BeiDou Navigation, artificial intelligence.

2.5.2.1　Actively promoting the development and application of IoT and establishing the IoT industrial system

The IoT is a new generation of intensive concentration and comprehensive application of information technology, with a powerful drive, strong pervasion and

---

[1] Hu Jintao, "Firmly March on the Path of Socialism with Chinese Characteristics and Strive to Complete the Building of a Moderately Prosperous Society in All Respect", *People's Daily*, Nov. 9, 2012.

[2] Xi Jinping, *Secure a Decisive Victory in Building a Moderately Prosperous Society in All Respects and Strive for the Great Success of Socialism with Chinese Characteristics for a New Era*, Beijing: People's Publishing House, 2017, pp. 21-22.

comprehensive benefits. The development and application of the IoT played a significant role in promoting industrial restructuring and upgrading the way of development. IoT was put into the first list of seven strategic emerging industries according to the Decision of the State Council on Accelerating the Fostering and Development of Strategic and Strategic Emerging Industries in order to accelerate the cultivation of new generation information technology for the country. It became a national development strategy and entered the stage of pilot application. In February 2013, the State Council released the Guiding Opinions on Promoting the Orderly and Healthy Development of the Internet of Things, pointing out to promote the establishment of IoT industry system with an internationally competitiveness, realize the wide application of IoT in various fields of economy and society, promote the transformation of production life and social management to the direction of intelligence, refinement and networking, so as to improve the level of national economy and social life informatization. Finally, IoT came to the commercial application stage and was spread nationwide.

2.5.2.2 Formulating innovative development measures for cloud computing and supporting key technology R&D and major project construction of cloud computing

The state cultivated new industries and new business models based on cloud computing, formulated policies and measures to promote the innovative development of cloud computing, fueled the in-depth application of cloud computing in economic production and social life, and made cloud data to facilitate start businesses and households. The state took the construction of IoT application demonstration project as a key and strategic project of emerging industries innovation and development in the 12th Five-Year Plan for National Economic and Social Development of People's Republic of China at the early stage in 2011. The state had taken measures to promote the innovation, promotion and application of cloud computing since the 18th CPC National Congress. The State Council released the Opinions on Promoting the Innovative Development of Cloud Computing and Cultivating New Business Forms of the Information Industry on January 6, 2015. The opinions was under the basic guidance of market-oriented, coordinated, innovation-driven and secured principles to continuously enhance the ability of cloud computing services and its independent innovation, explore new models of e-government cloud computing development, and strengthen the development and application of big data as well as the overall layout of cloud computing infrastructure, so as to improve the security capabilities of information technology.

2.5.2.3 Constructing artificial intelligence with first-mover advantages to cultivate new engine of economic development

Artificial intelligence (AI) has come to be a strategic technology leading the future economic development into a new stage of development driven by information technology and big data. The State Council released the Development Plan on the New Generation of Artificial Intelligence in July 2017, stating to build system of AI science and technology innovation and an intelligent infrastructure, seize new opportunities for the development of AI. and cultivate new engines for China's economic development. The state laid an layout for projects of major new-generation AI science and technology to promote the development of AI. The Ministry of Science and Technology of the People's Republic of China built an innovation platform to promote the development of a new generation of AI through overall planning. On November 15, 2017, the Ministry of Science and Technology announced the first list of national inclusive innovation platforms for a new generation of AI as follows, Autonomous driving of Baidu, city brain of AliCloud, medical imaging of Tencent, and intelligent voice system of iFLYTEK.[1]

2.5.3 More comprehensive and coordinated development of information infrastructure

2.5.3.1 Promoting the evolution and upgrading of information infrastructure and actively building a data-sharing platform

The improvement of information infrastructure is a key factor in the development of information technology for the country. The state had launched a number of initiatives since the 18th CPC National Congress to accelerate the evolution and upgrade of information infrastructure, speed up the construction of information and data platforms, and boost the comprehensive application and service capabilities of the national information infrastructure. Meanwhile, the state is proactively designing a data-sharing network and developing a complete information service chain on the basis of data accessibility, storage, processing, mining and open sharing.

---

[1] "The Full Launch of Plans for a New Generation of Artificial Intelligence Development", *Economic Information Daily*, Nov. 16, 2017.

The State Council released the 12th Five-Year Plan for Building National Capacity for Independent Innovation on January 15, 2013, proposing to lay a consolidation for science and technology innovation, to accelerate the construction of scientific data platforms, and to strengthen the construction of China's science and technology resource-sharing network. On February 23, 2013, the State Council rolled out the *Medium and Long-Term Plan for Key National Technology Infrastructure Construction* (2012-2030), proposing to build future network research facilities to address scientific and technological issues in the development of future networks and information systems so as to provide experimental verification support for the development of future network technologies. The Several Opinions of the State Council on Promoting Information Consumption and Expanding Domestic Demand was promulgated in August 2013, requiring to accelerate the evolution and upgrade of information infrastructure and provide a sound environment for information consumption.

2.5.3.2 Implementation of "Broadband China" strategy to promote the comprehensive, balanced and coordinated development of broadband networks

Broadband network is a strategic public infrastructure for economic and social development in the new era, playing a positively essential role in promoting information consumption and the transformation of production and development mode. The overall development of broadband network was an important strategic deployment of national informatization. It was since the reform and opening up in 1978 that China made achievements in expanding the coverage of broadband network, proceeding greatly in broadband technology and enhancing the application capacity. Nevertheless, China's broadband network had some fields to be improved, including defining its role in public infrastructure, balancing its layout in regional and urban-rural development, providing sufficient application services, contriving technical originality and creating favorable development environment.

The state put forward the "Broadband China" strategy for a more comprehensive, balanced and coordinated development of broadband networks The State Council rolled out the "Broadband China" Strategy and Its Implementation Plan on August 1, 2013, making the specific technical route and development schedule, including the stage of comprehensive speed-up (to the end of 2013), the stage of promotion and popularization (2014-2015), and the stage of optimization and upgradation (2016-2020). The plan was implemented to give the priority to promote the coordinated development of regional broadband networks as a key construction to coordinate the development of broadband networks in the eastern, central and western regions and rural areas.

The CPC Central Committee and the State Council carried out positive guidance and preferential policies for the coordinated development of information infrastructure between urban and rural areas and between different regions. At the Second Session of the 12th National People's Congress on March 5, 2014, Li Keqiang delivered a speech and emphasized the role of enhancing the economy driven by domestic demand as a main engine. He stressed, "We will promote information consumption; implement China's broadband strategy; speed up the development of 4G mobile communications; build 100M fiber optic networks in cities and extend broadband connectivity to rural villages; greatly increase the speed of the Internet." During a fact-finding trip of for the development and opening up in the west of China to Chongqing, from April 27 to 29, 2014, Li Keqiang stated to accelerate the development of broadband and other infrastructure in the western regions, so that information services and other modern services industry could also be attracted to the west to play the role of increasing job opportunities and drive income growth.

The program of national information infrastructure construction was in tandem with rural poverty alleviation so that people below the poverty line in rural areas could be provided more employment opportunities through the popularization and application of information networks and they could be given more access to online information in an effort to bridge the digital divide. In January 2014, the General Offices of the CPC Central Committee and the State Council issued the Opinions on Innovating New Mechanisms to Firmly Promote the Work of Poverty Aid Development in Rural Areas, pointing out that it was necessary to promote IT application in poor villages as a key work. It made a point to promote the establishment of incorporated villages in poverty-stricken areas to connect to the internet certified by administrative organs. Efforts would be intensified to eliminate the digital divide in order to promote the balance of development.

In order to strengthen spending on information goods and services, stimulate effective investment and reduce cost of start-ups, the General Office of the State Council released the Guiding Opinions on Accelerating the Construction of High-Speed Broadband Networks, Boosting Internet Speed and Lowering Internet Charges on May 16, 2015, proposing to significantly increase network rates, effectively reduce network tariffs and continuously improve service levels by accelerating infrastructure construction.

2.5.4 Promoting full integration of IT application with industrialization to build a strong manufacturing power

Since the founding of the People's Republic of China, especially the reform and opening up in 1978, China has established a comprehensive and independent industrial system, with the manufacturing industry continuing to develop and the level of industrialization keeping improved. However, Chinese manufacturing, compared to world's advanced manufacturing, is large but not yet strong in terms of independent innovation, resource utilization efficiency, the degree of information technology and so on. Since the 18th CPC National Congress, China has been promoting the deep integration of IT application and industrialization, using next-generation information technology to advance the transformation and upgrading of traditional manufacturing industries, and striving to build an advanced manufacturing industry with international competitiveness.

On May 8, 2015, the State Council issued Made in China 2025, the guide for China's manufacturing strategy during the coming decade for the purpose of China's large manufacturing to become strong within three decades. Three-Step Strategy for Economic Development to realize strategic manufacturing goals concentrated on accelerating the deep integration of next-generation information technology and manufacturing industry and gave priority to promoting smart manufacturing. First step: By 2025, China will strive to turn into a major manufacturing power in ten years. Second step: By 2035, Chinese manufacturing will reach an intermediate level among world manufacturing powers. Third step: By 2049, the centennial of the founding of New China, China's manufacturing sector status will become more consolidated and China will become the leader among the world's manufacturing powers. Made in China 2025 contributed to promote the full integration of next generation IT and industrialization and focused on the development of next-generation information technology industry, including integrated circuits and special equipment, communication equipment, operating systems and industrial software.

China insisted on market orientation, guiding enterprises to adapt to and lead the market, making breakthroughs in "Made in China + internet" in a fast way, and realizing Made in China to a medium-high level for a strong manufacturing power. While presiding over an executive meeting of the State Council on January 27, 2015, then Premier Li Keqiang called for promoting the integration of Made in China 2025 and "internet +", with a focus on advancing digitalization, network, smart manufacturing, accelerating the construction of automatic control and perception technology, industrial cloud and smart service platform, the industrial internet and other new foundations of manufacturing, so as to cultivate new models, new industries, and new products. On June 16, 2015, the State Council decided to establish a national leading group for a manufacturing power in order to promote the implementation of the manufacturing power strategy and strengthen the overall planning and policy coordination in relation to this work.

On May 13, 2016, the State Council issued the Guiding Opinions on Enhancing the Integrated Development of the Manufacturing Industry and the Internet, deploying the deepening of the integration and development of manufacturing industry and the internet, collaborating to promote the Made in China 2025 and "internet +" actions, supporting the cross-sectoral integration of manufacturing enterprises and internet enterprises, so as to cultivate new modes of integration between manufacturing and the internet, and accelerate the construction of manufacturing power. On May 19, 2016, the CPC Central Committee and the State Council issued the Outline of the Innovation-Driven Development Strategy of China, proposing to accelerate the deep integration of industrialization and informatization on the basis of technologies such as digitalization, networking, smart, and eco-friendly networks to enhance industrial competitiveness, to promote cross-sectoral innovation of emerging technologies in various fields, and to build a modern industrial technology system with reasonable structure, advanced management, as well as open, inclusive, independent, controllable and international competitiveness. In December 2017, China began to fully deploy the construction of Made in China 2025 national demonstrations with advancing this work by pilot, to explore new models and new paths of manufacturing transformation and upgrading. "Made in China" is transforming into "Intelligent Manufacturing in China", and China is moving forward from a manufacturer of quantity to one of the qualities on account of the next-generation information technology and the internet.

2.5.5 Promoting the innovative development of new information industries

New models of industries and new industries are emerging, including geomatics industry, digital content industry, and production-oriented service industries which become a new growth point of the economy with the innovative development of information technology. Emerging information industry plays an important role in accelerating the shift of growth model in economy, ensuring the wellbeing of the people, and improving their lives.

2.5.5.1   China is promoting the development of geographic information industry and digital content industry

China continues to expand the content of the information industry, extending the information industry in both scope and implication. At the early stage of information technology, China concentrated on the development of IT industry based on IT application and communication technology. China has been promoting the development of information content industry and fostering the new IT industry since the 21st century.

The Opinions of the General Office of the State Council on Promoting the Development of Geographic Information Industry was released on January 22, 2014, which focused on the promotion of remote sensing data acquisition and processing capabilities, the revitalization of geographic information equipment manufacturing, the improvement of geographic information software R&D and industrialization, the development of the integration of geographic information, navigation and positioning, as well as the acceleration of deeper applications of geographic information. On February 26, 2014, the Opinions of the State Council on Promoting the Integrated Development of Cultural Creativity and Design Services with Relevant Industries was released, encouraging to accelerate the development of digital content industry, to promote the digitalization and networking process of the production, dissemination and consumption of cultural products and services, to strengthen the content support, creativity and design enhancement of culture to the information industry, and to accelerate the cultivation of the new industry of two-way deep integration.[1]

2.5.5.2   Acceleration of the development of productive service industries to promote industrial restructuring and upgrading

China attaches importance to the innovative development of productive service industry, focuses on productive service industry to upgrade the structure of traditional industries, and accelerates the improvement of weak links and key areas in productive service industry.

China has released policies to promote logistics informatization, strengthen the application of Beidou navigation, IoT, cloud computing, big data, mobile internet and other advanced information technology in the application of logistics, drive the development of public information platform for transportation and logistics, advance effective docking of logistics information and public service information, realize

---

[1] The State Council, Opinions of the State Council on Promoting the Integrated Development of Cultural Creativity and Design Services with Revelant Industries, the Chinese Central Government's Official Website, Mar. 14, 2014, http://www.gov.cn/zhengce/content/2014 -03/14/content_8713.htm.

interconnectivity, propel the development of modern logistics, for the purpose of the coordinated development of modern logistics and manufacturing industry so as to boost the development of productive service industry, On September 12, 2014, the State Council issued the Medium-and Long-Term General Plan for the Development of the Logistics Industry (2014-2020) to focus on further improvement of the logistics information technology.

2.5.5.3 Promotion of the "internet +" to boost product and service innovation

Since the 18th CPC National Congress, China has made progress in internet technologies, industries, applications and cross-sectoral cooperation for the deep integration and innovative development of the internet and other industries. China is taking advantage of next-generation information technology such as the internet, IoT, cloud computing, to promote the transformation of production and management models and drive social and economic innovation and development. New industries have made great progress in "internet + " initiative in entrepreneurship and innovation, collaborative manufacturing, modern agriculture, inclusive finance, modern logistics, e-commerce, as well as artificial intelligence. On July 1, 2015, the State Council released the Guiding Opinions on Vigorously Advancing the "Internet +" Action, proposing to establish a networked, intelligent, service-oriented and collaborative "internet +" industrial ecosystem and giving rise to new economic growth areas in "internet +".

China supports the development of "internet +" service industry. The Several Opinions of the State Council on Accelerating the Development of the Modern Insurance Service Industry was released on August 10, 2014. The State Council called for the integration of new generation information technology and insurance service industry, encouraged innovation in insurance products and services, and proposed to support insurance companies to take good use of new technologies such as network, cloud computing, big data and mobile internet to promote innovation in sales channels and service models in the insurance industry.

China has promulgated policies to encourage innovation, regulated and guided the smooth development of "internet+" for the sound application market of "internet+". In July 2015, the People's Bank of China and other nine departments jointly released the Guiding Opinions on Promoting the Sound Development of Internet Finance. It put forward measures to encourage innovation, supported the steady development of internet finance, encouraged innovation in internet finance platforms, products and services to stimulate market vitality. It also encouraged practitioners to cooperate with each other to achieve complementary advantages, broaden financing channels for practitioners to improve the financing environment, adhered to streamline administration and delegate more powers of the government to provide quality services, implemented the improvement of the relevant financial and taxation policies, promoted the construction of credit infrastructure, and fostered supporting services system of the internet finance.

China is encouraging and giving supports to the development of "internet +" mass entrepreneurship and innovation platform. The State Council released the Guiding Opinions on Accelerating the Building of Supporting Platforms for Mass Entrepreneurship and Innovation on September 23, 2015, to encourage and support the rapid development of mass entrepreneurship and innovation supporting platforms based on the internet and other means, such as mass innovation, crowd sourcing, collective support and crowd funding. On May 18, 2016, the "Internet +" Artificial Intelligence Three Year Action and Implementation Plan was released jointly by the National Development and Reform Commission, the Ministry of Science and Technology, the Ministry of Industry and Information Technology, and the Central Network Information Office to boost the development of emerging AI industries, with a focus on the project to develop core technology R&D, industrialization, the public service platform of basic resources.

On October 26, 2015, General Office of the State Council issued the Opinions on Strengthening Control Over Acts of Rights Infringement and Counterfeiting in the Field of the Internet to promote the sound and sustainable development of internet finance and effectively take good use of the positive role of internet finance in supporting mass entrepreneurship and innovation. China is fostering a sound cyberspace environment with a focus on regulation and management to implement the responsibility of enterprises, to strengthen the cooperation on law enforcement and inspection, to improve long-term mechanisms, in response to the illegal and criminal acts of infringing intellectual property rights and selling counterfeit and shoddy goods on the internet. On April 12, 2016, the General Office of the State Council released the Implementation Plan for Special Rectification on Risks in Internet Finance, putting emphasis on peer-to-peer (P2P) network lending and equity crowd-funding business through asset management and cross-border financial business on the internet, third-party payment business, and advertisement in financial sector on the internet.

2.5.5.4 Positive deployment to promote the innovative development of e-commerce

E-commerce has become a new dynamic engine for economic growth in the new era. The state is proactively embracing an environment, and improving policies to explore multi-level and diversified ways of e-commerce development continuously and promote the development of e-commerce vigorously for the enhancement of the leading edge of e-commerce in China, as well as the consolidation of the integration of e-commerce and other industries.

During this period, China promoted the development of e-commerce by policies and measures, including reducing the barriers to entry, increasing financial and fiscal support, improving the regulatory and standard system, as well as strengthening the support of science and technology education. On May 7, 2015, the State Council issued the Opinions on Vigorously Development E-Commerce and Acceleration of Fostering of New Driving Forces for the Economy for a comprehensive deployment and integrated planning, proposing seven following policies to promote the innovative development of e-commerce. First, to create an inclusive environment for e-commerce development through tax reduction and financial services support. Second, to improve employment and entrepreneurship by strengthening personnel training. Third, advance traditional trade and circulation in enterprises and vast rural areas to develop e-commerce and realize transformation and upgrading through financial service innovation. Fourth, to support the construction of logistics and distribution terminals and smart logistics platform and to improve logistics infrastructure. Fifth, to strengthen international cooperation in e-commerce and to improve the efficiency of cross-border e-commerce customs, and to enhance the level of openness to the outside world. Sixth, to construct a security line of defense, to protect e-commerce network security, and to ensure e-commerce trade. Seventh, to improve the system of regulations and standards, to strengthen the construction of credit system, to strengthen science, technology and education support, and to ensure the development of e-commerce.[1] China is working hard take advantage of institutional safeguards to maintain fair competition in e-commerce enterprises, to protect the rights and interests of the workers, to prevent and combat crimes in the field of e-commerce, and to regulate the market and enhance security on the basis of continuously promoting the innovative development of e-commerce through the system.

Efforts have been intensified through links running eastward and westward to proactively promote e-commerce to take great advantage of in domestic and foreign trade activities so as to expand consumption, to promote industrial upgrading, and to

---

[1] The State Council, Opinions on Vigorously Development E-Commerce and Acceleration of Fostering of New Driving Forces for the Economy, the Chinese Central Government's Official Website, May 7, 2015, http: //www. gov.cn/zhengce/content/2015-05/07/content_9707.htm.

embrace new economic growth. The General Office of the State Council released the Opinions on Promoting the Sound Development of Distribution in Domestic Trade on October 24, 2014, proposing to promote the development of modern circulation by strengthening the construction of information technology, regulating and promoting the development of e-commerce, accelerating the development of logistics and distribution, and vigorously developing chain operations, so as to create convenient conditions for domestic information consumption. At the same time, China deployed to promote the healthy and rapid development of cross-border e-commerce proactively by taking use of "internet + foreign trade" to optimize imports and exports.

2.5.6　Overall upgrading of the e-government construction project

China has taken full advantage of platforms of the government websites in public information transparency to promote the development of e-government since the 18th CPC National Congress. China is carrying out the internet plus government services model to promote better information sharing between government departments, to provide more efficient services, to reduce charges of transaction, to promote the communication of government information more transparent, accessible and available, to open to the public, and to attract them to participate the construction of the government websites. The government promotes the integration of offline and online service platforms of government halls by optimizing online service processes, improving the government services, and constructing the platform and system of integrated data-sharing exchange.

The Chinese government has continuously improved its policies and plans via government websites in advancing the modernization of national governance system and capabilities in order to taking advantage of the major government information platform to make it open to the public. The Opinions on Strengthening the Development of Contents of Information on Government Websites was released by the General Office of the State Council on November 17, 2014. It focused on the principles of accomplishing the central task of economic development and serve the overall interests of the country. It also put people first to ensure the interests of the people, made itself open and transparent to the public, strengthened interactions between people and the government. It required more efforts should be made to accelerate reform and innovation of the government websites, attach importance on effectiveness, speed up the release and updating the information on time, interpret the policy of the government fully, make responses to social hotspots positively, strengthen interactive communication with the outside, broaden the website communication channels, create and improve the system for cooperation between different departments, establish ties and collaboration with the press and media, make the content of the government websites in foreign language standardized, coordinate the information mechanism, standardize the process of information release, reinforce the integration of online and offline, define the relationship between outsourcing services and other measures to strengthen the information release of government website, improve the communication capacity of government websites, and improve the supporting system of information content. The Detailed Rules for Implementing the Opinions on Comprehensively Promoting Open Government was promulgated on November 10, 2016 according to the General Office of the State Council. It required strengthening the construction of platforms, the management of government websites, the integration of sharing information resources accessible to other channels, so as to form an integrated government service network and enhance the clustering effect of websites.

The "internet + government services" model made its contribution to improve the administrative efficiency of the government and expand the public engagement in establishment of the government. On September 25, 2016, the State Council issued the Guiding Opinions on Accelerating the Promotion of the "Internet + Government Services" Work, proposing to build the internet plus government services model and a nationwide integrated network by 2020 with joint supports of the central government, all departments, the local government at the provincial level so as to improve government services wisdom significantly, make more intelligent government services, and provide more convenience and efficiency accessible to the public and enterprises. The Guidance on System Construction of the "Internet + Government Services" Technology was released according to the General Office of the State Council on December 20, 2016. It focused on a series of the "internet + government services" business models, including the supporting system, basic platform system, key security technology, evaluation and assessment system, in order to strengthen the national integration of "internet + government services" technology and service system design as a whole, to improve the level of online government services in all regions and departments, and to provide protection for the "internet + government services" technology and service system.

2.5.7　Making coordinated plans for the construction of network security and information technology in a unified way to build an internet power

A plan for building up strength in cyberspace was put forward by the CPC Central Committee and the State Council since the 18th CPC National Congress. To achieve modernization and a strong network driven by information technology plays an important role in implementing the Four-pronged Comprehensive Strategy[1] and is an assured choice to realize the Two Centenary Goals[2] and the great rejuvenation of the Chinese nation.

The Central Leading Group for Cyberspace Affairs (later renamed the Central Cyberspace Affair Commission) was established on February 27, 2014, and held the first meeting, Xi Jinping put emphasis on those efforts should be intensified to build, which was the first time to proposed the goal of building up strength in cyberspace for China. It called for moving toward the basic implementation of network infrastructure, enhancing independent innovation capacity significantly, as well as realizing the comprehensive development of information economy and the continuous progress of strong network security.[3] The 19th CPC National Congress reiterated to build an internet power and digital China in 2017.

In the process of building a strong cyber nation, China emphasizes the coordinated development of cybersecurity and informatization. Xi Jinping pointed out that, "Network security and information technology are like the two wings of a bird or the two wheels of a cart so that the government should make coordinated plans for both and implement them in a unified way while building an internet power with a focus on the coordinated development of network security and information technology for China."[4] The CPC Central Committee attached importance to cyber security, set up a leading group on cybersecurity and informatization, proposed to speed up legislation in the field of internet, and initiated maintaining cybersecurity while delivering a Report on the Work of the Government (2014). The National Security Law of the People's Republic of China, approved on July 1, 2015, put stress on setting cyberspace with the jurisdiction

---

[1] It refers to China's strategic plan for building socialism with Chinese characteristics, that is, to make comprehensive moves to complete a moderately prosperous society in all respects, to further reform, to advance the rule of law, and to strengthen Party self-governance. —*Tr*.

[2] The two goals are to complete a moderately prosperous society in all respects by the centenary of the CPC (founded in 1921), and to build China into a modern socialist country that is prosperous, strong, democratic, culturally advanced, and harmonious by the centenary of the People's Republic of China (founded in 1949). —*Tr*.

[3] [4] Xi Jinping, Working Hard to Build a Large Online Community into a Cyberpower for China. Xinhuanet, Feb. 27, 2014, http: //news.xinhuanet.com/ politics/2014 -02/27/c_119538788.htm.

of national sovereignty and safeguard the sovereignty of cyberspace. The Cybersecurity Law of the People's Republic of China was submitted to the 24th Session of the Standing Committee of the 12th National People's Congress for deliberation and approval and came into effect officially on November 7, 2016. China officially embarked on a stage of protecting network security in accordance with laws to safeguard the sovereignty of cyberspace, national security and social public interests, which marked that China's information security industry has entered a new era.

China focused on enhancing network management and strengthening the security defense capability in cyberspace at the course of building a strong network country. A leading group on informatization network security and informatization under the Ministry of Education was established on October 26, 2016, taking place of the leading group on informatization under the Ministry of Education and the office of promoting the application of information technology in education. The first plenary meeting of the leading group on informatization network security and informatization under the Ministry of Education was held in November 2016 to conduct a special study on securing information security with a focus on raising awareness of the work of network security and informatization.

2.5.8 Strengthening international cooperation in cybersecurity for a community with a shared future in cyberspace

Since the 18th CPC National Congress, the CPC Central Committee, with Xi Jinping at its core, has adhered to a sharing and opening strategy of development, strengthened international cybersecurity cooperation, and built international internet governance system proactively.

For four consecutive World Internet Conferences from 2014 to 2017, China has proposed to proactively promote internet governance, mutually respect cyber sovereignty, and join hands to build a community of destiny in cyberspace. The first World Internet Conference held in Wuzhen, Zhejiang Province, on November 19, 2014, was themed "an interconnected world shared and governed by all", through which China conveyed the concept of shared development to the world. China has always been people-centered and brought the benefit of development of the internet to all. China and other countries around the world have been deepening international cooperation, promoting the interconnection of internet facilities, strengthening cooperation and sharing of internet technologies, working together to foster a peaceful, secure, open and cooperative cyberspace, and putting in place a multilateral, democratic and transparent global internet governance system. Xi Jinping pointed out at the opening ceremony of the Second World Internet Conference in 2015, "Cyberspace is the common space of activities for mankind. The future of cyberspace should be in the hands of all countries. Countries should step up communication, broaden consensus and deepen cooperation to jointly build a community of shared future in cyberspace."[1] Xi Jinping proposed to deepen international cooperation in cyberspace and jointly build a community with a shared future in cyberspace while delivering a video speech at the Third World Internet Conference in 2016. Xi Jinping noted that the transformation of the global internet governance system had entered at a crucial juncture. As a result, building a community with a shared future in cyberspace was an increasing consensus of the international community while expressing a congratulation at the Fourth World Internet Conference in 2017.[2]

As a responsible power, China is taking the lead in building, governing and sharing the international internet. China has positively strengthened its cooperation with the United States on cybersecurity, achieving remarkable results and making important contributions to the promotion of international peace and security in cyberspace. Xi Jinping pointed out headquarters that a secure, stable and prosperous cyberspace was increasingly significant for peace and development in a country and the world, for which he advocated fostering a peaceful, secure, open and cooperative cyberspace while attending a meeting with representatives from both sides attending the eighth China-US Internet Industry Forum at Microsoft Corp on September 23, 2015. In 2015, the heads of state of China and the US reached a five-point consensus on cybersecurity cooperation. China and the US have established a dialogue on law enforcement and cybersecurity as one of four high-level dialogue mechanisms between China and the US. The two heads of China and the US reached a multilateral agreement once again during the visit of Donald Trump, then US President, on November 9, 2017. In terms of cybersecurity, China and the United States agreed to continue to implement the five-point consensus on cybersecurity cooperation between the two countries by taking advantage of the hotline mechanism for combating cybercrime to ensure cybersecurity. Both sides would further strengthen cooperation in cyber counter-terrorism and combated online child pornography, e-mail fraud, cyber theft of corporate intellectual property, as well as cybersecurity of key infrastructure.

---

[1] Xi Jinping, "Build a Community of Shared Future in Cyberspace Jointly", *Xinhua Daily Telegraph*, Dec. 17, 2015.

[2] Xi Jinping, "The Congratulatory Message to the Fourth World Internet Conference", *People's Daily*, Dec. 4, 2017.

Since the 18th CPC National Congress, the CPC Central Committee and the State Council have been implementing the strategy of cyber power and promoting the deep integration of IT and socio-economic development under the principles of promoting development in a coordinated manner, playing the role in leadership of innovation, driving development, bringing benefits to the people, improving win-win cooperation, and ensuring security. The General Offices of the CPC Central Committee and the State Council released the Outline of the National Informatization Development Strategy on July 27, 2016. It was a programmatic document to improve the 2006-2020 National Informatization Development Strategy in light of the new circumstance, playing an essential role in the national strategic system. It was a vital basis for the formulation of policies in the field of informatization.

The 13th Five-year Plan period is an important strategic opportunity period to build a new national competitive advantage, so the country has strengthened the overall planning, taken the initiative to lead the new wave of information revolution, vigorously enhanced the development capacity of information technology, focused on improving the level of economic and social information technology, and constantly optimized the development of information technology environment, so as to maintain network information security. A series of important documents were released successively, including the Outline of the 13th Five-Year Plan for the National Economic and Social Development of the People's Republic of China, the National Development Plan for Strategic Emerging Industries During the 13th Five-Year Plan Period, the 13th Five-Year Plan for National Informatization, and the 13th Five-Year Plan for Employment Promotion. The Central Committee of the CPC and the State Council, put forward a guideline of informatization according to circumstances from home and abroad. The guideline gave priority in 12 fields, including the pre-deployment of new generation information network technology, the construction and application of BeiDou Navigation system, the construction of application infrastructure, new smart city and online Silk Road, the sharing and opening of data resources, the "internet + government services", the informatization of beautiful China, poverty alleviation through the internet, prosperous network culture, online education for all, as well as health China information services.[1]

---

[1] The State Council, Notice on the Release of the 13th Five-Year Plan for National Informatization, the Chinese Central Government's Official Website, Dec. 15, 2016, http://www. gov.cn/zhengce/content/2016-12/27/content_5153411.htm.

Since the 18th CPC National Congress, China's information construction, under the guidance of Xi Jinping's important discourses on information technology in the new era, has made a series of significant achievements and presented new features. The CPC Central Committee and the State Council are promoting the "internet +" action proactively to achieve the "Broadband China" strategy fully, the implementation of the national big data strategy, significant agricultural modernization progress, deep integration of industrialization and information, as well as emerging new industries and new models of business. Xi Jinping proposed building a modernized economic system at the 19th CPC National Congress, strengthening structural reform on the supply side, and implementing rural revitalization strategies, all of which are based on the construction of information technology. Information technology has driven to promote industrial upgrading, improved people's livelihood, and become an important engine for China to achieve socialist modernization. The CPC Central Committee put people-centered development philosophy into practice, adhered to the concept of shared development, and formulated inclusive policies to bring the benefits of information development for all.

Chapter 3
The Achievements of China's Internet and Information Technology Development

The internet has become a key information infrastructure for all countries around the world in the information age, and its development has contributed to continuously transformation and upgrading of the economy and society. In recent years, China has accelerated the construction of network information infrastructure, expanded the coverage of broadband networks, increased the transmission and access capacity, enhanced the innovation capacity of broadband technology. With the increasing improvement of the level of internet application, new industries such as internet-based e-commerce have been flourishing. The Fifth Plenary Session of the 18th CPC Central Committee proposed the plan of building up China's strength in cyberspace, which accelerated the step of China's progress from scale to strength in cyberspace.

3.1   Course of development of the internet in China

China's internet application started in the 1980s. After the development of the past 30 years, China has made remarkable achievements and become a major cyber power that attracted the worldwide attention. At the Third China Internet Conference in 2004, the China Internet Network Information Center (CNNIC) launched the theme exhibition of China's Internet History Corridor, and divided the development course of internet in China into five phases based on the trajectory of its construction and application, including the exploration phase from 1987 to 1994, the build-up phase from 1993 to 1996, the start-up phase from 1996 to 1998, the internet booming phase from 1999 to 2002, and the prosperous and future phase after 2003.[1]

---

[1] China Internet Network Information Center, China Internet History Corridor, China Internet Network Information Center Website, Aug. 31, 2004. http://www.cnnic.cn/gywm/xwzx/rdxw/2004nrd/201207/t20120710_31400.htm.

Since 2004, the internet has experienced decades of golden development period, and the internet technology and application has changed dramatically. Therefore, we should actively deal with the development and changes of the internet and re-divide the stages of its 30 years of development. From the author's point of view, the internet in China has roughly gone through three stages of development since 1987, including the start-up phase, the development phase and the acceleration phase.

3.1.1   Phase Ⅰ: start-up phase from 1987 to 1993

According to the CNNIC, with the help of a research team at the Karlsruhe Institute of Technology in Germany in 1987, Professor Wang Yunfeng and Doctor Li Chengjiong built an e-mail node at the Institute of Computer Application (ICA) in Beijing and successfully sent an e-mail to Germany on September 20 with the message "across the Great Wall we can reach every corner in the world", marking the official start of the internet in China. On Novembcr 28, 1990, China accomplished the registration of its top-level domain name ".CN", which enabled China to have its own identity on the international internet, but the server of the top-level domain name was temporarily located at the Karlsruhe Institute of Technology, Germany. At the end of 1992, the construction of National Computing and Networking Facility of China (NCFC), including Chinese Academy of Sciences Network (CASNET), Tsinghua University Network (TUNET) and Peking University Network (PUNET) was all completed. In December 1993, the NCFC backbone project was completed, and used optical fiber lines to build up the backbone network and connect the network of Peking University, Tsinghua University and Chinese Academy of Sciences via the bridge.[1]

The internet application in China was marked by the beginning of sending e-mails. In the development period, China had not yet achieved a fully functional linking to the international internet, and until 1993, the NCFC backbone network could only achieve interconnection among three networks of the CASNET, TUNET and PUNET. Therefore, the Chinese internet did not achieve the real sense of application at this stage.

3.1.2   Phase Ⅱ: development phase from 1994 to 1998

With the connection of NCFC project to the internet in 1994 as a symbol, China achieved a fully functional interaction with the internet, thus opening up the full-featured internet service and realizing the real internet application service. Since 1994, China has become the country with a truly fully functional internet. Since then,

---

[1] China Internet Network Information Center, Chronology of Chinese Internet Development.

various internet application projects in China has been launched and expanded nationwide.

The Institute of High Energy Physics of the Chinese Academy of Sciences set up and launched the first WEB server in China on May 15, 1994. In March 1995, the Chinese Academy of Sciences completed the remote connection of four branches in Shanghai, Hefei, Wuhan and Nanjing, and the internet expanded its application to the whole country. National backbone network, HINANet, was completed and officially opened in January 1996, and it was also the first set of nationwide public computer internet network to provide services. Since then, the internet has fit into people's lives.[1]

3.1.3   Phase Ⅲ: acceleration phase (1999 to present)

Since 1999, with the opening of the satellite backbone of China Education and Research Network (CERNET) and the national internet intermodal center in Beijing, the operation speed of Chinese internet has increased dramatically. Marked by the completion of China Unicom's CDMA mobile communication network, China's mobile communication technology has developed into a new phase.

In this phase, China first introduced various policies to support the development of the internet. On August 1, 2013, the State Council issued the "Broadband China" Strategy and Its Implementation Plan, emphasizing the strengthening of strategic guidance and systematic deployment to promote the rapid and healthy development of broadband as a strategic public infrastructure, and setting the development goals for two phases of 2015 and 2020. In July 2015, the State Council issued the Guiding Opinions of the State Council on Vigorously Advancing the "Internet Plus" Action, aiming to drive the development of traditional industries through the internet and created a new form of economic and social development with the internet as the infrastructure and innovation elements. And in October 2015, the Fifth Plenary Session of the 18th CPC Central Committee considered and adopted the Proposals of the CPC Central Committee for Formulating the 13th Five-Year Plan for National Economic and Social Development, which proposed to implement the development strategy of national power and accelerate the construction of a new generation of high-speed, mobile, secure and ubiquitous information infrastructure.

With the support of national policies, the efficiency of internet application had

---

[1]   China Internet Network Information Center, Chronology of Chinese Internet Development.

been improving, and the scope of internet application had been broadening, with new models such as e-commerce, e-government and e-banking emerging. Currently, Chinese internet has entered a period of accelerated development and has begun to develop towards the IoT and the next generation internet.

With the deepening application of the internet, China began to actively deploy the development of the next-generation internet, and built the first Chinese next-generation exchange point DRAGONTAP in 2000. In August 2003, the State Council officially approved the launch of the "China Next Generation Internet" Strategic Programme and actively carried out pilot applications. On December 23, 2004, the IPv6 address of the national top-level domain name ".CN" server in China was successfully registered to the global domain name root server, and the national domain name system in China entered the next-generation internet.[1]

The IoT is an integration of the new generation of information technology, which enters the innovative development stage based on the internet. The IoT in China was initially known as a sensor network. At present, China is one of the four leading countries in international sensor network standardization, and the standardization of the IoT has reached the world's advanced level. The IoT is a representative of the new generation of information technology that China has focused on, and is also a strategic emerging industry that China has focused on and supported.

China has continued to strengthen the top-level design of IoT development, formulate development plans, and promote the R&D, promotion and application of IoT technology. According to the Decision of the State Council on Accelerating the Fostering and Development of Strategic Emerging Industries in 2010, the IoT became the first batch of strategic emerging industries cultivated by the state. In 2011, China set up a special fund for it to increase capital investment and promote its development. In the Report of the Work of the Government (2012) issued by the State Council, IoT was presented as an attachment, which was the first time that China officially defined its concept. Moreover, China proposed to actively establish an internationally competitive system of the IoT industry, and thus it was gradually moving towards the phase of industrialization development in 2013. The projects such as the 12th Five-Year Development Plan for the Internet of Things and the Outline of the 13th Five-Year Plan for the National Informatization were issued intensively, which focused on supporting the development of the IoT, clearly proposed action guidelines for the development of

---

[1] China Internet Network Information Center, Chronology of Chinese Internet Development.

the IoT, and implemented the IoT application demonstration project, thus promoting its deepening application and productivity transformation.

3.2 Development level of internet in China

With the support of national policies, China has made great achievements in the internet industry and become a pivotal internet power. As of June 30, 2008, the total number of internet users in China reached 253 million, ranking first in the world for the first time. On July 22, 2008, the number of ".CN" domain name registrations reached 12.188 million, becoming the world's top-level domain name for the first time. After nearly 10 more years of development, the scale of Chinese internet users amounted to 751 million by June 2017, and the internet popularity rate reached 54.3%.[1]

3.2.1 Continuous improvement of the network infrastructure in China

With the promulgation of 2006-2020 National Informatization Development Strategy and the implementation of the "Broadband China" strategy, China has made the improvement of comprehensive information infrastructure and promoted the network convergence, so as to realize the transformation to next-generation networks as the strategic focus on its information technology application. Besides, China has combined network infrastructure and industrial innovation, and also connected network upgrade with industrial innovation, so as to promote the accelerated development of the broadband infrastructure. At the strategic perspective, China has promoted the "network convergence" including telecommunications, radio and television, and internet services over a single broadband connection from the service, network and terminal levels, developed various forms of broadband access, and vigorously boosted the popularization and application of the internet. At the same time, the photoelectric sensing, RFID and other technologies should be applied to expand network functions and thus steadily make the transformation to the next-generation network.

In 2016, the Outline of the 13th Five-Year Plan for National Economic and Social Development of the People's Republic of China proposed to accelerate the construction of the new-generation information infrastructure of high speed, mobility, security and ubiquity, promote the widespread application of information network technologies, and expand the network economic space by improving the new generation of high-speed

---

[1] China Internet Network Information Center, CNNIC.

fiber optic network, building an advanced and ubiquitous wireless broadband network, accelerating the development and application of new information network technologies, and promoting the speed upgrade and cost reduction of broadband network. Under the guidance of the national strategic planning, China has been actively building a modern communication backbone network, accelerating the construction of the fourth generation of mobile communication (4G) network, promoting the fifth generation of mobile communication (5G) and the research of ultra-broadband key technology, and launching the 5G commercialization. The TD-LTE 4G mobile communication network with independent intellectual property rights has been a global leader in scale, and the third phase of 5G technology development trials is being actively deployed, which is the final step towards the 5G commercialization. China has also advanced the layout of the next-generation internet and promoted the full evolution to Internet Protocol Version 6 (IPv6).

By June 2017, the number of IPv4 addresses in China reached 338 million, and the number of IPv6 addresses accessed 21,283 blocks/32, both of which ranked second in the world. Meanwhile, the number of Chinese websites was 5.06 million, and the international export bandwidth reached 7,974,779 Mbps, an increase of 20.1% from the end of 2016. At present, China has built the world's largest 4G network and established 2.99 million base stations with 890 million users, and the total length of fiber optic cable lines has reached 30.41 million kilometers, ranking the first in the world.

3.2.2 Significant improvement in the level of internet access

According to The 1st China Statistical Report on Internet Development released by China Internet Network Information Center (CNNIC) in 1997, as of October 31, 1997, the number of internet computers in China was 299,000, of which only 49,000 were directly on the internet, and 250,000 were dial-up computers, with about 1,500 "WWW" sites. At that time, the number of internet users in China was 620,000, and most of them accessed the internet via dial-up. Internet users engaged in research, education, computer industry and students accounted for 54.7%, and the percentage of real consumer users was very small due to the problems such as slow internet speed and expensive charges.

With the support of national policies, the internet in China has developed rapidly in the past 20 years and the overall level has improved significantly. In July 2017, CNNIC resealed The 40th China Statistical Report on the Internet Development. According to the report, as of June 2017, there were 5.06 million websites in China, 751 million internet users, 201 million rural internet users, and 724 million cell phone users. The internet coverage rate in China increased year by year, and as of June 2017, the internet penetration rate was 54.3% (see Table 3-1 for details). Internet access was diversifying, and the use of computers, tablets, cell phones, TVs and other internet usage was generally increasing. The internet access rate was 55% for desktop computers, 36.5% for laptops, 28.7% for tablets, 26.7% for TVs, and 96.3% for cell phones.

Table 3-1   Basic data of internet development in China from 2007 to 2017

Item	Up to June, 2017	Up to June, 2015	Up to June, 2011	Up to June, 2007
Netizen scale (million person)	751	668	485	162
Scale of mobile netizen (million person)	724	594	318	—
Scale of rural netizen (million person)	201	186	131	32
Total number of websites (million)	5.06	3.57	1.83	1.31
Number of IPv4 addresses (million)	338	336	332	118
Number of IP addresses (blocks/32)	21,283	19,338	429	27
International export bandwidth (Mbps)	7,974,779	4,717,761	1,182,261.45	312,346
Internet popularity rate (%)	54.3	48.8	36.2	12.3

Source: China Internet Network Information Center, China Statistical Report on the Internet Development.

3.2.3   High-speed growth of internet applications

Currently, the application of the internet in China is becoming increasingly widespread and in-depth, and gradually shifting to the mobile internet. Digital technology represented by the internet is driving consumer upgrading as well as economic and social transformation and development. The overall size of internet applications for information acquisition, business transactions, financial services, and entertainment is experiencing growth.

Online news is one of the earliest internet applications developed on the internet in China. With the development of next-generation information technology, the information access applications such as online news has been improving. As of June 2017, there were 625 million internet news users in China, with 83.1% of internet users, of which 596 million were cell phone internet news users, accounting for 82.4% of cell phone internet users.

Transactions of business applications maintained high growth. By the end of June 2011, the scale of online shopping users reached 173 million, while by June 2017, it reached 514 million in China, including 480 million cell phone online shopping users. In the first half of 2017, the user scale of online shopping, online takeaway and online travel booking increased by 10.2%, 41.6% and 11.5% respectively, and the proportion of using cell phone payment in offline shopping reached 61.6%.

Internet applications have gradually shifted from business transactions to education, transportation and other aspects of life. Artificial intelligence technology has driven the rapid development of online education, and online car-hailing has become a common way for people to move around. The current user scale of online education, online car-hailing, online special or express car and shared bike reached 144 million, 278 million, 217 million and 106 million respectively. The financial internet has also become a new area of internet applications, and the scale of internet financing users has gradually increased. Up to June 2017, there were 126 million internet users purchasing internet finance products in China.[1]

At the same time, the scale of users of online entertainment applications was growing steadily, and the industry continued to develop towards formalization. By the end of June 2011, the scale of China's online game users was 311 million, and it grew to 422 million by June 2017 (see Table 3–2). Network entertainment applications further shifted to mobile, and in the first half of 2017, the growth rate of mobile network music, video, games and literature user increased above 4%, of which the growth rate of mobile network games reached 9.6%.[2]

Table 3–2   Development of internet applications in China from 2011 to 2017

Unit: 100 million

Item	Up to June, 2017	Up to June, 2015	Up to June, 2011
User scale of instant messaging	6.92	6.06	3.85
User scale of search engines	6.09	5.36	3.86
User scale of mobile search	5.93	4.54	—
User scale of online news	6.25	5.54	3.62
Scale of new mobile network users	5.96	4.59	—
User scale of online shopping	5.14	3.73	1.73
User scale of mobile phone online shopping	4.80	2.70	—
User scale of online travel booking	3.34	2.29	0.37
User scale of mobile travel booking	2.99	1.67	—
User scale of internet financing	1.26	0.78	0.56
User scale of Online payment	5.11	3.59	1.53
User scale of mobile payment	5.02	2.76	—

[1][2] Information based on the China Statistical Report on the Internet Development of China Internet Network Information Center.

continued

Item	Up to June, 2017	Up to June, 2015	Up to June, 2011
User scale of online game	4.22	3.80	3.11
User scale of mobile online game	3.85	2.67	—
User scale of online literature	3.53	2.84	1.95
User scale of monile online literature	3.27	2.49	—
User scale of online video user	5.65	4.61	3.01
User scale of mobile video user	5.25	3.54	—
User scale of online music	5.24	4.80	3.82
User scale of mobile online music	4.89	3.86	—
User scale of online education	1.44	—	—
User scale of mobile online education	1.20	—	—
User scale of online car-hailing	2.78	—	—
User scale of online car-hailing or express car	2.17	—	—
User scale of shared bikes	1.06	—	—
User scale of online takeaway	2.95	—	—
User scale of mobile online takeaway	2.74	—	—

Data Source: China Internet Network Information Center, China Statistical Report on the Internet Development.

Internet applications are gradually shifting to mobile, the mobile internet is developing rapidly, and the market share and user scale of smart wireless terminal devices are growing steadily. Smartphones and other mobile devices have become the main media carrier for people to obtain information, online shopping, entertainment and leisure. The efficient, timely and portable mobile internet has improved the efficiency of people's access to information, business transactions and electronic payments. Applications of entertainment and banking are the mainstream forms of mobile internet business, and their consumer groups are becoming broader and more diversified.

With the continuous improvement of internet infrastructure and the soundness of information security guarantee system, China's internet popularity rate has been increasing. The deeply integration of the internet with public livelihood services such as healthcare, education and transportation has further deepened the impact on individuals' ways of life. With the gradual popularization of mobile internet access devices, the increasing improvement of the network environment, and the growing richness of mobile internet application scenarios, three factors are working together to rapidly develop and strengthen the dominant position of mobile internet applications in China. And the internet has become a booster for improving people's livelihood and social well-being.

3.2.4   Rural internet as a new growth point

China's rural internet was growing rapidly, showing great potential for growth, although the overall level was lower than that of urban areas. The Survey Report on the Internet Usage in Chinese Rural Area (2007) shows that as of June 2007, the population of China's rural internet users exceeded 37 million, with a large gap between urban and rural areas, and the rural internet popularity rate was 5.1%; while the urban internet popularity rate in China was 21.6% during the same period.[1] After nearly 10 years of development, the speed of rural internet development increased significantly. The 2015 Rural Internet Development Status Research Report released in August 2016 showed that the population of China's rural internet users reached 195 million in 2015, accounting for 28.4%, the growth rate was twice that of the cities and towns; rural internet popularity rate was 32.31%, an increase of 2.38 percentage points higher than that of cities and towns; the population of rural search engine users is 152 million, with an annual growth rate of 16.9%. The search engine usage rate of rural internet users was 77.7%, an increase of 4.9 percentage points compared with the end of 2014.[2]

Instant messaging is the application with the highest usage rate among rural internet users. Up to December 2015, the population of rural internet users of instant messaging was 172 million, with an annual growth rate of 10.8%. In the development of rural internet, mobile phone internet users are growing faster. Among the 195 million rural internet users, mobile phone internet users account for 87.1% of the overall rural internet users, and the number of users using cell phones to access the internet has reached 170 million. The 40th China Statistical Report on Internet Development showed that until June 2017, rural internet users accounted for 26.7% of China's internet users, with a size of 201 million; at the level of universal access, the rural internet penetration rate rose from 28.3% in 2014 to 34.0% in 2017, but was still lower than that of urban areas by 35.4 percentage points.[3]

---

[1] China Internet Network Information Center, Survey Report on the Internet Usage in Chinese Rural Area (2007), China Internet Network Information Center Website, Sep. 7, 2007, http://www.cnnic.cn/hlwfzyj/hlwxzbg/ncbg/201206/t20120612_27435.htm.

[2] China Internet Network Information Center, *2015 Rural Internet Development Status Research Report*. China Internet Network Information Center Website, Aug. 29, 2016, http://www.cnnic.cn/hlwfzyj/hlwxzbg/ncbg/201608/t20160829_54453.htm.

[3] China Internet Network Information Center, *The 40th China Statistical Report on Internet Development*, China Internet Network Information Center Website, Aug. 3, 2017, http://www.cnnic net.cn/hlwfzyj/hlwxzbg/hlwtjbg/201708/P020170807351923262153.pdf.

Among the rural internet applications, rural e-commerce, mainly business transaction-type applications, is developing rapidly, and the usage rate of users is increasing year by year. Particularly in 2015, with the encouragement and support of national policies on "internet +", the user scale of business transaction applications in rural areas has grown significantly, with an annual growth rate of 19.8% in the scale of online shopping users. Because of the country's increased support for financial inclusion policies, the rural internet banking applications grew at a significant rate, with the size of online payment users reaching 93.2 million by the end of 2015, with an annual growth rate of 48.5% and a usage rate of 47.7%, and the population of online banking users reaching 71.61 million, with an annual growth rate of 25.6% and a usage rate of 36.6%.

3.3 The achievement of China's information technology development

Since the founding of the People's Republic of China, China's information technology has developed steadily, going through the preparation stage, accumulation stage, formal start-up stage, all-round development stage and accelerated development stage. According to the requirements of the development of the times, unified planning and organization, actively oriented to the market to develop guidelines and policies that meet the characteristics of different stages of development, the CPC Central Committee and the State Council would promote the country's information technology to a higher level of development. At present, China's information technology has entered a period of diversified, deep, all-round and highly effective development, becoming an important driving power for building a moderately prosperous society in all aspects and achieving the great rejuvenation of the Chinese nation.

Data from the State Information Center's about China Information Society Development Report 2016 showed that the national information society index grew at an average annual rate of 8.35% from 2007 to 2016, and China was in an accelerated transition from an industrial society to an information society. The results of an evaluation of countries around the world conducted by the China Internet Network Information Center showed that China's informatization has improved significantly, with the national informatization development index rising from 36th in 2012 to 25th in 2016. China's information development has been a global leader in terms of industry scale and application benefits. The informatization construction continued to advance the development of Chinese digital economy, which in 2016 accounted for 30.3% of GDP, ranking second in the world. The four key areas of China's information development including information economy, network society, online government and digital life have all entered a period of accelerated development, at the same time there are still problems such as unbalanced and insufficient development, obvious regional differences, and a growing digital divide between urban and rural areas.

3.3.1   Increasing improvement of comprehensive information infrastructure

In recent years, China's information and communication technology applications have deepened, the coverage area of broadband network has expanded, the internet popularity has increased significantly, and information networks have achieved leapfrog development. The data of the sixth China Broadband Popularity Status Report (third quarter of 2017) released by China Broadband Development Alliance showed that by the third quarter of 2017, the popularity rate of Chinese fixed broadband household had reached 72.5% and the popularity rate of mobile broadband users had reached 82.3%. Driven by the policy of building up strength in cyberspace, China has issued Several Opinions of the State Council on Promoting Information Consumption and Expanding Domestic Demand, the "Broadband China" Strategy and Its Implementation Plan and other policies and opinions to promote the development of the internet, the next-generation internet, fiber optic access and information infrastructure such as broadband wireless mobile communication so as to accelerate the evolution and upgrading of information network infrastructure in each region and the improvement of the network environment for information development. Currently, China ranks first in the world in terms of the internet and broadband access users, and the radio and television network has basically covered all administrative villages in the country. At the local level, the popularity rate of fixed broadband in Zhejiang Province ranked the first in China for reaching 89.1%, the popularity rate of Beijing's mobile broadband reached 129.9%, ranking the first in China.

The popularization of information networks benefited by the continuous development of communication network infrastructure such as fiber optic cables, switches and broadband. Since the implementation of reform and opening up policy, the total length of China's fiber optic cable has grown from nothing to a qualitative leap, from 1,212,358 km in 2000 to 24,863,348 km in 2015. The number of fixed long-distance telephone calls exchange capacity, bureau exchange capacity, mobile telephone calls exchange capacity, mobile telephone calls base stations, and the internet broadband access ports have increased year by year (see Table 3–3).

Table 3–3　　　　National communication network infrastructure development
from 1978 to 2015

Indicator	1978	1990	2000	2005	2010	2014	2015
Total length of fiber optic cable (km)	—	—	1,212,358	4,072,788	9,962,467	20,612,529	24,863,348
Total length of toll cable (km)	—	3,334	286,642	723,040	818,133	928,398	965,283
Fixed long-distance telephone calls interchanger capacity (roadside)	1,863	161,370	5,635,498	13,716,307	16,414,644	9,829,082	8,110,825
Local exchange capacity (ten thousand)	405.9	1,231.8	17,825.6	47,196.1	46,537.3	40,517.1	26,446.5
Mobile phone calls exchange capacity (ten thousand)	—	5.1	13,985.6	48,241.7	150,284.9	205,024.9	218,150
Mobile telephone calls base stations (ten thousand)	—	—	—	28.1	139.8	350.8	465.6
Internet broadband access ports (ten thousand)	—	—	—	4,874.7	18,781.1	40,546.1	57,709.4

Source: *China Statistical Yearbook* in previous years.

3.3.2　Constant improvement of industrial informatization

China's industrial technology innovation capacity has been significantly enhanced, and the innovative application of information technology has been accelerated to promote the transformation and upgrading of traditional industries. The level of informatization in the industrial field continues to improve, and the integration of informatization and industrialization has a deep development. With the implementation of the national development strategy of the new type of industrialization, informatization and industrialization are deeply integrated, and Made in China is gradually upgraded to smart manufacturing. Information technology in industrial R&D design, production management, marketing management, logistics distribution to deepen the application of traditional enterprises, which promoted traditional enterprises to transform modes of production.

In the period of R&D design link, dominant position of innovation of China's enterprises has gradually come to the fore, and the information technology innovation capacity has been improving. At present, R&D expenditure of Chinese enterprises continues to improve, and China has become the world's second largest R&D investment country. With abundant research funding support and under the guidance of the national policy of independent innovation, China has also continued to make great breakthrough in key core technologies, and supercomputers, quantum communications, BeiDou satellite Navigation and other technological levels were ranking among the top in the world. In process of manufacturing, some industries have adopted digitalization production tools to achieve informatization and intellectualization. At present, the popularity rate of China's digital design tools including aerospace, aviation, machinery, ships, automobiles, rail transportation equipment and other industries is more than 85%, and the computer numerical control (CNC) rate of key technological process such as iron and steel, petrochemicals, non-ferrous metals, coal, textiles, pharmaceuticals and other industries is more than 65%, the planning equipment rate of enterprise resource is more than 70%. Precision manufacturing, extreme manufacturing, agile manufacturing capabilities significantly improved.[1] In marketing and logistics sessions as well as based on the internet and the IoT, customer-centric personalized marketing, precise marketing methods and modern logistics systems have greatly improved the efficiency of the supply chain.

With the improvement of the industrial informatization and at the same time, the traditional manufacturing industry continues to transform and upgrade, emerging industries is also rapidly developing. With the support of information technology, labor productivity of high-tech industries such as medicine manufacturing industry, aerospace manufacturing, the manufacturing industry of electronic and telecommunications equipment, electronic computer and office equipment manufacturing, healthcare equipment and instrumentation manufacturing and others has increased significantly, and revenue and profits have also been a substantial increase. In 2007, the main business revenue of China's high-tech industry was RMB4,971.4 billion, which grew rapidly to RMB11,604.9 billion in 2013, and it was also 2.3 times that of 2007.[2]

---

[1] China Informatization Almanac of the Compilation Committee, *China Informatization Almanac 2015*, Beijing: Publishing House of Electronics Industry, 2016, p. 3.

[2] Ministry of Science and Technology of the People's Republic of China, Chinese High Technology Industry Database.

3.3.3 Rapid growth of electronic information industry

Since the implementation of the reform and opening-up policy and under the guidance of national policies, the scale of China's electronic information industry continues to grow, electronic information manufacturing and software industry have achieved growth, which contribute to China's significantly economic growth. The development of the electronic information industry provides a strong support for the improvement of the overall informatization in China.

First, the scale of the electronic information industry continues to expand and the proportion of the software industry continues to increase.

The number of electronic information enterprises in China is growing rapidly. Up to 2015, the number of enterprises in China's electronic information industry above the scale had reached 60,800, of which 19,900 were electronic information manufacturing enterprises and 40,900 were software and the service industry of information technology. This showed that software and the service industry of information technology had become the main enterprise type of China's electronic information industry. Electronic information enterprises are expanding its scale. In the meantime, the main business income and profits also increased year by year. The data released by the Ministry of Industry and Information Technology shows that the main business income of China's electronic information industry in 2007 was RMB5.6 trillion, of which the manufacturing industry above the scale was RMB4.54 trillion, accounting for a high proportion of 81%, while the main business income of the software industry was RMB583.4 billion, accounting for a lower proportion in only 10%. After 5 years of development, the sales revenue of China's electronic information industry had exceeded RMB10 trillion by 2012. The total revenue of China's electronic information industry reached RMB15.4 trillion by 2015, the income of electronic information manufacturing industry achieving the main business had reached RMB11.1 trillion, and the rapid development of software and the service industry of information technology, the income growth rate of software business was higher than the electronic information manufacturing industry about 9 percentage points, and its proportion also increased to about 28%.[1] By 2016, the main business income of China's electronic information industry was as high as RMB17 trillion, which was 1.55 times more than in 2012. Total profit of electronic information industry

---

[1] Ministry of Industry and Information Technology, 2015 Electronic Information Industry Statistical Bulletin, Website of Ministry of Industry and Information Technology of the People's Republic of China, Feb. 29, 2016, http://www.miit.gov.cn/n1146290/n1146402/n1146455/c4655529/content.html.

reached RMB1.3 trillion, which was 1.89 times that of 2012.[1] During the development of the electronic information industry, the main business income of the software industry grew at a higher rate, and the growth rate from 2007 to 2016 was higher than that of the electronic information manufacturing industry (see Table 3–4 for specific data).

Table 3–4   Development of China's electronic information industry from 2007 to 2016

Year	Main business income of electronic information industry (RMB trillion)	Growth (%)	Main business income of electronic information manufacturing industry above the scale (RMB trillion)	Growth (%)	Main business income of software industry (RMB trillion)	Growth (%)
2007	5.6		4.5		0.6	
2008	6.3	12.5	5.1	12.8	0.8	29.8
2010	7.8	29.5	6.4	24.1	1.3	31.3
2011	9.3	20.9	7.5	17.1	1.8	35.9
2012	11.0	16.7	8.5	13.0	2.5	28.5
2013	12.4	12.7	9.3	10.4	3.1	24.6
2014	14.0	13.0	10.3	9.8	3.7	20.2
2015	15.4	10.4	11.1	7.6	4.3	16.6
2016	17.0	11.6	12.1	8.4	4.9	14.9

Source: Ministry of Industry and Information Technology of the People's Republic of China, *Electronic Information Industry Statistical Bulletin* in previous years.

Second, China's foreign trade in the electronic information industry is developing rapidly, and the scale of import and export continues to rise.

Ministry of Industry and Information Technology data show that in 2008, the total import and export of electronic information products in China was US$885.4 billion, accounting for 35% of China's total foreign trade. Laptop computers, mobile communication equipment, integrated circuits and other electronic information products exported in larger quantities. In 2010, the value of China's electronic information products import and export exceeded US$1 trillion, reaching up to US$1,012.8 billion, and its year-over-year increase in the value of 31.2%. From 2008 to 2016, the value of import and export of electronic information products in China's total foreign trade import and export volume has remained at more than 30%. Since 2008, China's foreign trade in electronic information products to maintain a surplus, and the amount of exports

---

[1] Ministry of Industry and Information Technology, "Research Report on the Comprehensive Development Index of China's Electronic Information Industry", *China Electronics News*, Sep. 5, 2017.

continues to be greater than its imports. China's exports of electronic information products continue to expand, accounting for the proportion of China's total foreign exports has also been maintained at more than 33%. This shows that it is an important part of China's foreign trade exports to electronic information products, and is also the main force driving the growth of China's foreign trade (see Table 3–5 for specific data).

Table 3–5　　Import and export of electronic information products in China from 2008 to 2016

Years	Total import and export of electronic information products (US$100 million)	Proportion of total foreign trade (%)	Export of electronic information products (US$100 million)	Proportion of total exports (%)	Import volume of electronic information products (US$100 million)	Proportion of total imports (%)
2008	8,854	35.0	5,218	36.5	3,637	32.1
2010	10,128	34.1	5,912	37.5	4,216	30.2
2011	11,292	31.0	6,612	34.8	4,680	26.8
2012	11,868	30.7	6,980	34.1	4,888	26.9
2013	13,302	32.0	7,807	35.3	5,495	28.2
2014	13,237	30.8	7,897	33.5	5,340	27.1
2015	13,088	33.1	7,811	34.3	5,277	31.4
2016	12,245	33.2	7,210	34.4	5,035	31.7

Source: Ministry of Industry and Information Technology of the People's Republic of China, *Electronic Information Industry Statistical Bulletin* in previous years.

3.3.4　Steady development of agriculture and rural information technology

In recent years, with the opportunity of "Broadband China", "networks convergence", "broadband village access" and other projects, Chinese rural areas have accelerated the development and continuously improved the basic communication facilities, fiber optic broadband network and the construction of information infrastructure such as mobile communication network and broadcasting cable network. Village to Village Project of communications has made progress. By the end of 2014, the proportion of administrative villages with broadband has increased to 93.5%. From the view of internet popularity, rural areas have reached 31.6% in 2015, with an increase of 2.8 percentage points compared to 2014.[1]

---

[1] China Internet Network Information Center, 2015 Rural Internet Development Status Research Report. China Internet Network Information Center Website, Aug. 29, 2016, http://www.cnnic.cn/hlwfzyj/hlwxzbg/ncbg/201608/t20160829_54453.htm.

Intelligent production of agriculture has continuously improved. Since 2013, the Ministry of Agriculture has launched a remarkable regional agricultural IoT pilot project to promote the agricultural production intellectualization. In the monitoring of agricultural resources, it has been possible to use high-precision sensing equipment to obtain information on agricultural resources; in the aspect of monitoring of the agricultural ecological environment, it has been possible to use sensor sensing technology, information fusion transmission technology and internet technology to achieve automatic monitoring; in the aspect of agricultural production process, the intellectualization control of the production process has been realized; in the supervision of agricultural products quality, the whole process of information perception and transmission of agricultural products production and circulation has been realized.

The system of rural information service continues to improve. In recent years, the Ministry of Agriculture and the State Council Leading Group Office of Poverty Alleviation (now the National Rural Revitalization Administration) and other departments to promote e-commerce into rural areas, targeted poverty alleviation of e-commerce promotes the rapid development of rural information technology. The development of informatization from basic information inquiry and consultation, to business transactions, internet finance, and public services such as education, medical care and transportation has steadily increased. The rapid development of e-commerce for agricultural products has given a strong impetus to other links in the agricultural industry chain. In 2014, e-commerce transactions of agricultural products exceeded RMB80 billion, and by the end of 2014, the scale of rural internet users for online shopping reached 77.14 million, with an annual growth rate of 40.6%.

3.3.5   Accelerating the service industry transforming to the direction in information technology

The service industry has accelerated the transition to information technology, and the popularity rate of the service industry IT application has gradually increased. The contribution of new service industry based on information technology and the internet to the economy is further enhanced. Supply-side structural reform as well as innovative development has given birth to a number of new industries, new business forms and new models based on the internet, which have become new growth points for economic development. Based on the "internet +", e-commerce, modern logistics, sharing economy and new models such as makerspace, crowd-sourcing collective support and crowd-funding have greatly optimized the allocation of resources and significantly increased the contribution to economic growth.

E-commerce is growing at a high rate, and the increase in the number of e-commerce platforms and the improvement of the e-commerce service system has led to a comprehensive informatization of the economy and society. Since March 2010, group-buying websites have gradually emerged in China, and by the end of 2010, the number of Chinese online group-buying users was only 18.75 million. On the basis of the development of the internet, the development of China's e-commerce has rapidly growth. E-tailing transactions reached RMB1.85 trillion in 2013, surpassing the United States to become the world's largest retail market. In the first half of 2017, the scale of information service revenue reached RMB260 billion, accounting for 91.5% of business revenue. In the information service revenue, the e-commerce platform revenue was RMB107.4 billion, increasing to 42.9% year-on-year. E-commerce market pattern is basically stable, Beijing, Guangdong and Shanghai engaged in e-commerce enterprises in large numbers and large scale, e-commerce platform revenue accounted for nearly 80%.[1]

With the development of information technology and internet economy, traditional banking services are gradually networked, and new models of internet finance such as third-party payment, internet banking and crowd-funding have emerged. In September 1999, China Merchants Bank took the first lead in fully launching the online banking "one-stop service" in China, establishing a network banking service system and launching online personal banking business. With the rising of internet finance in 2013, internet finance products have enriched people's investment and financing channels and methods. In recent years, with the booming of e-commerce, the transaction scale of China's internet finance has gradually grown. Data from Zhiyan Consulting shows that in 2009, the scale of China's online banking transactions was only RMB36.7 trillion and quickly rose to RMB549.5 trillion, with an explosive growth in 2010. According to the industrial database of Econet, along with the boom of e-commerce, the scale of China's online banking transactions in 2016 was as high as RMB1,990.2 trillion more than a decade of development, including RMB467.5 trillion in the first quarter, RMB480.8 trillion in the second quarter, RMB505.6 trillion in the third quarter and RMB536.3 trillion in the fourth quarter. The third-party payment model has also entered a period of rapid development, with data from BigData-Research showing that the total payment transactions of third-party reached RMB58 trillion in 2016, an increase of 85.6% year-on-year. With the development and popularization application of mobile terminal

---

[1] Bu Xuan, "The Growth Rate of China's Internet Business Revenue Steadily Increased in the First Half of the Year", *China Electronics News*, Aug. 8, 2017.

devices, internet finance has gradually shifted to mobile, and the scale of mobile payment transactions in China was RMB38.6 trillion in 2016, accounting for 66.5% of the total transaction value. The transaction model of the internet finance is constantly enriched and innovated, which enhances the liquidity of funds, reduces transaction costs, improves transaction efficiency and provides strong support for the development of the national economy.

3.3.6   The comprehensive development of information society

Information technology, information network and other information resources are continuously deepening their applications in all aspects of life such as education, culture, healthcare and transportation, promoting the formation and development of an intelligent society, digital city and smarter planet, and also facilitating the transformation of our society into an information society. New social platforms such as WeChat and Weibo have changed people's communication way; online shopping and payment have gradually become more convenient, and online ordering has become a fashionable part of people's lives; online registration, electronic medical records, and electronic healthcare bills have improved the efficiency of healthcare; distance education and online courses have continuously expanded the way of education and increased the diversity of education; the sharing economy such as shared-bikes, car rental, and credit lending has emerged and provides unlimited convenience to people's lives. Supported by the country's strong mobile communication capabilities and accurately satellite positioning system, shared-bikes has become a universally popular mode of travel in China, prompting the development of China's shared economy. By the end of 2016, the overall number of users in China's shared-bikes market had reached 18.86 million. The Statistical report from the State Information Center indicates, the number of people involved in sharing economy activities in China exceeded 600 million in 2016, with a financing scale of about RMB171 billion, an increase of 130% year-on-year; the high growth of financing scale has contributed to the prosperity of China's sharing economy market, with a transaction volume of RMB3,452 billion in 2016, an increase of 103% year-on-year.

The Ministry of Education launches the "three connections and two platforms" project to promote the development of education informatization. The "three connections" refer to broadband network for schools, quality resources for classes, and network learning space for all, and the "two platforms" refer to the national public platform for education resources and the national public service platform for education management. The construction project of "three connections and two platforms" has increased the number of the broadband access to all types of schools, expanded learning space, and provided students with more learning resources.

In the field of cultural informatization, the resource sharing project of cultural information has been effective, and a six-level public digital cultural service network covering urban and rural areas has been basically built. Meanwhile, the national public digital culture support platform, the national digital library and other informatization cultural platforms are gradually developing and improving. Information technology has been integrated into every aspect of social life, and information technology has developed towards universal access, providing intelligent solutions for people's education, healthcare, transportation, etc.

Chapter 4
The Development Path of China's Industrial Informatization

Since the 1970s, the third wave of the information revolution has had a significant impact on economy, politics, society, culture and other aspects of life. In this context, the economy and society have been continuously transformed and upgraded. From the perspective of the industrial development process, the Western developed countries began informatization after the basic completion of industrialization. As a developing country, China, due to the late start of industrialization, seized the opportunity to develop information technology in the middle of industrialization with great efforts, thus forming the development path to the integration of informatization and industrialization with Chinese characteristics.

4.1 Basic problems of the integration of informatization and industrialization

4.1.1 Basic connotation of the integration of informatization and industrialization

The integration of informatization and industrialization refers to integrated development of the two. However, due to the different understanding towards informatization and industrialization in academic circles, the basic connotation of the integration of informatization and industrialization is defined differently.

Some experts believed that the misunderstanding of industrialization and informatization may lead to animosity instead of integration. "The integration of informatization and industrialization is obviously not only for industry or the secondary industry. Traditional sectors of the national economy, including primary industries such as agriculture, forestry, animal husbandry, side-line production and fishery, secondary industries such as manufacturing, extraction, metallurgy and construction, and tertiary industries such as education, healthcare, banking, communications, transportation, commerce and tourism, all bear the task of integrating information technology with industrialization in the process of industrialization."[1]

Some experts further pointed out that, "the integration of informatization and industrialization is to make full use of information technology and information resources, and combine them with the industrial production mode, thus accelerating the development and upgrading of industrialization, and promoting the transformation of the industrial economy to the information economy".[2] The integration of informatization and industrialization includes both the information application of industrial production and the informatization of agriculture and service industries that provide support for it.

Therefore, the industrialization cannot be narrowly understood as the industrialization of the secondary industry, that is, the manufacturing industry, but should include the primary and tertiary industries that support the development of the secondary industry from the perspective of the national economic system. However, the major focus and penetration point in the integration process is still the manufacturing industry. Each industry cannot be developed without the manufacturing industry, and the informatization of this industry is the driving force to radiate and drive the informatization of the whole national economy.

From the perspective of the driving force of economic development, some experts believe that "the integration of informatization and industrialization is a process of increasing information literacy of workers, accelerating the pace of the intellectualization of traditional energy conversion tools, making information an equally vital social resource and production factor as energy and materials, and triggering the changes of industrial structure, production modes, organization methods, and lifestyle".[3] Information has become an important driving force for economic transformation and development, and an indispensable production factor in the production process. As production factors, information technology and information resources have become the key to achieve big development strides in productive forces.

In terms of the process and the level of integration, some scholars pointed out that the essence of the integration is the industrial integration, while the application of IT in industries, is a process. On the basis of information resources and information environment construction, and under the guarantee of regulations, policies, security and standards,

[1] Zhou Hongren, *On Informatization,* Beijing: People's Publishing House, 2008, p. 284.

[2] Zou Sheng, *Ten Lectures on Informatization*, Beijing: Publishing House of Electronics Industry, 2009, p. 66.

[3] Zhou Zixue, *The Integration of Informatization and Industrialization: Exploration a Road of Optimization of Industrial Structure,* Beijing: Publishing House of Electronics Industry, 2010, p. 7.

the high-tech technologies represented by information technology penetrate and integrate in the whole life cycle of industrial infrastructure, industrial technology, industrial products, industrial equipment, industrial management, industrial market environment and other levels, so as to form a comprehensive, integrated and innovative modern industrial technology, new production and business models, sustainable development models and emerging industries. As a result, the industrial competitiveness, innovation capacity and industrial quality are comprehensively improved, and eventually move towards the integration of the IT application strategy and industrialization strategy, with mutual coordination and coherence, thus forming a complete and unified new industrialization strategy.[1] Here summarizes the three levels of the integration of informatization and industrialization, namely, the micro enterprise level, the medium industry level, and the macro social level. The integration from the micro enterprise level to the medium industry level and then to the macro social level is a gradual process. It starts from the informatization of the micro enterprises to realize the informatization of the whole industrial chain of enterprise research and development, production, operation and service, extends to the medium level to realize the transformation and upgrading of industrial structure, and finally realizes the comprehensive informatization of the economic society.

According to the author, the integration of informatization and industrialization is a process of economic development, which takes information technology and information resources as the driving force and the informatization of the whole industrial chain, such as R&D, production, operation and management of micro enterprises, as the core, so as to promote the transformation of production methods and the upgrading of industrial structure and finally realize the transformation from industrial society to information society. The innovation of information technology and the development of industrial technology are conducted collaboratively, and the information technology penetrates into the industrial field in an all-round way. The informatization of enterprises, industries and countries is synchronous, and the informatization of the economic, political, cultural and social fields is mutually reinforcing.

From the perspective of the driving forces, information technology and various information resources such as the internet are the driving forces and support to realize the integration of informatization and industrialization. New industrialization road can only be provided with lasting power by strengthening investment in R&D and

---

[1] Wu Cheng, *Integrated Strategic Research on Informatization and Industrialization: Reviews, Status Quo and Foresight of China's Informatization*, Beijing: Science Press, 2013, p. 23.

continuously realizing information technology innovation, especially by making breakthroughs in new generation information technology such as IoT and cloud computing. In terms of the integration breadth, informatization refers to various fields related to industrial production, involving R&D and designing, producing process, operation and management, customer service and other products' lifecycle and every relative step in the industry chain. The integration of informatization and industrialization specifically includes the technology integration, process integration, management integration, and product integration. From the view of the integration subject, the micro enterprises are the source of technological innovation and the real handlers of informatization. In terms of the pillar industry, the integration of manufacturing industry and informatization is the core for the integration of informatization and industrialization, which radiates and drives the informatization of agriculture, services and other related industries. The informatization of the manufacturing industry is the important support for a new path of industrialization in the process of integrating informatization and industrialization in China.

4.1.2 Significance of the integration of informatization and industrialization

4.1.2.1 Promoting economic transformation and upgrading to improve economic efficiency

With the economic development and the continuous improvement of industrialization level, China has become a world manufacturing power. However, in the international division of labor system, Chinese manufacturing industry mainly occupies the labor-intensive and resource-intensive low-end links, with low value-added products. Under the background of economic globalization, China can only improve the added value of products and economic benefits by seizing the opportunity of informatization, promoting the upgrading of industrial structure through IT innovation, and improving the level of product informatization and intellectualization.

4.1.2.2 Achieving energy conservation and emission reduction to promote the green economic development

Green development is the theme of economic development in the world today. It is important to adhere to the concept of saving resources and protecting the environment and build a resource-saving and environment-friendly society in economic development. Labor-intensive and resource-intensive industries with high pollution and high energy consumption can no longer meet the needs of economic development. In this regard, it is necessary to improve the technological content of these industries, raise the level of intellectualization in industrialized production, and drive industrialization with IT application, so as to realize the integration of IT application and industrialization. The widespread application of information technology and information network can help improve the efficiency of resource utilization, streamline the industrial chain, and reduce energy consumption per unit production, so as to achieve the goal of low-carbon-based economic growth.

4.1.2.3   Improving enterprise efficiency and participating in international competition

Flexible production and personalized manufacturing can be realized by making use of information technology and information network, and market demand and customer orders can be obtained in a timely manner through customer relationship management. By utilizing office automation, management links and procedures can be reduced, and working efficiency can be improved. Production efficiency can be improved by employing intelligent equipment, while by using information technology, the entire product supply chain can be supervised, and the whole product life cycle can be effectively managed. The integration of informatization and industrialization can improve the production and operation efficiency of enterprises, reduce the cost of each link of the product value chain, and thus improve the advantage of enterprises participating in international competition.

4.1.2.4   Revitalizing the real economy and enhancing the quality advantage

The real economy is the key point to achieve socialist modernization and establish a modern industrial system. It is a firm foundation for facilitating China's economy to win the initiative in global competition. The development of modern socialist industry must put quality first and give priority to performance. New dynamic energy has to be actively cultivated and grown to revitalize the real economy and improve the quality of industrial development, and IT is undoubtedly a new element and a new driving force to improve the quality of economic development. Revitalizing the real economy through informatization and establishing an industrial system with sustainable competitiveness will promote the transformation of China's economy from speed-based growth to quality-based growth.

The integration of informatization and industrialization is beneficial to improve the technological content of industrial production equipment and the informatization level of products, thus enhancing the quality advantage of economic development in China. The integration can also reduce the costs of operation, resources and labor of enterprises, improves the quality of workers, and lays the foundation for the improvement of industrial quality.

4.1.2.5 Facilitating the all–round development of human beings and the comprehensive progress of society

During the construction of informatization, China has always put people first, taken the people-centered approach as the development strategy, and satisfied the aspirations of people for a better life as the goal. The IT influences the industrial production and ultimately improves the quality of the products, which helps to meet the needs of the people. The integration and development of informatization and industrialization can not only promote industrial transformation and improve economic efficiency, but also equip entrepreneurs and workers with IT, improve the quality of workers, cultivate a knowledgeable and innovative labor force, and foster the all-round development of human beings.

In socialist modernization, China has adhered to the Five-Sphere Integrated Plan, and combined IT application with economic, political, cultural, social and ecological civilization construction, so as to provide the impetus for building a moderately prosperous society in all respects. The informatization gradually penetrates into various fields of economy while promoting the optimization and upgrading of industrial structure, and ultimately promotes the overall progress of the society.

4.2 Development course and key links of the integration of informatization and industrialization

4.2.1 Formation and evolution of the integration of informatization and industrialization

The economic development for over 70 years after the founding of the People's Republic of China is the history of industrial restructuring, optimization and upgrading from a large agricultural country to a large industrial country and then to an industrial power. In the process of optimizing and upgrading the industrial structure, China has encountered many problems and challenges. However, under the leadership of the CPC Central Committee and the State Council, the Chinese people of all ethnic groups have always adhered to Marxism, and have combined with China's development reality to explore a new approach to industrialization that conforms to the basic conditions of the primary stage of socialism with Chinese characteristics and actively integrate into economic globalization.

The industrialization process in China is characterized by three important stages, including the stage of giving priority to the development of heavy industry, the stage of coordinated development of heavy and light industry, and the stage of new industrialization development.

4.2.1.1   The first stage (1949–1978): the stage of giving priority to the development of heavy industry in a closed environment

In view of the complex situation of weak industrial base, backward technology and international sanctions before 1949, the New China implemented an industrialization strategy that prioritized the development of heavy industry with the goal of the Four Modernizations under the guidance of the Soviet model after its founding. In 1953, China initiated its First Five-year Plan to concentrate on developing heavy industry, which laid a primary foundation for national industrialization and the modernization of national defense. In this stage, the economy of China focused on the development of labor-intensive industries with low technological level and lower level of informatization. The industrial base was weak when China began to promote industrialization, and the proportion of the modern industry in China's total industrial and agricultural output was low. In this particular historical condition and environment, China pursued a strategy of prioritizing the development of heavy industry, seeking to accumulate funds for China's industrialization through the price scissors between industry and agriculture.

4.2.1.2   The second stage (1979–2000): the stage of coordinated development of light and heavy industries under open environment

In 1978, after the convening of the Third Plenary Session of the 11th CPC Central Committee, the focus of the CPC's work was shifted to construction of socialist modernization, and the development strategy of focusing on economic construction promoted the continuous restructuring of the national economy. After the Central Economic Work Conference in 1979, the development of heavy industry was gradually slowed down. Thereafter, the State Council proposed the vigorous development of consumer goods production, the coordinated development of agriculture, light industry and heavy industry, and the continuous optimization and upgrading of industrial structure. On the Fourth Session of the Fifth National People's Congress in November 1981, the policy of opening to the outside world and strengthening international economic and technological exchanges was put forward. China started to implement the development strategy of "bringing in" and "going global" simultaneously, and continuously introduced technology and foreign investment. During this period, China seized the opportunity of the development of the world information revolution to effectively promote the improvement of industrial informatization and the growth of the national economy. With the adjustment of national industrialization development strategy, China's industrial structure was constantly optimized and upgraded. The ratio of output value among the three industries was 50.5%:20.9%:28.6% by 1952, and 16.4%:50.2%:33.4% by 2000.[1]

4.2.1.3 The third stage (after 2000): the stage of a new approach to industrialization

In the process of industrialization, environmental pollution and resource depletion have become increasingly prominent, and labor-intensive and resource-intensive economic growth modes are no longer adapted to the needs of economic development. The problem of low-level structural surplus emerged in China in the 1990s, with a major imbalance between the industrial structure and the demand structure, and an increasingly prominent challenge between the people's growing material and cultural needs and inadequate level of development. For a long time, the main reason for the low productivity of labor in China, and a huge gap between economic efficiency and the world's advanced level is its backward production technology and low technology content of technical equipment. With a higher proportion of labor-intensive low-value-added products, and a very low market share of technology- intensive high-value-added products. Following the rapid economic growth, domestic resources have encountered serious challenges. High input and energy consumption are not only unsustainable, but also cause serious environmental pollution and lead to ecological degradation. Facing the complex background, the CPC Central Committee and the State Council actively explore the idea of industrial development and develop new dynamic energy for economic development. Information technology application has undoubtedly become the key to adjust industrial structure and realize economic transformation and upgrading.

Since the beginning of the 21st century, China has begun to take a new path of industrialization in line with the characteristics of the times. On the Fifth Plenary Session of the 15th CPC Central Committee, the strategic idea that drives the industrialization with information technology application was firstly put forward. This strategic thinking in the 16th CPC National Congress developed into a new trail to

---

[1] Li Xingshan, *Theory and Practice of the Socialist Market Economy*, Beijing: Central Party School Press, 2004, p. 443.

industrialization with information technology application to drive industrialization, and industrialization to promote information technology application. The 17th CPC National Congress proposed to vigorously promote the integration of informatization and industrialization. The 18th CPC National Congress put forward to promote the deep integration of informatization and industrialization and promote the synchronized development of industrialization, informatization, urbanization and agricultural modernization. The 19th CPC National Congress further pointed out the need to promote the simultaneous development of new industrialization, informatization, urbanization and agricultural modernization.

In the process of industrialization, China has given strong support to the integration of industrialization and informatization: ranging from driving and promoting industrialization with informatization to integration of informatization and industrialization and then to their deep integration. It can be seen that informatization is a strategic initiative to promote China's industrial transformation and upgrading, and is a booster to realize China's industrial modernization. In the construction socialist modernization, China proposed to develop a modern industrial system, which should not only fully exert the advantages of human resources, but also seize the opportunity of the development of the information revolution to achieve technological innovation, improve the content of science and technology, increase economic efficiency, at the same time reduce resource consumption and environmental pollution, and establish a resource-saving, environmentally friendly society. The penetration and integration of information technology in all aspects of industrial production will help revitalize the equipment manufacturing industry, accelerate the elimination of backward production capacity and promote the upgrading of traditional industries.

Through the integration of informatization and industrialization, China's industry in the global value chain has continued to move from low value-added links to high value-added links. To develop information technology with great efforts and improve the development level of informatization, which can help reduce production and operation costs, reduce environmental pollution, and to realize the development of an intelligence in a green and sustainable manner.

4.2.2　Key links of the integration of informatization and industrialization

The integration and development of informatization and industrialization cannot be promoted in a wholesale manner and accomplished at one stroke, but should start from the key links and proceed gradually. Information technology is the core driving force of informatization. Hence, in the process of promoting integration of informatization and industrialization, priority should be given to promoting the penetration of information technology into traditional industrial production areas. Enabling the integration of information technology and industrial technology, also to actively develop strategic new industries based on information technology. As a core of the internet, information infrastructure is an important strategic resource for information technology application. Therefore, in the process of integration of informatization and industrialization, the improvement and development of information network is also regarded as a key link.

4.2.2.1 To accelerate independent innovation in information technology, achieve technological integration, and promote the transformation and upgrading of traditional industries

One of the strategic focuses of China's development of informatization is using information technology to transform and upgrade traditional industries, and taking information technology as the driving force to realize the transformation over high energy consumption, high material consumption and high pollution industries. The innovation and application of information technology is a key point for transformation and upgrading of traditional industries. With the rapid development of global information technology and the fierce competition among countries around the world, relying on imported technology cannot bring high and lasting economic benefits. The key information technology independent innovation is the magic weapon to win in the wave of information technology. The 2006-2020 National Informatization Development Strategy clearly proposes that China should implement independent innovation plan for key information technology that involves the independent development capability in key areas such as integrated circuits (especially central processor chips), system software, key application software, and independent controllable key equipment. To target the frontier of international innovation, increase investment, focus on breakthroughs, and gradually grasp the initiative of industrial development. In mobile communications, digital TV, next-generation networks, radio frequency identification and other fields with a research and development base and broad market prospects, priority is given to the use of standards with independent intellectual property rights to accelerate the development, promotion and application of products and drive industrial development.[1]

---

[1] The Compilation Committee of China Informatization Almanac, *China Informatization Almanac 2015,* Beijing: Publishing House of Electronics Industry, 2016, p. 386.

Innovation in information technology is crucial, however, it is more important to achieve the integration and development of information technology and industrial technology. In the process of industrialization development, the new generation of information technology must meet the actual needs of industrial production. It is necessary to integrate information technology into industrial technology and realize the informatization of industrial technology. The integration of information technology and industrial technology should be strengthened in the application, and promote the continuous transformation of technology into actual productivity. Transform the traditional production modes with high pollution and high energy consumption; reduce its energy and material consumption per unit of product, and promote energy conservation and emission reduction in enterprises; improve the efficiency of resource utilization and reduce resource waste; promote green production and intelligent production; develop circular economy to achieve transformation, upgrading and sustainable development. The integration, innovation and development of information technology and industrial technology will help realize the transformation of the economic development mode from resource-intensive and labor-intensive to technology-intensive, especially information technology-intensive, thus improving the quality of economic growth.

4.2.2.2 Based on the new generation of information technology, to vigorously develop emerging industries and foster new models

In the integration and development of information technology and industrialization, especially the deep integration of new-generation information technology and manufacturing, China is constantly cultivating emerging forms of businesses, new business models and economic growth points with high added value and strong driving capacity. Constantly breakthroughs have been made in 3D printing, big data, supported by information technology, the electronic information industry and communications industry are rapidly formed. At the same time, e-commerce, network crowdsourcing, collaborative design and other new business models have emerged, further promoting the transformation of economic development.

In the process of integration of information technology and industrialization development, China should not only strengthen the transformation and upgrading of traditional industries by using information technology, but also vigorously develop new industries. To seize the opportunity of the new generation of information technology continues to innovate and upgrade, and to actively promote the transformation of traditional industries from production-based manufacturing to service-based manufacturing, and vigorously develop high-end value-added services to provide new growth points for the realization of industrial modernization. Since new industries based on a new generation of information technology are an important driving force for industrial modernization, the development of new industries and the cultivation of new models should be an important part in the process of integration of informatization and industrialization.

4.2.2.3 To improve the information internet, China will realize the coordinated development of the internet, mobile internet and IoT

Information network is an important infrastructure to realize the integration of informatization and industrialization. It is very important to realize industrial modernization to have information network with fast transmission speed, widespread driving areas and complete application functions. In the strategic focus of information development, China proposes to improve the comprehensive information infrastructure, promote network integration, optimize network structure, improve network speed, realize the integration of telecommunications, radio and television, and internet services and steadily realize the transformation to the next generation network.

Strengthening information network construction and promoting network integration can effectively reduce costs, achieve optimal allocation of resources and information sharing, and create a good environment for information technology application development. China has ranked first in the world in terms of the scale of internet applications, internet access and broadband access users, and gradually increased the application and penetration of mobile internet and IoT. Based on the internet, mobile internet and IoT, the smooth network and information sharing of all links in the industrial production chain can help improve industrial production efficiency, optimize supply chain management and customer relationship management, and improve service quality and efficiency.

With the development of the wireless broadband technology, the application scope and extent of the mobile internet have been gradually raised and become another driving force for economic growth. At present, the popularization rate of mobile internet is very high in China. The integration of mobile internet and traditional industries has continuously generated new business models and patterns. Based on the flexibility of the mobile internet, consumers can seamlessly participate in the production of enterprises through mobile clients, convey and feedback consumer information to all links of the industry chain in a timely manner, which will realize consumer-driven personalized production and services. The IoT is a representative of the new generation of information technology. Through wireless radio frequency technology, it realizes intelligent production and management of industry, which helps to realize the informatization of each link of the product value chain and the whole supply chain, and greatly improves production and operational efficiency. Therefore, the innovative development and in-depth application of mobile internet and IoT have become the key link of the integration of the informatization and industrialization.

4.3   Integration of informatization and industrialization based on the whole production chain

Michael Porter, a leading American strategist, broke down the various types of value-creating and cost-generating activities in a given industry into nine strategically interrelated activities, including five basic activities and four supporting activities. This activity involves enterprise production, sales, inbound logistics, outbound logistics, and after-sales service. Supporting activities involve personnel, planning, research and development, and procurement. Its basic and supporting activities constitute the value chain of a company. The integration of informatization and industrialization involves each link of the industrial value chain.

The integration of informatization and industrialization is a process of gradual development from the primary stage to the advanced stage. At the primary stage of industrial informatization, information technology is only applied in individual industries and individual enterprises of a production unit. Information technology in industrial production is only to play a supporting and auxiliary role. High-quality, comprehensive information technology and management talents are lacking, and the economic efficiency of enterprises is limited. The advanced stage of industrial informatization is based on the integration of informatization and industrialization of the whole industrial chain of enterprises. Information technology is widely penetrated in every aspect of industrial production, enterprise business processes are optimized, production equipment and production processes are mainly driven by information technology, business operations and management are tending to the development of automation and digitalization. And the technological content of the final product and the added value of the product are significantly improved.

In the process of promoting the development of deep integration of informatization and industrialization, China has accelerated the development of the integration of information technology and manufacturing technology, promoted the integrated application of information technology in the whole process of enterprise research and development design, manufacturing, operation management, sales and service and the whole industrial chain, and realized the informatization of the whole life cycle management of products, customer relationship management and supply chain management system.

4.3.1   IT application in R&D and design

The innovation capability of research, development and design is the core competitiveness of the enterprises. Enterprises can only be invincible in the fierce market competition by having core technology and independent intellectual property rights in product development and design. The application of information resources such as information technology and information networks can enhance the R&D and design capabilities of enterprises and improve their efficiency. Enterprises use new generation information technology such as big data and cloud computing to collect and select massive data in a timely manner, optimize analysis and simulation testing in virtual reality, realize network collaborative design, improve enterprise independent innovation capability and R&D efficiency, and provide core guarantee for the optimization and upgrading of the industrial chain.

Computer-aided design (CAD), product data management (PDM), and various intelligent software have become fairly typical intelligent R&D and design tools. Computer-aided design is a process in which computers and graphic equipment are used to assist designers in the design process, such as computing, information storage and graphic production. By applying computer-aided design, rapid retrieval, processing and handling of data graphics can be realized to improve design capability and efficiency. Most enterprises in Guangdong Province have adopted computer-aided design. In the electromechanical industry, more than 90% of enterprises have adopted two-dimensional computer-aided design, and more than 60% have adopted three-dimensional computer-aided design.[1] The PDM is a tool to assist staff in managing product data and the product development process, enabling the management of all data and information

---

[1] Zou Sheng, *Ten Lectures on Informatization,* Beijing: Publishing House of Electronics Industry, 2009, p. 66.

related to product production, achieving efficient use of documents, data and drawings, and improving R&D and design efficiency.

The information technology application of R&D design has promoted the continuous innovation of China's core technologies in key areas. A major breakthrough has been achieved in such areas as supercomputers, BeiDou satellite navigation, and high-speed railroad equipment. At present, China's self-developed "Sunway TaihuLight" Supercomputer has become the world's fastest supercomputer in terms of computing speed. The Overview of the IoT led by China became the first international standards of the IoT issued by the International Telecommunication Union, and TD-LTE led by China became the international standard of the fourth generation of mobile communication. In 2015, the number of accepted invention patent applications in China surpassed one million. Informatization in research, development and design, R&D and design informatization and technological innovation promote each other and are developed collaboratively, providing important support for stable economic growth. According to the data from the National Development and Reform Commission, during the 12th Five-year Plan period, the average annual growth rate of seven strategic emerging industries, including new-generation information technology, was nearly 20%, which was twice the growth rate of GDP and drove GDP growth of about 1.4%, becoming an important driving force for economic transformation and upgrading.[1]

4.3.2　IT application in production and manufacturing

Informatization in manufacturing is mainly reflected in two aspects: the informatization of production equipment and the informatization of production process.

4.3.2.1　Intellectualization of the production equipment

In June 2015, during his inspection of Ministry of Industry and Information Technology, China Nuclear Power Engineering Co., Ltd., Li Keqiang stressed the need to promote the manufacturing industry from large to strong, not only in the field of general consumer goods, but also in the high technology content of major equipment and other advanced manufacturing fields to strive for the first. Production equipment, as the infrastructure of industrial production, is the key to improving productivity. Information technology embedded in manufacturing equipment to achieve the intelligence of production equipment, can better promote the transformation and

---

[1] National Manufacturing Strategy Advisory Committee, *2016 Blue Book on Made in China 2025*, Beijing: Publishing House of Electronics Industry, 2016, p. 20.

upgrading of enterprises and improve their competitiveness.

High-grade CNC machine tools and robots are representatives of intelligent production equipment and have become the strategic focus of today's global manufacturing competition. China's CNC machine tools in the past 10 years have entered a period of rapid development, large CNC machine tools to fill the gaps in the domestic strategy, machine tool output CNC rate and the market share of CNC machine tools with independent intellectual property rights have increased year by year, Shenyang Machine Tool Group Co., Ltd. and Dalian Machine Tool Group Corporation have been among the world's top five machine tools. China's high-grade CNC machine tool research and development level continues to improve, CNC precision grinding machines, CNC gear processing machine tools, super heavy CNC vertical turning and cannons processing machine tools, special CNC axial wheel groove cannons, high-grade heavy metal cutting machine tools, high-grade special processing machine tools, high-grade CNC systems and other automotive machines with independent intellectual property rights and reach the international leading level. Global market share of over 30% for covering parts stamping lines.[1]

In his congratulatory letter to the World Robot Conference, Chinese President Xi Jinping pointed out: "With the continuous integration of information technology and industrialization, the intelligent industry represented by robotics has flourished and become an important symbol of technological innovation in the present era."[2] In the process of the development of the deep integration of the two, robots as intelligent production tools to assist humans to become an important tool to improve the efficiency of industrial production, the robot in the manufacturing industry is increasingly widely used. China already has a certain international competitiveness in the development and production of industrial robots.

4.3.2.2 Automation and flexibility of production process

Continuous improvement in the level of intelligence of production equipment provides the conditions for automation and flexibility of the production process. High-grade CNC machine tools, robots and other intelligent equipment have greatly improved the degree and level of automation of the production process, shortened production time, reduced production costs, and improved the efficiency of resource

---

[1] National Manufacturing Strategy Advisory Committee, *2016 Blue Book on Made in China 2025*, Beijing: Publishing House of Electronics Industry, 2016, p. 79.

[2] Xi Jinping, Congratulatory Letter to the World Robot Conference 2015, Xinhuanet, Nov. 23, 2015, http：// news.xinhuanet.com/fortune/2015-11/23/c_1117229738.htm.

utilization and production efficiency. Intelligent manufacturing (IM) systems, which are composed of intelligent machines and equipment and human experts, can skillfully perform production scheduling, process control, and picking and assembly in production, improving the efficiency and level of production management while enabling supervision and management of the entire production process.

Information technology provides the conditions for personalized customization and flexible production. In the process of deep integration of information technology and industrialization, production enterprises use information technology and information networks to understand customers' individual needs in a timely manner, collect market information, establish a flexible production system oriented to market demand, and reduce enterprise production costs. Enterprises use information technology and networks such as computers, the internet, big data and cloud computing to establish customer databases and interface with customers to keep abreast of changes in customer demand, realize customized production and improve operational efficiency. For example, Haier Group has seized the opportunity of the information revolution to explore and practice Haier's concept of win-win business model (*Ren Dan He Yi* model), shifting from product-oriented to user-oriented and all user-centered. Based on information technology, Haier established the Haier customized platform, pioneering three customization modes involve modular customization, crowd innovation customization, exclusive customization to meet users' various personalized needs. Haier production lines are flexibly produced according to customers' individual needs, realizing mutual benefits under the customization ecology.

4.3.3   IT application in enterprise operation and management

In business operation and management, more and more enterprises are using information technology and information networks to establish modern management methods supported by information resources and to realize the in-depth development of integration of informatization and industrialization. The enterprise resource planning (ERP), supply chain management (SCM), office automation (OA), customer relationship management (CRM), management information system (MIS), and other information systems have eliminated redundant links and optimized business processes through digital and intelligent management operations, realizing business process reengineering and optimizing resource allocation. The use of management information systems in enterprises can ultimately achieve precise management, reduce costs and energy consumption, and improve the efficiency of the enterprise as a whole.

The ERP is an integrated enterprise supply chain management platform, which is an enterprise management software with information technology as the core and highly integrated material resource management, financial resource management, human resource management and information resource management, with the advantages of being systematic, open, integrated and high efficiency. Based on the ERP system, data is fully shared among various systems within the company, thus helping to improve the efficiency of collecting and using data for each business and optimizing business processes and management procedures. Using enterprise resource planning system, enterprises can completely integrate logistics, capital flow, business flow and information flow in one platform. Thus, it can avoid duplication and ineffective work, and realize automation of business management.

The SCM is an information system that integrates all the activities of a company which is mainly responsible for the procurement of raw materials to the sale of products to the end user in a seamless process. With the supply chain management system, transactions between all links of the enterprise supply chain can be carried out according to the standardized process of the system. Timely communication of product supply-related information through the information platform can shorten order processing time, reduce the negotiation time between various business stakeholders, reduce procurement costs and improve inventory turnover.

Enterprises are able to achieve a paperless office model based on computer hardware, software and network platforms by using office automation systems. China's OA system has been gradually developed and matured since the first office automation planning meeting in 1985.

The CRM is a system platform that integrates marketing and customer service activities based on the concept of customer-centric management and the use of modern information technology and network databases. Customer relationship management systems generally include marketing management systems, customer service systems, call centers and other subsystems. Through these information systems, companies provide personalized services to meet customer needs, improve customer satisfaction, and cultivate customer loyalty.

Under the condition of open economic globalization, enterprises improve the efficiency of production, operation, management and service to strengthen the connection with the world market. Through information technology and network platform, they integrate the advantageous resources inside and outside the enterprise, optimize the enterprise business process, innovate the management mode, streamline the organization, and implement flat management. As a result, it can effectively reduce energy consumption, material consumption and human resource consumption, improve overall operational efficiency and enhance international competitiveness.

4.3.4　IT application in marketing service

Information technology application is an important means to improve the efficiency of supply chain. In the process of deep integration of informatization and industrialization, all links in the supply chain have gradually realized informatization, intelligence and automation, and the ability of enterprises to capture market information and response speed has increased remarkably. The development of e-commerce and modern logistics has improved the enterprises' marketing and service capability.

Enterprises carry out procurement, sales, logistics, customer service, financial services and other activities through electronic means. With the help of information network to realize the coordinated development of logistics, commercial flow, capital flow, information flow, etc., and to enhance market response speed and optimize customer service quality. Purchasing through e-commerce platform, enterprises evaluate and screen suppliers by using big data and cloud computing. As well as shorten purchasing time and improve the efficiency of incoming goods by processing, supervising and managing orders in a timely manner. Enterprises establish management information systems and distribution systems through e-commerce platforms to track orders in a timely manner and to accurately follow the changes in customer and capital flows to improve marketing accuracy. Through the e-commerce platform for customer management, enterprises can capture customer feedback on products instantly, provide services on products and usage quickly, grasp changes in customer needs promptly, thus provide a basis for business management decisions, and establish a marketing and production method centered on customer needs. With the development of information network, e-commerce services penetrate the whole process of enterprise business activities. Enterprises gradually turn to full e-commerce and establish an efficient and smooth supply chain.

In terms of logistics, China has established a modern logistics industry based on the automatic identification technology, data acquisition technology, tracking and positioning technology, electronic data interchange, electronic payment technology and other information technology. The third-party logistics, the fourth-party logistics, logistics park and other modern logistics models continue to be developed and improved. With the help of information system, enterprises can monitor and process the transportation service, storage service, delivery service, loading and unloading service and packaging service of goods in real time, so as to shorten and optimize the supply chain, and effectively integrate resources and reduce logistics costs.

4.4 Exploration on the transformation from "Made in China" to "Intelligent Manufacturing in China"

Building up China's strength in manufacturing development and achieving the transformation from "Made in China" to "Intelligent Manufacturing in China" are the strategic deployments put forward by the CPC Central Committee and the State Council based on the development situation at home and abroad. China has coordinated planning, solidly promoted various efforts to build a strong manufacturing country, innovated the policy environment, and promoted the integration of information technology, the internet and manufacturing. It will not only consolidate and enhance traditional advantages, but also accelerate the cultivation of new dynamic energy. Driven by information technology, the development momentum of China's manufacturing industry has been transformed, and the structure has been optimized and the quality has been gradually improved. With the deep integration of informatization and industrialization, "Made in China" is realizing the transformation to intelligent manufacturing.

4.4.1 Development situation of "Made in China"

4.4.1.1 Comprehensive competitiveness is constantly increasing

Since the reform and opening up in 1978, China has successfully undertaken the third international industrial transfer and vigorously developed the manufacturing industry by taking advantage of labor force and resources to introduce industrial capital. Since the beginning of the 21st century, China's industrial added value has increased year by year, expanding from RMB19.16 trillion in 2011 to RMB22.9 trillion in 2015. The industrial output and production level are already among the world's highest, and the comprehensive strength of the manufacturing industry has increased significantly. According to the data of IHS, an American consulting company, China's manufacturing industry accounted for only 2.7% of the world's total in 1990. By 2010, this proportion surpassed that of the United States, reaching 19.8%, making China the world's largest manufacturing country. By 2014, this proportion jumped to 22% (see Table 4–1). China ranks first in the world in terms of the industrial scale of seven industries, including textiles, electric power equipment, transportation and tobacco. The output of more than 220 major industrial products ranks first in the world, and the output of crude steel accounts for nearly 50% of the world's total.[1]

Table 4-1   Changes in the global share of China's manufacturing output value   Unit: %

Number	Year	Global Share
1	1990	2.70
2	2000	6.00
3	2007	13.20
4	2010	19.80
5	2014	22.00

Source: Series interpretation data of Made in China 2025.

4.4.1.2   Significant improvement has been made in technology development and innovation capabilities

In order to improve the ability of independent innovation, China continuously strengthens policy guidance and support, gradually establishes a market-oriented innovation system with enterprises as the main body and the combination of industry, university and research, as well as increases research and development investment. According to the data of the National Bureau of Statistics, by 2015, China has become the second largest R&D investment country only second to the United States, and the proportion of R&D expenditure in GDP has reached the level of the moderately developed countries. China's investment capacity in high-tech industries has been significantly enhanced. In 2000, the state arranged six major special projects for high-tech industrialization in the fields of information technology, biotechnology and new materials, with a total investment of only RMB13.1 billion. In 2015, the national investment in the high-tech industry was as high as RMB3,259.8 billion, which further increased to RMB3,774.7 billion in 2016, an increase of 15.8% over 2015.

The enhancement of research and development capabilities has contributed to continuous innovation in industry technology. From 2012 to 2017, the number of invention patent applications in China has ranked first in the world for six years in a row. The "Crust 1" 10K ultra-deep scientific drilling rig has made significant breakthroughs in

---

[1] Ministry of Industry and Information Technology, Interpretation No. 2 of Made in China 2025: China's Manufacturing Development Enters a New Stage, the Website of Ministry of Industry and Information Technology, May 19, 2015, http://www.miit.gov.cn/n1146295/n1146295/n1652858/n1653018/c3780661/content.html.

deep drilling technology and intelligent mining technology. China's deep-water semi-submersible drilling unit (HYSY-981) has been the world's top.[1] In 2017, the total number of China's supercomputers in the Top 500 surpassed the United States, ranking first in the world. Among them, China's "Sunway TaihuLight" and "Tianhe-2" are among the top two in terms of computing speed. The "Sunway TaihuLight", located in the National Supercomputing Center in Wuxi, China, sustained Linpack performance is 93.01 petaflops, making it the fastest supercomputer in the world. The Linpack performance of Tianhe-2 is 33.86 petaflops, ranking second in the world. On November 17, 2017, the application of nonlinear earthquake model based on the supercomputing system of "Sunway TaihuLight" won the Gordon Bell Prize, the highest award in the international field of high-performance computing application.[2] China has built the world's first long-distance quantum communication backbone network, and the Quantum Experiments at Space Scale "Micius" has been successfully launched. The Gaofen-2 satellite has promoted the accuracy of civil remote sensing to sub-meter high resolution, and the BeiDou Navigation Satellite System with independent intellectual property rights has also entered a new era of global networking. The "Great Intelligence" independently developed by China became the world's first certified smart ship.

4.4.1.3 New progress has been made in industrial optimization and upgrading

In recent years, with the development and change of national industrial policies, China's traditional industrial structure has been continuously optimized and upgraded, and the production mode of enterprises has also changed from factor-driven to innovation-driven. With the deepening of supply-side structural reform, China has launched several reform measures to gradually eliminate backward production capacity and accelerate the transformation and upgrading of traditional industries. Seven strategic emerging industries—energy conservation and environmental protection, new-generation information technology, biotechnology, high-end equipment manufacturing, new energy, new materials and new-energy vehicles—have become the main driving force for economic growth. The level of high-tech manufacturing industries has been continuously enhanced, including medicine, aviation and aerospace equipment, electronic and telecommunications equipment, computer and office equipment, medical equipment and instruments, and information chemicals. And the added value of these industries

---

[1] He Ying, "Ideas for the Construction of China's Manufacturing Innovation Index System", *China Industry Review*, 2015(9), pp. 52-60.

[2] "Chinese Supercomputer Project Wins 2017 ACM Gordon Bell Prize", *People's Daily*, Nov. 18, 2017.

increased gradually. According to the data of the National Bureau of Statistics, since 2010, the growth rate of added value in China's high-tech manufacturing industry has kept above 10% (see Table 4–2). In 2015, it increased by 10.2%, accounting for 11.8% of the added value of industrial enterprises above designated size.[1] In 2016, the added value of China's strategic emerging industries grew by 10.5%, and the value added of high-tech industries grew by 10.8% over the previous year, which was 4.8 percentage points faster than the industries above designated size, and accounted for 12.4% of the added value of industries above designated size, an increase of 0.6 percentage points over the previous year.[2]

Table 4–2   Value added of high-tech manufacturing industry
in China from 2010 to 2016   Unit: %

Year	Growth rate of the added value in high-tech manufacturing industry	Proportion of industrial added value above designated size
2016	10.8	12.4
2015	10.2	11.8
2014	12.3	10.6
2013	11.8	—
2012	12.2	—
2011	16.5	—
2010	16.6	—

Source: Statistical Communiqué on the National Economic and Social Development issued by National Bureau of Statistics of China in previous years.

4.4.2   New challenges for "Made in China"

After more than 40 years development of reform and opening up, China has grown into a major manufacturing country in the world. However, China's manufacturing has always been large but not strong, with problems such as low independent innovation capacity, low brand value and weakened competitiveness of traditional comparative advantages.

---

[1] National Bureau of Statistics of the People's Republic of China: Statistical Communiqué of the People's Republic of China on the 2015 National Economic and Social Development, the Website of National Bureau of Statistics of the People's Republic of China, Feb. 29, 2016, http://www.stats.gov.cn/tjsj/zxfb/201602/t2016 0229_1323991.html.

[2] National Bureau of Statistics of the People's Republic of China: Statistical Communiqué of the People's Republic of China on the 2016 National Economic and Social Development, the Website of National Bureau of Statistics of the People's Republic of China, Feb. 28, 2017, http://www.stats.gov.cn/tjsj/zxfb/201702/t2017 0228_1467424.html.

4.4.2.1 The capacity for independent innovation is insufficient, and China is at the low end of the global value chain

The core technology and high-end equipment of China's manufacturing industry have a high degree of external dependence, with insufficient independent innovation capabilities and low profit levels. Taking manufacturing of electronic products, clothing and toys as examples, in the international division of labor dominated by developed capitalist countries, "Made in China" manufacturing is mainly focused on original equipment manufacturer (OEM) assembly and the production of non-core parts of products. China is locked in the low value-added link of the product value chain by virtue of its comparative advantage of labor force, while the high value-added links, such as technology development, R&D design, and marketing management, are occupied by the developed capitalist countries that dominate the international division of labor. Most Chinese enterprises are classified into the manufacturing link that has the lowest added value, the most consumption of resources, the most serious damage of environment, and the exploited laborers, while other links with higher added value are basically in the hands of enterprises in Europe and the United States.

American Mattel's Barbie doll is such a typical product. In the whole production chain, China is in the manufacturing link of the Barbie doll's international division of labor, and the profit shared is very low. "In the US market, the retail price of China's export of Barbie doll is US$9.99, while the import price at US customs is only US$2. The price difference of US$8 is taken away by the US as the added value of intelligence. Of the remaining US$2, US$1 is for transportation and management fees, and 65 cents pays for the cost of importing raw materials. China only gets 35 cents for processing fees."[1] Thus, in a ten-dollar value chain, the labor cost of manufacturing is only 35 cents. The domination and control of "cheap labor" by "developed capital" supported by technology has become a "bottleneck" for the development of China's manufacturing.

Similarly, the OEM production of electronic products is also a representative of China's manufacturing. From laptops to cell phones, China takes advantage of its rich labor force to occupy the production of non-core parts of electronic products and the production of complete machine assembly. The value-added of products and profits is very low. In addition, in order to grab the market, many Chinese manufacturers are competing at low cost by suppressing labor wages, further reducing labor's share of profits. Apple's products are typical examples in international productive specialization.

---

[1] Li Guangdou, "The Most 'Profitable' Toy in the World", *China Clothing News*, Mar. 11, 2011.

Its design, production, and assembly services are distributed in different countries around the world. The capital-intensive links such as the design and manufacturing of key chips containing core technologies are occupied by manufacturers in the United States, Japan, Republic of Korea and other countries. While Chinese manufacturers such as Foxconn occupy labor-intensive manufacturing links such as OEM assembly. Apple's net profit in 2015 reached US$53.394 billion. In such a high profit, the profit shared by Chinese workers who are part of the production chain is very low.

4.4.2.2   Traditional comparative advantages are gradually losing their dividends

Although the profit of the processing and manufacturing link in the international division of labor is very low, in this link, the undeveloped peripheral countries with the comparative advantage of labor force are also in fierce competition. Taking advantage of the third international industrial transfer, China entered the global value chain at the low end, becoming a manufacturing power with the advantages of cheap labor and resources. However, in the 21st century, with the gradual disappearance of China's demographic dividend and the rising labor costs, the capital of multinational corporations gradually withdrew from China and turned to cheaper countries such as Vietnam and Mexico, and some enterprises withdrew their capital from China, and the world entered the fourth wave of international industrial transfer. The world entered the fourth international industrial transfer. The reason why capital was transferred from China to Vietnam and other countries stems from the nature of capital to pursue surplus value or profit maximization. Capital is constantly searching for cheaper labor value around the world to further reduce variable capital expenditures.

In addition, China's manufacturing industry also has problems such as low utilization efficiency of resources and energy, prominent environmental pollution, unreasonable industrial structure, backward development of high-end equipment manufacturing and producer services, and low degree of industrial internationalization.

4.4.3   Strategic measures to develop "Intelligent Manufacturing in China"

Since the financial crisis, the global economy has entered a period of deep adjustment. China is actively looking for new economic growth points. With innovation as the driving force, China cultivates competitive advantages with the help of information technology innovation, vigorously develop intelligent manufacturing and emerging economy industries, and seize the strategic commanding heights of global manufacturing.

Faced with the deficiencies in independent innovation capability, resource utilization efficiency, industrial structure level, informatization level, quality and efficiency, etc., China actively seizes the development opportunities of the information technology revolution and implements a manufacturing power strategy in accordance with the Four-pronged Comprehensive Strategy to develop "Intelligent Manufacturing in China". Intelligent manufacturing is a general term for advanced manufacturing processes, systems and models. It incorporates the new generation of information technology into all aspects of manufacturing activities, such as design, production, management and service, with functions such as autonomous perception of the depth of information, intelligent optimization and self-determination, and precise control of self-execution.[1] The former Premier Li Keqiang pointed out that, "We will promote the extensive application of information technologies in industrialization, develop and utilize networking, digitalization, and smart technologies, and work to develop certain key areas first and make breakthroughs in these areas."[2] In October 2015, the Fifth Plenary Sessions of the 18th Central Committee of the CPC adopted the Proposal of the CPC Central Committee for Formulating the 13th Five-Year Plan for National Economic and Social Development, which states accelerate the construction of a manufacturing power, implement intelligent manufacturing projects, and build a new manufacturing system.

4.4.3.1 China formulated the Made in China 2025 action plan[3]

In 2015, the State Council issued Made in China 2025, emphasizing the deep integration of the new generation of information technology and manufacturing, and the establishment of new modes of production, industrial patterns, business models and economic growth points. This is the first ten-year action plan for China to build up its strength in manufacturing development. China has formulated the three-step strategy to achieve the goal of building up China's strength in manufacturing development.

First Step, from 2015 to 2025, China will enter the ranks of buiding up its strength in manufacturing development. Efforts should be made to continuously strengthen the

---

[1] Shanghai Municipal Commission of Economy and Informatization, Implementation Opinions on Accelerating the Development of Intelligent Manufacturing to Boost the Construction of Global Science and Technology Innovation Center in Shanghai, the Website of Shanghai Municipal People's Government, Aug. 21, 2015, http://www.shanghai.gov.cn/nw2/nw2314/nw2319/nw10800/mw11408/nw32865/u26aw44622.html.

[2] Li Keqiang, Report on the Work of the Government Delivered at the Third Session of the 12th National People's Congress of the People's Republic of China, Mar. 5, 2015, the Chinese Central Government's Official Website, Mar. 16, 2015. http://www.gov.cn/guowuyuan/2015-03/16/content_2835101.htm.

[3] China Informatization Almanac Compilation Committee, *China Informatization Almanac 2015*, Beijing: Publishing House of Electronics Industry, 2016, pp. 366-379.

integration of industrialization and informatization, master the core technologies in key areas, accelerate the building of digitized, networked and intelligent manufacturing, so China can basically realize industrialization by 2020. By 2025, the integration of industrialization and informatization will reach a new level, and a number of multinational corporations and industrial clusters with strong international competitiveness will be formed. And China's position in the global industrial division of labor and the value chain will increase significantly. The national action plan puts forward specific indicators for the integration of industrialization and industrialization (see Table 4–3).

Table 4–3   Main indicators of the integration of informatization and industrialization of manufacturing in 2020 and 2025   Unit: %

Indicator	2013	2015	2020	2025
Popularity of broadband networks	37	50	70	82
Popularity of tools for digital R&D and design	52	58	72	84
Rate of numerical control on key processes	27	33	50	64

Source: The State Council, Made in China 2025.

Second step, from 2025 to 2035, China will reach the middle level of the manufacturing powers. By 2035, China will achieve full industrialization and greatly enhance its innovation capacity. The advantageous industries will form global leadership in innovation.

Third step, from 2035 to 2049, China's comprehensive strength will enter the forefront of the world's manufacturing powers. By the 100th anniversary of the founding of the People's Republic of China, the main areas of the manufacturing will have innovation leadership and obvious competitive advantages, and the leading technology system and industrial system in the world will be established.

To build up China's strength in manufacturing development, China must follow a new path of industrialization with Chinese characteristics, accelerate the deep integration of the new generation of information technology and manufacturing, promote the replacement of old drivers of growth with new ones, and vigorously promote "intelligent manufacturing". The CPC Central Committee and the State Council attach great importance to it, and have clearly defined the strategic focus and core tasks. Made in China 2025 has put forward nine strategic tasks and focus, including improving the innovation capacity of China's manufacturing, promoting the deep integration of informatization and industrialization, enhance basic industrial capabilities, strengthen the building of quality brands, comprehensively implement green manufacturing, advance the development of key areas, further promote the structural adjustment of the manufacturing, actively develop service-oriented manufacturing and producer services, improve the international development level of the manufacturing. China has put forward various measures to promote the transformation and upgrading of China's manufacturing, improve the core competitiveness of manufacturing, and ultimately achieve the strategic goal of building up China's strength in manufacturing development.

(1) *Perfecting the manufacturing innovation system, implementing the science and technology innovation projects, and improving the innovation capacity of manufacturing*

Made in China 2025 proposes to establish and perfect a manufacturing innovation system, a combination of government, industry, university and research with enterprises as the main body and market as the guidance. China will implement science and technology innovation projects to improve the innovation capacity of manufacturing.

First, advocate the research and development of core technologies, improve innovative design capabilities and actively promoting the industrialization of scientific and technological achievements. China strengthens the dominant position of enterprises in innovation, carries out major national science and technology projects, and supports research and development of core technologies through science and technology programs. China develops all kinds of innovative design education, establishes national industrial design awards, improves innovative design capabilities, strengthens the research and development of key common technologies in the design field, and overcomes common technologies such as informatization design, process integrated design, complex process and system design. China establishes and improves the information release and sharing platform of scientific and technological achievements, improves the incentive mechanism for the transformation of scientific and technological achievements, and continuously promotes the industrialization of scientific and technological achievements.

Second, improve the innovation system of manufacturing, accelerate the establishment of manufacturing innovation network with innovation center as the core carrier, public service platform and engineering data center as important support, build manufacturing engineering data center in key fields, in order to provide open and sharing service of innovation knowledge and engineering data for enterprises. China vigorously develops manufacturing innovation projects. Around the common requirements for innovative development of the new generation of information technology, intelligent manufacturing, and additive manufacturing, China has built industrial technology research bases, aiming to build about 15 by 2025 and about 40 by 2035.

(2) *Promoting the integrated development of the new generation of information technology and manufacturing technology, and vigorously promoting intelligent manufacturing*

The deep integration of information technology and manufacturing technology is the key to the transformation and upgrading of China's manufacturing. China has formulated policies to vigorously promote technology integration, develop intelligent equipment and products, promote intelligent production processes, and realize intelligent manufacturing.

First, promoting the intellectualization of equipment and products. With the new generation of information technology as the driving force, efforts should be made to accelerate the development of intelligent manufacturing technology standards, establish intelligent manufacturing industry alliances, carry out integrated innovation and engineering application of the integration of the new generation of information technology and manufacturing equipment, develop smart products and autonomously controllable smart devices, and realize industrialization. The key intelligent manufacturing equipment and products that China is actively developing mainly include intelligent equipment such as high-grade digital machine tools, industrial robots, and additive manufacturing equipment, as well as intelligent core devices such as new type sensors, intelligent measuring instruments, industrial control systems, servo motors and drives, and reducers.

Second, actively promoting the intellectualization of the manufacturing process. Relying on advantageous industries, China will build intelligent factories and digital workshops in key fields, closely focusing on the intellectualization of key processes, the replacement of key positions by robots, the intelligent optimization and control of production processes, and the optimization of supply chain. China will accelerate the application of human-computer intelligent interaction, industrial robots, intelligent logistics management, additive manufacturing and other technologies and equipment in the production process to promote the simulation optimization of manufacturing processes, digital control, real-time monitoring of state information and adaptive control. China has proposed to actively rely on advantage industries, and strive to achieve full intellectualization in key areas of manufacturing by 2025, reducing the operation cost of pilot demonstration projects by 50%, shortening product life cycle by 50%, and reducing the rate of defective products by 50%.

(3) *Relying on information infrastructure such as the internet to vigorously develop "internet + manufacturing"*

Enterprises rely on the industrial internet, big data and other platforms to achieve changes in research and development, production and management model. China has proposed to take consumer demand as the guide, improve innovation vitality, and develop new manufacturing models such as personalized customization, crowd-sourcing design, and cloud manufacturing based on the internet.

Based on the internet, China will develop personalized customization with consumer demand as the core and driving force, establish customer databases to respond to the dynamic demand of consumers in a timely manner, and force the supply chain of enterprises to set production on demand, reduce inventory and reduce costs. On the basis of the IoT, network collaboration models such as intelligent monitoring, remote diagnostic management and traceability of the whole industrial chain will be cultivated to achieve lean management and improve resource allocation efficiency.

Promoting the development of intelligent manufacturing with industrial cloud. Through industrial cloud, large-scale scattered information technology resources will be integrated and shared to achieve social services and reduce the cost of enterprise informatization. The application of industrial cloud can greatly promote the application of industrial software in R&D design, technological process, production equipment, process control and other aspects, promote automatic control and intelligent control of the entire production process, and accelerate the establishment of modern production system.

(4) *Vigorously develop strategic emerging industries based on the new generation of information technology*

The new generation of information technology is mainly focused on big data, cloud computing, communication networks, IoT, triple-network convergence, new flat-panel displays, high-performance integrated circuits, and high-end software.[1] In the process of building a strong manufacturing country, relying on the new generation of information technology, China will vigorously develop the information technology industries such as integrated circuits and special equipment, information and communication equipment, operating systems and industrial software, and promote the systematic development and large-scale application of the new generation of information technology.

---

[1] Xia Yanna, Zhao Sheng, *China Manufacturing 2025: Industrial Internet Opens New Industrial Revolution*, Beijing: China Machine Press, 2016, p. 179.

China focuses on developing the new generation of information technology industry (including integrated circuit and special equipment, information and communications equipment, operating systems and industrial software), high-grade digital machine tools and robots, aerospace equipment, marine engineering equipment and high-tech ships, advanced rail transportation equipment, energy saving and new energy vehicles, electronic equipment, agricultural machinery equipment, new materials, biological medicine and high performance medical device, all of which will foster new economic growth points, optimize the industrial structure, and promote economic transformation and upgrading.

(5) *Actively carrying out service-oriented manufacturing and promoting the coordinated development of manufacturing and service*

The coordinated development of manufacturing and service is the inevitable trend of the development of intelligent manufacturing. China actively promotes the extension of industries from processing and manufacturing links to high-end links such as cooperative R&D, joint design, marketing and brand cultivation, so as to extend the enterprise value chain, promote the transformation of production-oriented manufacturing to service-oriented manufacturing, and foster the development of producer services such as e-commerce, modern logistics and internet finance.

By expanding value-added services and increasing investment in service links, enterprises develop personalized customization services, internet precision marketing, online support services and total life cycle management to realize business process reengineering and develop service-oriented manufacturing. Through information technology and the internet, China will accelerate the development of producer services, carry out e-commerce, mobile electronic commerce, online customization and other modes, develop modern logistics service outsourcing, financial leasing, after-sales service, brand building and other productive services, and focus on the development of modern service industries such as R&D and design, information, logistics, commerce and finance. At the same time, China will rely on the internet to carry out services with high value-added, such as network collaborative design, precision marketing, value-added service innovation and media brand promotion.

(6) *Optimizing the development layout, and promoting the coordinated development of large, medium and small enterprises as well as manufacturing industries in the eastern, central, and western regions of China*

First, promoting the structural adjustment of the manufacturing to achieve the coordinated development of large enterprises and small and medium-sized enterprises (SMEs). Firstly, with advantageous enterprises as the leader and main body, efforts should be made to foster the cooperation between enterprises, improve the scale and intensive operation level of enterprises, and cultivate competitive enterprise groups. Secondly, stimulating the vitality of SMEs to promote them to focus on market segmentation and improve their unique competitiveness. China will guide the coordinated development of large enterprises and SMEs, and achieve win-win cooperation through professional division of labor.

Second, promoting the structural adjustment of the manufacturing, and promoting the coordinated development of manufacturing industries in the eastern, central, and western regions of China. China will optimize the spatial distribution of manufacturing development in accordance with regional advantages and local conditions to promote the coordinated development of the eastern coastal areas and the central and western regions. In the eastern coastal region, China will actively promote the coordinated development of industries in the Beijing-Tianjin-Hebei region and the Yangtze River Economic Belt. At the same time, a national industrial transfer information service platform will be established to actively guide the rational and orderly transfer of industries to the central and western regions, injecting vitality into the development of manufacturing in the central and western regions.

(7) *Giving full play to the advantages of the system, deepening the reform of the mechanism, and improving financial and fiscal support policies*

China is accelerating the deepening of the reform of the administrative examination and approval system, reforming the technological innovation management system and the mechanism of project funding allocation, achievement evaluation and transformation, innovating the government management method, actively deepening the reform of state-owned enterprises, and creating a fair market competition environment for the construction of a manufacturing power.

The state emphasizes the need to deepen reform in the financial sector to broaden financing channels and actively leverage the advantages of policy finance, development finance and commercial finance to guide risk investment and private equity investment. It also encourages eligible manufacturing to carry out securitization pilots by loans and leased assets, which will promote the transformation and upgrading of manufacturing through financial leasing.

In terms of fiscal levy policy, through the cooperation between the government and social capital, China will guide financial funds to focus on intelligent manufacturing, the development of key basic materials, core basic spare parts and components, advanced fundamental techniques, and basic industrial technologies, high-end equipment and other key areas, and implement tax policies conducive to the transformation and upgrading of manufacturing to reduce the burden on enterprises.

4.4.3.2   Local version of Made in China 2025

After the State Council released Made in China 2025, Jiangsu, Fujian, Guangdong, Hebei, Beijing, Zhejiang, Shandong and other provinces have issued documents, putting forward specific guiding suggestions and quantitative targets for developing Made in China and building a manufacturing power, all of which promote the integrated development of manufacturing and the internet, and accelerate the transformation from "Made in China" to "Created in China" and "Intelligent Manufacturing in China".

In June 2015, Jiangsu Province first issued the Program of Action on Made in China 2025 in Jiangsu Province, which put forward specific action measures for the development and construction of Jiangsu's manufacturing in the next ten years, and set the overall goal of building a domestic leading and internationally influential manufacturing province by 2025

In July 2015, Fujian Province issued the Action Plan for the Implementation of Made in China 2025 in Fujian Province and Opinions of the People's Government of Fujian Province of China on Further Accelerating Industrial Transformation and Upgrading, proposing that the motive force of the development of manufacturing in Fujian should be turned from factors to innovation, so as to promote the upgrading of industrial structure in Fujian.

In August 2015, Shanghai issued the Implementation Opinions on Accelerating the Development of Intelligent Manufacturing to Boost the Construction of Global Science and Technology Innovation Center in Shanghai, which focuses on the application layer, equipment layer, network layer and platform layer to implement five major projects, including intelligent manufacturing application demonstration, independent breakthrough, standard support, platform creation and carrier construction.

In September 2015, Guangdong Province issued the Opinions on Implementing Made in China 2025. Combined with the Intelligent Manufacturing Development Plan of Guangdong Province (2015-2025), it promotes the transformation and upgrading of manufacturing with the deep integration of the new generation of information technology and manufacturing as the breakthrough point and with intelligent manufacturing as the core.

In November 2015, Hebei Province issued the Implementation Opinions on Further Promoting Made in China 2025, which focuses on building ten major projects for the development of manufacturing, including technological upgrading, strong foundation for manufacturing, manufacturing innovation center construction, collaborative innovation of the industrial chain, intelligent manufacturing, "internet + collaborative manufacturing", green manufacturing, coordinated development of manufacturing and service, the "Double-thousand Project" (to implement over 1,000 key projects and to achieve a total investment of over RMB100 billion during the 14th Five-year Plan Period), and international cooperation with superior production capacity.

In December 2015, Beijing issued the Program of Action on Made in China 2025 in Beijing, proposing eight new industrial ecological special projects for the development of intelligent manufacturing, including new energy intelligent vehicles, integrated circuits, intelligent manufacturing systems and services, autonomous controllable information systems, cloud computing and big data, the new generation of mobile internet, the new generation of health treatment and services, and general aviation and satellite applications.

In December 2015, Zhejiang Province issued the Program of Action on Made in China 2025 in Zhejiang Province, and Tianjin also issued the Practice Plan for Building a National Advanced Manufacturing R&D Base in Tianjin (2015-2020). In March 2016, Shandong Province issued the Program of Action on Made in China 2025 in Shandong Province. At the same time, Henan, Hubei, Hunan, Anhui, Jiangxi, Shanxi and other provinces in central China, as well as Sichuan, Yunnan, Gansu, Guizhou, Qinghai and other provinces in western China also issued action programs and planning, and established a number of supporting policies and measures to actively undertake industrial transfer, adjust the industrial structure, deepen the innovation drive, promote the deep integration of informatization and industrialization, and build a modern industrial system.

All provinces fully realize the importance of the development of manufacturing to economic growth. Based on the market demand, they adhere to the problem-oriented and put forward action guide for intelligent manufacturing with clear objectives and strong operability according to local conditions. The policy priorities of all provinces mainly include the following aspects:

First, improving the support system of intelligent manufacturing, and promoting the upgrading of enterprises' intellectualization. The establishment of a comprehensive support system of intelligent manufacturing is the key to achieving intelligent upgrading of enterprises. In the Program of Action on Made in China 2025 in Jiangsu Province, Jiangsu Province clearly stated that it is necessary to improve the industrial information infrastructure of "network + cloud + terminal" (industrial broadband network, industrial cloud, and industrial intelligent terminal), and build industrial internet with low latency, high reliability, and wide coverage; at the same time, organize and carry out the "enterprise to enterprise" broadband projects for large and medium-sized enterprises, high-bandwidth dedicated line services for industrial enterprises and production service enterprises, and optimize "industrial cloud", "enterprise cloud", and "e-enterprise cloud" of small and medium-sized enterprises, so as to provide basic services for intelligent manufacturing.

To promote the intelligent upgrading of enterprises, Shanghai proposed to promote the coordinated development of intelligent manufacturing in application layer, equipment layer, network layer and platform layer, and build intelligent manufacturing application demonstration project, intelligent equipment independent breakthrough project, intelligent manufacturing standard support project, intelligent manufacturing platform creation project, and intelligent manufacturing carrier construction project.

Second, vigorously developing the "internet + manufacturing" to promote the transformation of manufacturing services. By promoting the integration and innovation of the internet and manufacturing, the level of intelligent development of enterprises will be improved. In the development of "internet + manufacturing" strategy, Jiangsu Province has proposed to implement the industrial internet integration innovation plan to promote the integrated and interconnected development of the next generation internet, mobile internet, IoT and cloud computing. The government encourages enterprises to develop new manufacturing models based on the internet, such as personalized customization, crowd-sourcing design, and cloud computing, and encourages enterprises to carry out personalized manufacturing and precision marketing by using big data. The government supports enterprises to carry out internet-based services and business model innovation, provides intelligent vertical services both online and offline, and develops high value-added services such as product design, operation and maintenance, retail distribution, and brand management.

Third, strengthening the construction of service function areas and public service platforms to promote intelligent collaboration across the whole industry chain. The service function areas and public service platforms are the basic platforms to realize information and data sharing and promote the coordinated development of the whole industry chain. Jiangsu Province has proposed to accelerate the construction of China Industrial Design Service Center and Jiangsu Industrial Design International Cooperation Platform, build an intelligent logistics demonstration base with logistics carriers such as intelligent management and dispatch center, intelligent logistics and distribution center, intelligent logistics port, intelligent monitoring and intelligent perceptual guidance platform, and build a logistics public information platform that provides regional and industry-wide supply chain services.

In the Implementation Opinions on Accelerating the Development of Intelligent Manufacturing in Shanghai to Promote the Construction of Global Science and Technology Innovation Center, Shanghai clearly proposed that it is necessary to accelerate the development of unified development platforms for intelligent manufacturing basic software and engineering software, and create innovation centers, inspection and testing centers, maker spaces, industrial supply and demand docking and information services, talent training bases, cloud services for industrial enterprises, information system security supervision and other service platforms in the field of intelligent manufacturing, which will promote the intelligent collaboration of the whole industrial chain.

Fourth, developing strategic emerging industries and building modern industrial clusters. The development of strategic emerging industries is the key to the transformation and upgrading of enterprises, and is the new growth point of the economy. Jiangsu Province proposed to actively develop strategic emerging industries and promote the intensive and concentrated development of industries. Efforts should be made to create international advantageous industrial clusters such as high-end intelligent equipment, software and the new generation of information technology, new energy materials and applications, green low-carbon energy conservation and environmental protection, branded textile and garment, medicine and health, modern logistics, science and technology services, and business services.

Zhejiang Province proposed to promote the transformation and upgrading of the massive economy to intelligent industrial clusters. It will implement the "internet +" industrial cluster development initiative, carry out trials for smart industrial clusters, and foster a number of information engineering companies to support the transformation of information application in industrial clusters. It will also actively promote the extension of industrial clusters to develop high-end equipment, and cultivate a number of high-end equipment industry clusters with information technology equipment, robots, modern agricultural intelligent equipment as the main body.

Fifth, establishing national demonstration zones for the development of intelligent manufacturing, and making full use of the selected units to promote work in the entire area. The intelligent transformation of traditional industries cannot be achieved overnight and fully coordinated. All provinces and cities should act according to local conditions and give priority to the development of advantage industries. Starting with individual projects that are expected to help spur larger-scale regional cooperative development, China will gradually promote it through pilot demonstration areas. Shanghai proposed to implement a batch of smart manufacturing pilot demonstration projects in industries and industrial parks with better basic conditions in Shanghai, build intelligent manufacturing application demonstration projects, so as to promote intelligent application of enterprises, and encourage state-owned enterprises to take the lead in intelligent upgrading and transformation.

Guangdong Province proposed to build national demonstration areas for the development of intelligent manufacturing. Selecting clusters or parks where the R&D and manufacturing of intelligent equipment and key components and parts, as well as intelligent manufacturing system integration and application service industries are relatively concentrated, it aims to establish about 10 intelligent manufacturing demonstration bases, and actively establish demonstration areas for the development of the robot industry.

Sixth, actively developing special manufacturing projects combined with the advantages of local resources. The difference in resource advantages in various regions determines the difference in the key industries for the development of intelligent manufacturing in various provinces and cities. In its development strategy, Zhejiang Province takes 11 industries as the focus of industrial development. In addition to the industries such as robot, intelligent equipment, new energy, new materials, Internet of Things and industrial software, it also takes green petrochemical industry and fashion light textile industry as the key development industries in combination with the local resource advantages. It focuses on promoting the construction of Zhoushan green petrochemical base and Zhenhai refining and chemical integration projects, and strives to build facing-port petrochemical ecological industry clusters with the aim of building a world-class modern green petrochemical base. Utilizing the existing industrial advantages, Zhejiang Province vigorously develops fashion light textile industry and silk products, and uses information technology to improve the design of fashion products.

Zhejiang Province initiated local industrial restructuring, transforming the province's extensive and inefficient growth pattern, and encouraged leading enterprises from outside the province to invest in Zhejiang. Zhejiang also built smart factories and facilitates the reutilization of idle resources such as vacant buildings and factories. It has been vigorously cultivating well-known companies, well-known brands and well-known entrepreneurs. It deeply promotes the quality upgrading of manufacturing, implements innovative cultivation project of micro, small and medium-sized enterprises, and cultivates new economic growth points and innovation engines.

Seventh, innovating the fiscal and financial policies to support the development of the micro, small and medium-sized enterprises. All provinces actively implement various national preferential policies, and provide support for the transformation of traditional enterprises in terms of taxation and finance. Jiangsu Province has established the Jiangsu Industrial and Information Industry Investment Fund of about RMB30 billion, focusing on supporting the upgrading of manufacturing and the integration of industrialization and informatization. Shanghai innovates financial services, guides the venture capital guidance fund, angel investment fund, industrial investment fund and other funds created by the government to give key support to intelligent manufacturing, and encourages social venture capital and equity investment to be put into the field of intelligent manufacturing. Guangdong Province has innovated and improved the investment and financing mechanism of micro, small, and medium-sized enterprises, and implemented special policies to promote the scale of these enterprises. Priority will be given to financing guarantee, preferential taxes and fees, financial support, counseling and training, and burden reduction for enterprises. Shandong Province innovates financing services for small and medium-sized enterprises, establishes award and compensation mechanism for loans for small and micro enterprises, actively promotes small and medium-sized enterprises to issue collective notes, collective bonds, collective trust and private placement bonds, and lists financing on the New Third Board and the provincial equity market, so as to attract more social capital to invest in small and medium-sized enterprises.

Eighth, the innovation ability is constantly enhanced, and the integration of industrialization and informatization has become the core strategic goal. The transformation and upgrading of the industrial structure of China's manufacturing must be based on information technology to promote the transformation of the driving force of economic growth from factor-driven to innovation-driven and to improve the intelligent level of production. For example, based on the principle of high-end leadership and intelligent support, Jiangsu Province proposed to deepen the integrated application of informatization and network technology, improve the level of intelligent manufacturing, accelerate the development of strategic emerging industries, and transform and upgrade traditional industries. It is expected that by 2025, Jiangsu Province will develop and apply 100 first piece (set) of major equipment to fill in gaps in domestic equipment by 50%; significantly improve the numerical control rate of enterprise machining and the application rate of high-end numerical control equipment, and the autonomous supporting rate of intelligent devices such as industrial robots and additive manufacturing equipment will reach more than 80%; cultivate 20 high-end equipment manufacturing feature and demonstration industrial base; basically build a complete intelligent manufacturing innovation system to widely promote intelligent manufacturing. The indicators of innovation ability and the integration of informatization and industrialization for Jiangsu Province to build a manufacturing power (see Table 4–4).

Table 4–4   Main indicators of building up its strength in manufacturing development in Jiangsu Province

Category	Indicator	2015	2020	2025
Innovation capability	The proportion of internal R&D expenditures in main business revenue of industrial enterprises above designated size (%)	1.02	1.30	1.70
	The number of scientific and technical personnel per 10,000 employees in enterprises (person)	80	90	100
	The number of invention patents granted per RMB10 billion output value of industrial enterprises (piece)	52	87	120
The integration of informatization and industrialization	Overall index of the integration of informatization and industrialization	94	98	105
	Popularity of tools for digital R&D and design (%)	67	75	85
	Numerical control rate of key process manufacturing equipment (%)	35	52	70
	Integrated coverage rate of production, supply, marketing and financial management (%)	20	30	40

Source: The website of the Economic and Information Commission of Jiangsu Province, the Program of Action on Made in China 2025 in Jiangsu Province.

Guangdong Province proposed to build national demonstration areas for the development of intelligent manufacturing and intelligent manufacturing industry clusters with international competitiveness. In order to achieve this goal, Guangdong Province put forward specific quantitative indicators on the development of intelligent equipment. By 2020, the added value of intelligent equipment industry reaches RMB400 billion, the output value of robots and related supporting industries reaches RMB100 billion, and the number of robots in the manufacturing industry reaches 100; by 2025, the intellectualization of the manufacturing industry will penetrate deeply, and the integrated application of information technology in manufacturing enterprises above designated size will reach the domestic leading level.[1]

4.5 Main progress of the integration of informatization and industrialization

Vigorously promoting the deep integration of informatization and industrialization is a strategic measure to promote China's economic transformation and upgrading, reshape new advantages in international competition, and build up China's strength in manufacturing development. The development of the industrial informatization in China is mainly reflected in the degree of the integration of informatization and industrialization. Sorting out the main progress of the integration of informatization and industrialization and analyzing the level of integration can provide a comprehensive and objective grasp of the development level of China's industrial informatization, and at the same time help to find existing problems so that various policies and measures can be adjusted in a timely manner.

4.5.1 The overall level of the integration of informatization and industrialization has improved significantly

Since the launching of the integrated development strategy of informatization and industrialization at the 17th CPC National Congress, the state, industries and enterprises have coordinated to advance it, and the national-level pilot zones of the integration of informatization and industrialization have played a good leading role. The coverage of the integration of informatization and industrialization continues to expand, the level of industrial informatization has improved significantly, and economic benefits have increased significantly.

The level of the integration of informatization and industrialization is mainly reflected in the basic environment and practical application of the industrial informatization. In terms of the basic environment of the industrial informatization, the construction of information infrastructure has been gradually improved, and network resources such as the internet and mobile internet have continued to be developed and improved. The information service platforms for small and medium-sized enterprises

---

[1] People's Government of Guangdong Province, Opinions on Implementing Made in China 2025 of the People's Government of Guangdong Province, the Website of the Guangdong Provincial Commission of Economy and Informatization, Sep. 25, 2015.

have also become the important information resources for enterprises' transformation and upgrading. As of the end of September 2017, internet companies had developed a total of 41.95 million broadband access users, up 43.4% year on year. In terms of industrial applications, informatization has become an important catalyst in the development of new industrialization. Information technology, information networks, and information resources have penetrated into the entire product life cycle of enterprises, including equipment production, production processes, and marketing services. Informatization is in R&D and design. The application level of information technology in R&D and design, manufacturing, marketing management, customer service, procurement, logistics and other links has been increasing year by year. Modern modes of production such as enterprise resource planning based on information technology and the internet, production process execution systems for manufacturing enterprises, product life cycle management, software configuration management, e-commerce, and intelligent manufacturing, have gradually taken shape. In terms of application benefit, with the continuous improvement of information infrastructure, the degree of information application in the production process of enterprises has increased year by year, and the comprehensive benefits are gradually emerging, with the application benefit index jumping from 57.47 in 2011 to 83.25 in 2015.[1] The improvement of the level of informatization has reduced production costs and resource consumption, increased labor productivity, and promoted the continuous increase of the main business income of enterprises.

In short, for the development of the industrial informatization, the CPC Central Committee and the State Council have made unified planning and deployment, and formulated policies and measures. China gives priority to the improvement of information infrastructure and gives full play to the comprehensive advantages of China's internet, so as to promote the development of information technology in industry from local applications to integrated applications and significantly improve application benefits. The Center for China Information Industry Development has set up a set of indicators for the integration of informatization and industrialization to evaluate the development level of the integration of informatization and industrialization. The results show that since 2011, the overall index of the integration of informatization and industrialization has been on the rise, and the integration of informatization and industrialization has entered a period of rapid development (see Table 4–5).

---

[1] China Center for Information Industry Development, *The Blue Book on the Integration of Informatization and Industrialization in China (2015)*, Beijing: People's Publishing House, 2016.

Table 4–5   Comparison of the various indexes of the integration of informatization
and industrialization from 2011 to 2015

Year	Basic environment index	Increment	Industrial application index	Increment	Application benefit index	Increment	Total index	Increment
2011	52.93	—	50.26	—	57.47	—	52.73	—
2012	58.36	5.43	56.13	5.87	65.65	8.18	59.07	6.34
2013	64.87	6.51	57.34	1.21	68.27	2.62	61.95	2.88
2014	71.71	6.84	59.7	2.36	73.43	5.16	66.14	4.19
2015	75.38	3.67	66.04	6.34	83.25	9.82	72.68	6.54

Source: Center for China Information Industry Development.

4.5.2   Electronic information industry has become an important force for industrial growth

With the in-depth development of the integration of informatization and industrialization, China's electronic information industry has accelerated its innovative development, opening up new space for economic growth. In the process of the industrial informatization, the contribution of electronic information industry to the national economy is increasing day by day, and its growth rate ranks first among all industrial sectors, becoming an important force in leading the industrial growth. The strong support of national policies has promoted the deep integration of electronic information industry and traditional manufacturing. China has continuously increased capital input in the information industry. The investment fund for the integrated circuit industry, the special fund for industrial transformation and upgrading, and the investment fund for the advanced manufacturing industry have played an obvious driving role, and the innovation of electronic information technology has been continuously strengthened. The amount of investment received by the electronic information industry has grown rapidly. The number of electronic information industries above designated size has increased year by year. The total sales revenue and main business income have increased significantly. Among them, the software business has developed well, which has effectively promoted the development of other industries.

With the support of the national policies, the overall efficiency of the electronic information industry is gradually improving. In 2012, the sales revenue of China's electronic information industry exceeded RMB10 trillion, reaching RMB11 trillion, an increase of more than 15%. The software industry achieved revenue of RMB2,502.2

billion, with a year-on-year increase of 28.5%.[1] The degree of integration between the software industry and the manufacturing industry has also gradually deepened, the growth rate of embedded system software has accelerated, and the revenue of software and the service industry of information technology has increased year by year, further enhancing the penetration of the traditional manufacturing industry. In 2015, the electronic information industry added RMB965.89 billion in fixed assets, up 20.6% year on year. With the increase of investment scale, the number of enterprises above designated size in the electronic information industry reached 60,800, including 19,900 enterprises in the electronic information manufacturing and 40,900 enterprises in the software and information technology service industry. By 2016, the added value of the electronic information manufacturing above designated size increased by 10% year-on-year, 4 percentage points faster than the growth rate of all industries above designated size, and its share in the added value of industries above designated size increased to 7.5%. In recent years, the development level of the electronic information manufacturing industry has gradually increased, becoming an important contributor to industrial growth (see Table 4–6 for specific data).

Table 4–6   Development of China's electronic information manufacturing industry from 2008 to 2016

Year	Investment in fixed assets of projects above RMB500,000 in electronic information industry (RMB100 million)	Investment growth rate (%)	Main business income of electronic information manufacturing industry (RMB100 million)	Software industry revenue (RMB100 million)
2008	3,529.0	—	51,253	7,573
2009	4,147.0	17.5	51,305	9,513
2010	5,993.0	44.5	63,645	13,589
2011	8,183.0	36.5	74,909	18,849
2012	9,592.0	17.2	84,619	25,022
2013	10,828.0	12.9	93,202	30,587
2014	12,065.0	11.4	102,988	37,026
2015	13,775.3	14.1	111,318	43,000
2016	15,951.8	15.8	120,668	49,000

Source: The website of Ministry of Industry and Information Technology, and the Statistical Communiqué on Electronic Information Industry in previous years.

---

[1] Ministry of Industry and Information Technology, Statistical Communiqué on the Electronic Information Industry in 2012, the Website of Ministry of Industry and Information Technology of the People's Republic of China, Feb. 5, 2013. http://www.miit.gov.cn/n1146312/n1146904/n1648355/c3335511/content.html.

In 2017, the investment in fixed assets of projects over RMB5 million in the electronic information manufacturing increased by 25.3% year-on-year, hitting a new high in the past five years. The growth rate accelerated by 9.5% year-on-year, maintaining a high growth rate of more than 20% for 10 consecutive months. Driven by huge investment, the added value of the electronic information manufacturing above designated size increased by 13.8% year-on-year, 7.2 percentage points faster than the growth rate of all industries above designated size.[1]

4.5.3 The enterprises' comprehensive informatization has achieved remarkable results

Enterprises are the microscopic subjects of information application, and are the main force in promoting industrial modernization. At present, the enterprise informatization based on the whole industry chain has made great progress, the level of the enterprise informatization has significantly improved, and the effect of improving the quality and efficiency of enterprises is remarkable. In the process of exploring the integration of informatization and industrialization, China is constantly exploring new models. In 2009, for the first time, China approved the establishment of eight national-level pilot areas for the integration of industrialization and informatization, including Shanghai, Chongqing, and the Pearl River Delta, so as to explore the application model of information technology in traditional industries. The establishment of the comprehensive pilot zones has effectively promoted the development of the enterprise informatization.

Informatization in R&D and design promotes the gradual enhancement of the innovation capabilities of enterprises. A technological innovation system with enterprises as the main body and with a combination of government, industry, university and research has been basically established. China has formulated various policies to vigorously promote informatization in R&D and design, and the R&D expenditure has gradually increased and the innovation capability of enterprises has significantly improved. In terms of technological innovation, China supports qualified private enterprises to establish national technological innovation centers, giving full play to the dominant position of enterprises of various types and further enhancing their innovation capabilities. During the 12th Five-year Plan period, the proportion of R&D expenditure of industrial enterprises above designated size exceeded 0.85% of the main business income, the popularity of digital design in large and medium-sized enterprises increased

---

[1] Website of Ministry of Industry and Information Technology.

by 23.5%, and the average annual growth rate of invention patents in ten key areas, such as new-generation information technology and high-grade digital machine tools, exceeded 23%.[1]

Driven by major national projects, such as the national defense science and technology industry foundation project, the equipment manufacturing capacity has been continuously improved, and intelligent equipment has become an important tool for enterprises to produce. The intelligent level of complete sets of equipment has been significantly improved, and the numerical control rate of key technological processes in major industries has exceeded 70%. Intelligent equipment, such as high-grade digital machine tools, industrial robots, and new smart terminals, enjoys a sound momentum of development. The large-scale, fast and efficient press line and the automated production line of automotive welding based on industrial robots have reached the world advanced level. More and more enterprises have introduced robot production lines and implemented the "machine substitution" plan to build smart workshops and smart factories in various forms. Industrial robots have promoted the continuous improvement of enterprise intelligent production, and the current market share of domestic robots in China has risen to 25%. According to the survey data of Gaogong Industry Institute (GGII), in 2013, China surpassed Japan to become the world's largest industrial robot application market. In 2014, China added 56,000 new industrial robots in the Chinese market, accounting for 25% of the global market.[2] In 2015, 75,000 new industrial robots were added to the Chinese market, accounting for 28.4% of the global market.[3] Data from the China Robot Industry Alliance shows that the total sales volume of China's industrial robots in 2016 reached 88,900, an increase of 26.6% over 2015. According to the statistics of the Ministry of Industry and Information Technology, in 2017, China's industrial robots continued to maintain a rapid growth trend, with output exceeding 100,000 units for the first time, and international competitiveness continued to increase.

China has actively promoted the implementation of standards for the integrated management system of informatization and industrialization, and selected national, provincial and municipal-level implementation pilot enterprises in batches. By the end of 2015, more than 2,000 enterprises have carried out the practical application of

---

[1] Website of Ministry of Industry and Information Technology.

[2] Gaogong Industry Institute, Global and Chinese Industrial Robotics Market Research Report in 2015 (the third Edition), the website of Gaogong Industry Institute, Aug. 17, 2015. http://www.gg-robot.com.

[3] Gaogong Industry Institute, Research Report on Robotics Industry Development in 2016, the Website of Gaogong Industry Institute, Apr. 18, 2016. http://www.gg-robot.com.

standards for the integrated management system of informatization and industrialization. The implementation of standards for the integrated management system of informatization and industrialization promotes enterprises to establish a more obvious competitive advantage in lean management, risk control and supply chain coordination.

Industrial e-commerce, precision marketing and other modes have brought about great changes in the way enterprises operate. At present, some enterprises in China have established e-commerce of the whole industry chain, integrating buyers, suppliers, manufacturers and sellers, realizing business cooperation between the upstream and downstream of the industry chain, and reducing the procurement cost and marketing cost of enterprises. Based on big data and industrial cloud, more and more enterprises begin to implement precision marketing and develop personalized customization mode. Red Collar Group in Qingdao, Shandong province launched the first clothing personalized customization platform in China to actively respond to customer needs.

With the in-depth promotion of the integration of informatization and industrialization, the competitiveness of enterprises has increased significantly. The comprehensive strength of some enterprises has been among the world's first camp. During the 12th Five-year Plan period, 56 manufacturing enterprises in China entered the world's top 500, 11 construction machinery enterprises entered the world's top 50, and 4 internet enterprises and 2 integrated circuit design enterprises entered the world's top 10.[1] A number of key national projects have been gradually implemented, including the demonstration project of industrial strong foundation engineering, the basic public service platform of industrial technology, the national big data comprehensive test zone, and the intelligent manufacturing project. In 2016, China's first national manufacturing innovation center, the National Battery Innovation Center, was established.

In recent years, the deep integration of informatization and industrialization has achieved some results. Intelligent manufacturing has become the primary way for enterprises to transform and upgrade. Faced with the complex and huge system engineering of intelligent manufacturing, China has made overall planning and promoted it systematically. China attaches great importance to pilot demonstration work, so as to promote the larger-scale development. China adheres to a market-oriented approach, encourages enterprises to play a leading role in the market, and actively enhances basic

---

[1] China is the World's Top Manufacturing and Network Country During the 12th Five-Year Plan, the Website of China News, Dec. 24, 2015. http:// www.chinanews.com/cj/2015/12-24/7686860.shtml.

information security, so as to guide enterprises to embark on a path of intelligent manufacturing development with Chinese characteristics.

From a national perspective, the information infrastructure network is gradually improving, and the national special funds are also increasing year by year. The intelligent production capacity supported by information technology and the internet is gradually increasing, and the added value of the industrial chain continues to increase. "Made in China" is gradually changing to "Intelligent Manufacturing in China", and the manufacturing model is changing from supply-oriented to demand-oriented. With the continuous expansion of the application scope of e-commerce, it has become an important way for enterprises to integrate supply chains and improve production efficiency, and new models and new business forms have gradually taken shape. However, in the process of building the new industrialization road, the regional development is not balanced, and the informatization level in the eastern, central and western regions is obviously different. The provinces with a higher level of integration of informatization and industrialization are concentrated in the eastern coastal areas of China, while the central and western regions, especially the southwest region, have a lower degree of integration of informatization and industrialization, and lag behind in the development of informatization, with obvious regional differences.

4.6   Development practice of the integration of informatization and industrialization

In the process of the integration and development of informatization and industrialization, some Chinese enterprises seized the strategic opportunities of "Made in China 2025" and "internet +", and implemented the transformation and upgrading from traditional manufacturing to intelligent manufacturing. They transform from production-based manufacturing to service-oriented manufacturing, and gradually move to the middle and high end of the industrial chain, achieving great economic benefits and accumulating valuable industry experience. Baosteel Group, Haier Group, and Red Collar Group actively integrate into the information age and innovative "internet +" thinking, achieving the transformation and upgrading of the enterprises by using information technology to develop intelligent manufacturing.

4.6.1 Baowu (formerly Baosteel) Group explores "industry + internet" model[1]

4.6.1.1 An overview of the development of Baowu Group

Founded in 1978, Baosteel Group Co., Ltd. gradually develops into an integrated iron and steel complex which is the most modernized in China with the reform and openingup. Focusing on the common development of manufacturing, service, finance and real estate, the Group has been named one of the top 500 enterprises in China and in the world for many years. In 2016, Baosteel Group merged with Wuhan Iron and Steel Group. Baosteel Group Co., Ltd. was renamed as China Baowu Iron and Steel Group Co., Ltd., becoming a world-class super steel enterprise. In 2016, Baowu Group ranked first in China's steel industry, with an operating revenue of RMB307.2 billion and a profit of RMB7.02 billion. The group's industrial structure is based on the steel industry, producing steel products with high technology content and high added value. The products include plain carbon steel, stainless steel, and special steel. The group implements a diversified development strategy, expanding the industrial chain and promoting the coordinated development of the industries based on the steel industry. At the same time, the company actively develop producer services, such as e-commerce, logistics, processing, data, resource services, information technology, and engineering, transforming to service-oriented manufacturing.

4.6.1.2 Baowu Group's "internet + steel" model

(1) *The construction of enterprise information system of Baowu Group*

As early as 1985, the former Baosteel Group established the first steelmaking production performance database based on the self-developed central data processor and network computer. Since the mid-1990s, the group has developed a management system of production and sales and a total management system of equipment maintenance, both covers all the production lines of the company. The enterprise integrates the original management system of spare parts and materials, and develops metallurgical ERP system, which realizes the computer tracking management of the whole process of enterprise production such as contract signing, product delivery, financial settlement, and customer service. Entering the 21st century, the group has actively utilized e-commerce and internet technology to extend its internal information system to both customers and suppliers, and establish a supply chain management system centered on customer needs.

---

[1] Source: Baowu Group website; Zhou Xiaohu, Chen Fen, *Information Management Case*: *Chinese Enterprise Study*, Beijing: Economy & Management Publishing House, 2014, pp.73-89.

The group actively explores the "internet + steel" model to promote the coordinated development of the steel industry and the e-commerce platform. Around the leading steel industry, the group has built an integrated information network service system covering R&D and design, big data analysis, intelligent manufacturing, steel trading, supply chain finance, logistics and distribution. The group has a well-functioning e-commerce platform, and the "Baosteel Online" network platform uses the internet as a medium to respond to users' needs quickly and timely. At the same time, Baosteel has also developed a data warehouse system and an enterprise workflow management system to build a complete data exchange and sharing platform for the enterprise.

(2) *Baowu Group's operation management information system and e-commerce platform*

Baowu Group actively develops informatization and establishes information systems for enterprise production and management, forming a complete system consisting of basic automation, process control system, production control system and information management system. The management information system of Baowu Group involves the conclusion of enterprise contracts, production planning, inlet and outlet management, receipt and delivery, etc., realizing the informatization, networking and intelligence of the whole industrial chain of the enterprise. By integrating contracts, planning and logistics through the information systems, the group has achieved resource information sharing in all aspects of enterprise production, improved management efficiency, reduced costs, shortened cycle times and sped up response to users and markets.

Based on the internet and computer technology, the group started the construction of an e-commerce platform in 2000 and has established an e-commerce system throughout the group, forming an online steel industry ecosystem. The e-commerce platform provides service support for enterprises from product booking, contract tracking, sales logistics, financial settlement, after-sales service and other aspects. Using "Baosteel Online", customers can timely check information related to their contracts, production process, ex-factory code list, ex-factory bill of lading, warranty and logistics dynamics, etc. Baosteel's procurement e-commerce platform provides the group with a networked service that integrates procurement, bidding and tendering, online consultation, interactive discussion and other services. In 2009, the "Special Steel Sub-item of Phase II Project of Integrated Sales and Logistics Control System" was officially launched. So far, the e-commerce platform has achieved full coverage of the group's steel products. In 2012, the group started to implement mobile electronic commerce services and launched mobile marketing services on mobile phones.

Baowu Group's management information system and e-commerce platform provide an open and shared infrastructure for technological innovation, realizing the coordinated development of production, research and sales; provide an open platform for fair and just procurement business, realizing green and efficient procurement; and provide an information platform for consultation, communication and feedback for consumers, realizing consumer-centered precision marketing.

As the most competitive steel enterprise in China, Baowu Group has realized the integrated development of informatization and industrialization. It continuously explores the development road of the new type of industrialization, vigorously develops enterprise informatization, and improves enterprise production efficiency as well as international competitiveness. The group's enterprise information construction practice has become an example of enterprise information construction in China's steel industry.

4.6.2 Haier Group integrates into the "internet +" thinking and transforms to the networked strategy stage[1]

4.6.2.1 Course of development of Haier Group

Founded in 1984 in Qingdao, Shandong Province, Haier Group is an integrator of total home appliance solutions focusing on the production of home appliances. In 1984, Zhang Ruimin was appointed as the director of Qingdao Refrigerator Factory, which was already insolvent and on the verge of bankruptcy. After that, Haier has always been innovation-driven and customer demand-centered, developing from a small collective factory that was insolvent and on the verge of bankruptcy into one of the world's largest manufacturers of household appliances.

Since its establishment in 1984, Haier Group has gone through five stages of development. From 1984 to 1991 was the famous brand strategy stage, creating the first brand of refrigerators; from 1991 to 1998 was the diversification strategy stage, creating the first brand of home appliances; from 1998 to 2005 was the international strategic development stage, creating the international brand; from 2005 to 2012 was the stage of globalization strategy development, creating the first brand of global white goods. From 2012 to now is the networked strategy development stage, creating a management model for the internet era. After more than 30 years of development, the enterprise has continuously reformed and innovated its management model. It has developed from an independent management team to a business unit system, a market

---

[1] Official Website of Haier, http://www.haier.com/cn/.

chain, and then to a win-win model of "RendanHeYi". The inverted triangle organization model has been realized and a win-win ecosystem of co-creation has been established. In the process of development, Haier is committed to becoming "a enterprise of the times". At every stage of development, it constantly innovates thinking and management models according to the changes of the times, and insists on taking people as the core. In 2005, it put forward "RendanHeyi" to realize innovative development of the business model of the enterprise.

4.6.2.2 Haier Group's "internet +" business model

In the process of development, Haier Group has integrated internet thinking to continuously explore new business models in the internet era, and innovate "internet +" models such as ecological user platform, ecological resource platform, Haier interconnection factory, Haier creative platform, creator lab, open innovation platform and Haier customized platform, achieving emerging industries such as "internet + industry", "internet + business", "internet + finance", "internet + housing", "internet + culture", and constantly transforming to the networked strategic stage.

(1) *Establishing Haier Open Partnership Ecosystem (HOPE) platform and exploring open innovation development mode*

Haier practices the basic concept of "the world is our R&D center". In the 1990s, it began to explore the development model of open innovation and established the open innovation platform HOPE. Haier Group has realized the zero-distance interaction of global users, creators and innovation resources through information technology and the internet, and realized the transformation and development of the enterprise: from product-centered to user-centered; from leadership decision to user decision; from series process to parallel process; from independent development to interactive innovation by using global wisdom.

Through the HOPE platform, the enterprise gathers all kinds of innovative scheme providers with technical, creative and design talents, innovates schemes through interactive design and other ways, and cooperates with various global innovation platforms to achieve resource coverage of the whole industry chain from prototyping, technical schemes, structural design, rapid modeling and limited-run trial production, so it can meet customers' individual needs.

HOPE platform has seven core capabilities, including user demand interaction and insight, global technical resource monitoring, global resource network, cross- discipline expert team, big data precision matching, professional domain knowledge and professional demand disassembly, and definition. Haier Group integrates global resources through the HOPE platform to provide low-cost, convenient and comprehensive services and support for small and micro enterprises, realizing the win-win sharing of the ecosystem. Haier's "Natural Wind" air conditioner was created and incubated through the HOPE platform. In January 2016, Haier's air conditioning R&D department released the creator project on the HOPE platform. After the technology demand was released, the platform used big data technology to automatically screen, analyze and evaluate the project, and finally two R&D institutions reached a technology cooperation agreement with Haier. In August 2016, Haier's "Natural Wind" air conditioner was successfully launched on the market. As of November 2016, more than 200 small and micro enterprises have been started on the Haier Group platform, more than 30 small and micro enterprises have successfully introduced venture capital, and 14 small and micro enterprises have been valued at more than RMB100 million.[1]

(2) *Haier Interconnection Factory realizes intelligent production*

Haier innovates the model of transparent factory and full interconnection through interconnected factory. Users can customize according to their individual needs through Haier interconnection factory. The customization mode is divided into crowd innovation customization, exclusive customization and modular customization. After the customization is completed, orders can be placed via the internet, and the orders automatically generated by the system are directly connected to the factory, realizing an efficient supply chain with real-time reception, zero delay, and zero intermediate links. Haier interconnection factory uses a number of world-leading technologies developed independently to achieve intelligent manufacturing. In the manufacturing process, users can apply to view the real-time production process. The connected factory visualizes the whole process from order placement, module procurement, intelligent assembly to logistics and installation, and users can track the order status and watch the production screen at any time through the internet.

In the process of intelligent production, Haier continuously innovates intelligent logistics systems to optimize the supply chain. Haier's ultra-long air logistics is a fully automated transport system created by Haier. It can automatically identify the materials needed by the production line and deliver them in place according to the order execution. The length of the entire transportation line is equivalent to the length of a cable from Lhasa to the top of Mount Qomolangma, effectively solving Haier's

---

[1] Xinhua News Agency, the Publicity Department of the Qingdao Municipal Committee of the Communist Party of China, *Decoding Made in Qingdao*, Qingdao: Qingdao Publishing House, 2017, pp. 216-218.

semi-finished product logistics problem. Traditional enterprises rely on forklifts to transport on the ground, and people carry them on their shoulders. This process requires about 40 people, which is time-consuming and labor-intensive. Haier Group uses information technology to achieve unmanned transport, that is, all workpieces do not fall to the ground, and intelligent and accurate sorting and distribution are realized. This eliminates quality damage caused by wrong or missed loading and turnover, and improves the logistics efficiency.

Haier's Zhengzhou Air-Conditioning Interconnection Factory has established an intelligent unmanned line for evacuation and perfusion, realizing precise production. This is the world's first intelligent unmanned line for evacuation and filling. The vacuum of the refrigeration system is twice higher than that of the industry, and the control accuracy of filling weight is 10 times higher than that of the industry. It has achieved zero error of parameters and zero release of defects.

Shenyang Refrigerator Interconnection Factory has innovated the U-shaped shell sheet metal forming line. Through quick mold-changing technology and real-time mixing technology, the production cycle of personalized shells has been shortened by 80%, and it supports the simultaneous production of 4 series of products. The whole production line of Shenyang Refrigerator Interconnection Factory is interconnected, efficient and flexible. Users' orders are automatically arranged to the machine, and quality and production information are visible throughout the whole process, which truly realizes the transparency of the factory.

The Foshan Washing Machine Interconnection Factory has innovated laser monitoring of the inner cylinder to improve product quality. The factory uses the world's leading laser measure technique to achieve 100% detection of the inner drum of the washing machine, and realizes the traceability of the detection data throughout the product life cycle, which improves the customer experience.

Through the "internet +" model, Haier Group has successfully transformed and achieved steady growth. In 2015, Haier's global turnover reached RMB188.7 billion, with a profit of RMB18 billion. From 2007 to now, Haier's compound annual growth rate of profit reached 33%, becoming a model for the deep integration of informatization and industrialization in Chinese home appliance enterprises. According to data from Euromonitor International, the world's authoritative market research agency, Haier's brand retail volume of large household appliances in 2016 ranked first in the world for the eighth time. In 2016, Haier entered the Global Brands Top100 for two consecutive years, and was included in the *Fortune* 2016 "Most Admired Chinese Companies" list, ranking first in the electronics category and entering the top three on the list.

4.6.3   Red Tollar Group innovates the C2M business model of "internet + manufacturing"[1]

4.6.3.1   Course of development of Red Collar Group

Founded in 1995, Red Collar Group was once a traditional garment enterprise in Qingdao. It mainly produced suits, pants, shirts, casual wear and apparel series products. Red Collar Group is a brand enterprise in the traditional manufacturing industry, which has been awarded the honorary titles of "China Famous Brand", "Shandong Famous Brand", "National Inspection-free Product", etc. The trademark of "Red Collar" is also a China's well-known trademark.

In the process of development, Red Collar seizes the opportunities of informatization development, and use information technology and industrial big data to drive intelligent manufacturing and the transformation and upgrading of the enterprise. After decades of exploration, Red Collar has successfully launched a global platform for personalized customization in the internet era—a global apparel customization supplier platform to develop intelligent manufacturing. Red Collar Group has transformed itself from a traditional enterprise focusing on mass manufacturing to an internet platform enterprise with "personalized mass customization oriented by consumer demand". In 2007, Qingdao Kutesmart Co., Ltd. was established. The traditional business model of Red Collar Group has been upgraded to the intelligent Cotte Yolan. Now its brands are divided into platform brands and product brands. The platform brands include the "Red Collar Magic Factory" C2M customized platform and RCMTM supplier customized platform. The product brands include "CAMEO", "Red Collar" clothing brands and SDE. The business model of Cotte Yolan has achieved rapid success. In 2011, it was rated as the Consumer Satisfaction Unit of Qingdao City. In 2013 it was rated as Qingdao Famous Trademark. In 2014, it became an e-commerce demonstration enterprise in Shandong Province, and in 2015 it became the "Intelligent Manufacturing Pilot Demonstration Project" unit of the Ministry of Industry and Information Technology. In 2012, Wu Bangguo, then Chairman of the Standing Committee of the National People's Congress of the PRC, inspected the Red Collar Group's achievements in the integration of industrialization and informatization, and fully affirmed the idea of transformation and

---

[1] The website of Redcollar Group, Xinhua News Agency, the Publicity Department of the Qingdao Municipal Committee of the Communist Party of China, *Decoding Made in Qingdao*, Qingdao: Qingdao Publishing House, 2017.

upgrading of Red Collar Group and the intelligent, personalized customization production model. He believed that Redcollar deeply promotes the integration of informatization and industrialization, improves the ability of independent innovation, and embarks on a new path of industrialization in China's apparel industry.

Based on the deep integration of informatization and industrialization, Cotte Yolan has established a global apparel customization supplier platform to promote the digitalization, globalization and platform development of garment customization and realize the production process reengineering, enterprise organization reengineering and office automation transformation. And it has established a complete system of IoT and created a new "source point theory of management thought" to achieve the overall transformation of the enterprise from platform to product, and to thought. The demand-driven business model of Cotte Yolan has significantly improved the production efficiency of the enterprise, shortening the production cycle by 40%, reducing raw material inventory by 80%, reducing production costs by 30% and reducing design costs by 90%. The intelligent production has brought great economic benefits to the enterprise. From 2012 to 2016, the enterprise output value increased by more than 100% for five consecutive years, and the profit margin reached more than 25%.

4.6.3.2 Intelligent mode of Cotte Yolan

(1) *Demand-driven C2M platform*

Red Collar Group has developed its own online customized and direct sales platform—C2M platform (customer to manufactory, which means consumer demand drives factory to effectively supply). It established a business model driven by consumer demand and directly met by manufacturers. Manufacturers no longer rely on middlemen, agents and channels to dominate sales, and consumers can customize a wide range of products online through C2M platforms. By downloading and registering the Cotte App, users can directly place orders for personalized needs to factories, select product styles, processes and raw materials online, and generate orders after online payment. This realizes data-driven and networked operation from product customization, transaction, payment, design, manufacturing process, production process, post-processing to logistics and distribution, and after-sales service. Based on the information application platform, Cotte Yolan realizes the full process of customization in seven working days: customers design their own products according to their personalized needs, and after measuring and placing orders, it will complete the plate making and drawing on the first day, the cutting on the second day, the sewing on the third and fourth day, the ironing and inspecting on the fifth day, the matching, packaging and putting in storage on the sixth day, and logistics and delivery on the seventh day.

Through the C2M platform, enterprises truly achieve personalized customization with zero inventory and on-demand production, which optimizes the supply chain, reduces production costs, and improves production efficiency. At present, a single production unit of Red Collar produces 1.5 million sets of customized garments annually. The product categories that enterprises can customize on the C2M platform cover the full range of men's and women's formal wear products over 3 years old. Consumers can design their own styles and freely choose from more than 30,000 fabrics and accessories. Red Collar Group has established intelligent solutions based on the whole life cycle of products and personalized customization of the whole industrial chain, leading the new business forms of internet-based, consumer-driven enterprise manufacturing.

(2) *Data-driven intelligent factory*

With a high degree of integration of industrialization and informatization, Cotte Yolan has established a data-driven intelligent production workshop and assembly line, realizing the intellectualization of the whole process, such as intelligent research and development, intelligent cutting, intelligent manufacturing, intelligent inspection, intelligent warehousing and intelligent supporting. Consumers submit their personalized demands through the C2M platform. The order data is automatically entered into the various databases of Cotte Yolan, including the version database, style database, raw material database and process database. With the help of information technology and the internet, order information is transformed into production tasks by means of instruction push and transmitted to each production unit for manufacturing. In the smart factory, data is transmitted and shared through the enterprise information system. Each product has its own electronic chip, and each worker can read the order information through the terminal device to carry out personalized production. The data-driven smart factory efficiently integrates the supply chain, realizes the synergy of the whole industry chain and improves the production efficiency of the smart assembly line.

(3) *Innovation-driven development meets individual needs*

In the process of transformation, Red Collar Group has formed the source point theory of management thought which supports the new model of the enterprise. The source point theory means that all behaviors take demand as the source point and are driven by source demand to realize the integration and collaboration of value chain resources and finally meet the demand of source point. The source point theory of management thought has been implemented in Red Collar Group. Enterprises transform the traditional bureaucratic department into a platform to provide resources, which breaks the original departments and hierarchies, and realizes the self-organization model based on consumer demand. The enterprise carries out cellular remodelling of the organization, and every position on the enterprise platform is a cell. The cells are aggregated according to the needs of consumers, and the aggregated cells will work around the source point and complete various works in the industrial chain with high quality and high efficiency.

Red Collar Group continues to innovate modes of production. It independently develops patented measuring tools and measuring methods, using 3D laser measuring instruments to automatically collect 22 sizes of 19 parts of the human body. The input of the user's body type data drives the synchronized changes of nearly 10,000 data within the system. It can meet the individual design needs of 113 special body shape features such as hunchback, convex belly and drop hip.

Red Collar Group has realized the intellectualization and informatization from products to platforms, and to ideas. While successfully transforming and upgrading itself, the enterprise also outputs the source point theory of management thought to help traditional enterprises achieve the transformation and upgrading at the organizational and ideological level. Red Collar integrates the personalized modes of production represented by the "zero inventory model of selling before production" and the "direct sales model of factory customization driven by consumer demand" into the solutions for the transformation and upgrading of traditional enterprises. Through coding and procedure, it creates the source point theory of data engineering (SDE), including the direct sales portals of personalized customization on the consumer side of the C2M platform, data models and intelligent logic algorithms on the big data platform, a developing path to industrialization and informatization in China flexible manufacturing solutions of personalized customization on the manufacturing side of the factory, and organizational process reengineering solutions. The business model and management thought of Red Collar Group have become a successful model for manufacturing transformation and upgrading. More than 20 industries have signed up for the source point theory of data engineering, and more than 10,000 enterprises, including Huawei, Alibaba and Haier, have come to learn from it.

Red Collar model is a representative of organic combination of manufacturing and e-commerce in the internet era, achieving a deep integration of informatization and industrialization. Red Collar Group continues to innovate the intelligent and personalized customization production model in garment industry, opening up a new trail to industrialization of China's garment industry driven by innovation.

Chapter 5
The Development Path of China's Agricultural Informatization

The Industrial Revolution has pushed agriculture to transform from traditional to mechanical and chemical, while the information revolution has made agriculture more intelligent and digital. On the path of informatization in China, the issues related to agriculture, rural areas and rural people play a key role in this process, with agriculture being the core of these issues. Agricultural informatization is the basic way to improve the comprehensive production capacity of agriculture and promote the increase of rural people's income, and is also an inevitable part for achieving agricultural modernization.

5.1　Basic issues of agricultural informatization

5.1.1　Content of agricultural informatization

5.1.1.1　Agricultural informatization

Agricultural informatization is the process of transforming traditional agriculture and the modes of production by using information technology, and the only way to develop modern agriculture. In the process of agricultural modernization, we should arm agriculture with IT, improve it with information networks and information resources, promote it with modern ideas and modern management methods, thus improving agricultural labor productivity and market competitiveness.

In a narrow sense, agricultural informatization refers to the penetration and application of IT in agricultural production, operation, management and service, including agricultural production equipment informatization, agricultural production process intellectualization, agricultural product management informatization and agricultural management informatization. In a broad sense, agricultural informatization covers a wide range of agricultural production informatization, management informatization, informatization of agricultural product quality traceability, agricultural e-commerce platform construction, construction of agricultural information service platform, agricultural database.

5.1.1.2　Whole-process agricultural informatization

In 2014, China put forward the idea of agricultural informatization, released the No. 1 Central Document for 2014, entitled Several Opinions of the CPC Central Committee and the State Council on Comprehensively Deepening Agricultural Reform to Promote Agricultural Modernization, proposed to achieve agricultural whole process informatization with the focus on IoT in agriculture and precision equipment.[1] In 2016, the No. 1 Central Document entitled Several Opinions of the CPC Central Committee and the State Council on the Implementation of New Concepts on the Development and the Acceleration of the Agricultural Modernization for the Realization of the Moderate Prosperity in All Respects states promoting the transformation and upgrading of the whole agricultural industry chain by using modern information technologies such as IoT, cloud computing, big data and mobile internet. Therefore, whole-process agricultural informatization based on the whole industry chain has pointed out the direction of developing agricultural informatization. The whole-process agricultural informatization is the informatization of the total elements, the whole process and the entire industry of agriculture. The modern communication technologies, such as big data, IoT technology, precision equipment and cloud computing, are integrated into all aspects of agricultural production, so as to make full use of their fast, convenient and intelligent advantages to fully perceive the various production and circulation elements of agriculture and to realize the digitization, intellectualization, precision and scientific management of agricultural production.[2]

In the national development strategy of agricultural informatization, the whole-process agricultural informatization mainly includes four parts of agricultural production informatization, agricultural operation informatization, agricultural management informatization, and agricultural service informatization.

Agricultural production informatization refers to the integration and application of modern information technology in the process of agricultural production. The application of information technology represented by the IoT in agricultural production has

[1] Several Opinions of the CPC Central Committee and the State Council on Comprehensively Deepening Agricultural Reform to Promote Agricultural Modernization, Chinese Central Government's Official Website, Jan. 19, 2014, https://www.gov.cn/jrzg/2014-01/19/content_2570454.htm.

[2] Kong Fantao, Zhang Jianhua and Wu Jianzhai et al., *Research on the Development of Agriculture Whole Process Informatization*, Beijing: Science Press, 2015, p. 27.

advanced the achievement of intelligent production.

Agricultural operation informatization refers to the participation and application of information technology in the process of agricultural operation, mainly including the two major aspects of purchasing and marketing as well as logistics. E-commerce platforms related to agriculture provide important channels for purchasing and selling agricultural products, and the IoT in modern logistics enables the monitoring and tracing of agricultural products.

Agricultural management informatization includes agricultural affairs informatization and the informatization for farm households to manage agricultural production. Farm households aim to transform traditional agricultural management methods by using modern information technology, while the government strives to strengthen the construction of government information resources and improve the efficiency of agricultural administrative management through the information management platform. Agricultural management informatization is mainly manifested in the construction of e-government standard and regulations system, agricultural monitoring and early warning, market supervision of agricultural products and production means, construction of emergency command sites, and informatization provided by agricultural science and technology market information.

Agricultural service informatization refers to the application of information technology in the process of agricultural services, including the construction of agricultural and rural information infrastructure, the informatization of agricultural information resource services, and the informatization of farmer skill training.

5.1.2　Informatization of agriculture, rural areas and rural people

As a large agricultural country, China has a strategic goal of promoting farmers' income, agricultural development and rural stability to make development of agriculture, rural areas and rural people. Farmers are the organizers and managers of agricultural production, while the rural areas are the residence of farmers. The development of the three needs to be promoted in coordination. Therefore, the agricultural informatization cannot be separated from the informatization of rural areas and farmers, and the informatization in agriculture, rural areas, and farms promote and develop together.

Agricultural informatization is the primary task and strategic focus of rural informatization. Agricultural informatization has promoted the improvement of agricultural production efficiency and farmers' income, and the increase in farmers' income is the prerequisite and foundation for the informatization of rural areas and farmers.

Rural informatization refers to the process of application and promotion of modern information technology in agricultural production, farmers' lives and social management, and it covers three major components of agricultural production informatization, farmers' lives informatization and rural management informatization. Zhou Hongren (2008) has put forward eight strategic priorities for rural informatization, including developing modern agriculture, boosting rural economy, increasing farmers' income, realizing the transfer of rural surplus labor, building modern rural information infrastructure, improving rural informatization education, vigorously training rural cadres, and establishing a modern rural management system.[1] Li Daoliang (2010) summarized the content of rural informatization as rural informatization development environment, rural informatization infrastructure, rural informatization resources, rural informatization service system, and thematic applications of rural informatization.[2] Rural informatization is the influence and application of modern information technology in economy, politics, society, and culture, and is the concentrated embodiment of informatization in the economic and social fields in rural areas.

Farmer informatization means that farmers receive informatization education and training, master the relevant knowledge of modern information technology and information networks, improve their ability to obtain and use information, and ultimately employ informatization methods to organize production and arrange life. Therefore, rural informatization education is the key to farmers' informatization. Informatization education should be developed and popularized in rural areas to constantly improve the level of rural informatization education, arm the minds of farmers with information technology and knowledge, thus narrowing the digital divide. The development of rural informatization education can provide a team of high-quality technical talents for the development of agricultural informatization, thereby accelerating the realization of agricultural modernization. A sound rural informatization service system is the basic element for the effective connection between farmers and modern agriculture. Therefore, agricultural informatization, farmer informatization and rural informatization are inseparable and develop collaboratively, and they are the key tasks of establishing modern agriculture and new socialist countryside.

5.1.3　Significance of agricultural informatization

The promotion and application of modern information technology in agriculture

---

[1] Zhou Hongren, *On Informatization*, Beijing: People's Publishing House, 2008, p. 343.

[2] Li Daoliang, *Rural Informatization and Digital Agriculture*, Beijing: China Agriculture & Building Press, 2010, pp. 2-4.

has improved the efficiency of agricultural production, operation, management and the utilization rate of agricultural resources, which is beneficial to establish a modern agricultural system and effectively solve issues related to agriculture, rural areas and rural people. Agricultural informatization is the only way for agricultural modernization, an objective requirement for taking a new path to industrialization, and an effective means for building a new socialist countryside and achieving the goal of building a moderately prosperous society in all respects.

5.1.3.1 Establishing a modern agricultural system to promote the transformation and upgrading of traditional agriculture

The rapid development of information technology and the innovative application of the internet have brought new development opportunities for agricultural informatization. The information technology and the internet have penetrated into all aspects of agricultural production and operation, giving rise to the development model of "information technology + agriculture" and "internet + agriculture", and promoting the transformation of modes of agricultural production, management, operation and services. The informatization of the entire agricultural industry chain has improved the level of intellectualization of agricultural production equipment and strengthened the ability to supervise and manage the agricultural production and operation process, thereby helping to establish an intelligent and efficient modern agricultural production system and promote agricultural productivity. The application of information technology in agricultural production has changed the extensive production mode with backward technology and low efficiency, and also promoted the transformation of traditional agriculture to modern and high-efficiency agriculture.

5.1.3.2 Improving resource utilization efficiency to promote the development of green agriculture

The popularization and application of information technology in agricultural production have optimized the supply chain and improved the resource utilization of each link, thereby helping to reduce the energy consumption per unit of production and promoting the green and low-carbon development of agriculture. The new generation of information technology such as artificial intelligence has improved the scientific and technological content of agricultural grain seeds and ensured the quality and safety of agricultural products. The application of information technology has freed field planting and aquaculture and animal husbandry from the impact of the natural environment, reduced production risks and decreased resource waste. Farm households accurately understand the planting environment and breeding environment through information technology, and implement precise fertilization, spraying, irrigation and feeding in accordance with the type of soil and the quality of water resources, thereby reducing the waste of agricultural production materials such as chemical fertilizers and pesticides. Information technology has increased the scientific and technological content of agricultural production machinery, helping to reduce the carbon emissions in the operation of the machinery and promoting the development of low-carbon and green agriculture.

5.1.3.3   Broadening the ways for farmers to increase income

The modern agricultural production system supported by information technology has broadened the ways for farmers to increase their income. Firstly, the penetration of information technology in all aspects of agricultural production has improved agricultural production efficiency, reduced production costs, and increased agricultural production profits and farmers' income. Secondly, the "internet +" has changed the way of agricultural operations. Through the development of agricultural e-commerce, farmers have effectively connected agricultural production materials, agricultural products and the market, reducing costs, improving the efficiency of agricultural market circulation, realizing precision procurement and precision marketing, and enhancing the profit development space. Thirdly, the internet has provided farmers with a platform for innovation and entrepreneurship, and has continuously created a large number of jobs, effectively solving the problem of surplus rural labor. The "internet + modern agriculture" development model has realized the sharing and win-win situation of agriculture, rural areas, farmers. It has built an intelligent, efficient, and green modern agricultural ecosystem.

5.1.3.4   Conducive to narrowing the digital divide and implementing the rural revitalization strategy

The application of information technology and information networks in agriculture, rural areas, and rural people has not only improved agricultural production efficiency, but also improved rural people's ability to master and apply information technology, cultivated new socialist rural people, improved rural people's quality, and promoted socialism. With the progress in building a new socialist countryside, the urban-rural gap and the digital divide continue to narrow. A complete comprehensive information infrastructure has improved the capabilities and levels of agricultural technical services, financial insurance, logistics and other comprehensive agricultural services, and created a good environment for comprehensive informatization of agriculture, rural areas, and rural people.

5.2 Innovative initiatives in China's agricultural informatization

At present, China has entered a new period of integrating the development of industrialization, informatization, urbanization and agricultural modernization. China is actively formulating policies and measures to promote the coordinated development of industrialization, informatization, urbanization, and agricultural modernization. Without agricultural informatization, there would be no agricultural modernization. Information technology and the internet are key factors to improve agricultural production efficiency and accelerate the pace of agricultural modernization. In 1994, the state proposed the Golden Agriculture Project. In 1996, the National Rural Economic Information Work Conference proposed "rural informatization" and established the first national agricultural information network—China Agricultural Information Network. Although the construction of agricultural informatization started late, the CPC Central Committee and the State Council attach great importance to agriculture and promote the construction of agricultural informatization by strengthening the top-level design, creating a good policy environment for the development of modern agriculture.

5.2.1 Top-level design of agricultural informatization

5.2.1.1 No. 1 Central Document has pointed out the direction for agricultural informatization

Since entering the 21st century, the CPC Central Committee and the State Council have attached great importance to the work of agricultural and rural informatization, constantly strengthen the strategic and political guidance of agricultural informatization to promote the process of transforming agriculture mode from traditional to modern. Since 2004, the issue of agricultural informatization was mentioned every year in the No. 1 Central Document. The document has been expanding and improving by the changes from the use of information technology to improve agricultural science and technology innovation capacity to the use of the internet to develop new modes of agricultural production and circulation, from the use of information technology to upgrade agricultural equipment to the upgrading and transformation of the entire agricultural industry chain, from the active promotion of agricultural informatization to the comprehensive promotion of rural informatization.

(1) *Beginning with improving the ability of information services*

At the beginning of the 21st century, a number of problems became more and more serious, such as the slow growth of the national per capita net income of farmers for many years and the continuous widening of the income gap between urban and rural residents. In response to these problems, in early 2004, the Opinions of the CPC Central Committee and the State Council Concerning Several Policies on Promoting the Increase of Farmers' Income calls for greater capabilities of agricultural production information services by the relevant central and local departments to increase farmers' income. The opinions pointed out that the relevant departments must closely track the monitoring and timely notification of domestic and international market supply and demand, policies and regulations and epidemics, inspection and quarantine standards and other developments, to provide information services for agricultural export enterprises.[1] China provides information services to farmers' professional cooperative organizations and agricultural export enterprises through various measures to improve the income levels of farmers and enterprises continuously.

In the No. 1 Central Document for 2005, entitled Opinions of the CPC Central Committee and the State Council on Further Strengthening Rural Work and Enhancing Comprehensive Agricultural Production Capacity, clearly states the concept of strengthening the construction of agricultural informatization, proposes the idea of strengthening agricultural informatization construction from the aspects such as agricultural technology, agricultural management, and ways of distribution. The concrete measures of it include: speeding up research on high-tech such as biotechnology and information technology, and improving agricultural science and technology innovation capabilities. Encouraging the development of modern logistics, chain operations, e-commerce and other new business formats and circulation methods, and speeding up the circulation of agricultural products. Enhance transaction functions through the development of brokers, agricultural product auctions, and online transactions.

(2) *China began to pay attention to the construction project of comprehensive agricultural information service platform*

Since the release of the No. 1 Central Document for 2006, entitled Several Opinions of the CPC Central Committee and the State Council on Promoting the Construction

---

[1] Opinions of the CPC Central Committee and the State Council Concerning Several Policies on Promoting the Increase of Farmers' Income, Chinese Central Government's Official Website, Dec. 31, 2003, http://www.gov.cn/test/2005-07/04/content_11870.htm.

of a New Socialist Countryside, China began to shift the focus of IT adoption in agriculture from the application of agricultural information technology to the construction of a comprehensive agricultural information service platform, in order to accelerate the progress of constructing a modern circulation system and a rural public service network. China has proposed the issue that actively promotes the construction of agricultural information technology, makes full use of and integrate information resources related to agriculture, strengthens information services such as radio, television and telecommunications for rural areas, and focuses on the Golden Agricultural Project and the construction of a comprehensive agricultural information service platform project.[1]

China attaches great importance to the construction of agricultural informatization projects. It takes the Golden Agricultural Project, Rural Informatization Demonstration Project and Rural Comprehensive Information Service Project as the key projects of agricultural informatization construction. The No. 1 Central Document for 2007, entitled Several Opinions of the CPC Central Committee of the Communist Party of China and the State Council on Actively Developing Modern Agriculture and Steadily Promoting the Construction of a New Socialist Countryside, proposed that to build the standard public agricultural database, in-depth implemented the demonstration projects of rural informatization, speed up the construction of "new rural modern circulation network" and "rural information services in commerce" and other projects. China would continue to improve the construction of comprehensive agricultural information service platforms.

(3) *Coordinating the development of information technology in agriculture and rural areas*

With the development of agricultural informatization, the CPC Central Committee and the State Council began to combine the development of modern agriculture and the construction of a new socialist countryside to collaboratively promote the construction of an integrated rural information infrastructure. The No. 1 Central Documents for 2008 and 2009, entitled Several Opinions of the CPC Central Committee and the State Council on Effectively Strengthening Agricultural Infrastructure and Further Promoting Agricultural Development and Increasing Farmers' Income, and Several Opinions of the CPC Central Committee and the State Council on Promoting Stable Development of

---

[1] Several Opinions of the CPC Central Committee and the State Council on Promoting the Construction of a New Socialist Countryside, Chinese Central Government's Official Website, Dec. 31, 2005, http: //www.gov.cn/ gongbao/content/2006/content_254151.htm.

Agriculture and Sustained Income Growth of Farmers, contains the following views that we should improve the rural information service system, accelerate the construction of rural infrastructure, promote the demonstration of rural information technology and rural business information services and other projects, and vigorously develop rural information technology.

The No. 1 Central Document for 2010, entitled Opinions of the CPC Central Committee and the State Council on Exerting Greater Efforts in the Overall Planning of Urban and Rural Development and Further Solidifying the Foundation for Agricultural and Rural Development, proposed vigorously develop e-commerce and other modern circulation methods, support the construction of new rural modern circulation network of supply and marketing cooperatives to create conditions for the development of rural markets. At the same time, China should strengthen the monitoring of market dynamics and information services to improve the agricultural market system.

With the great importance of water for agricultural development, water information technology plays an important role in the development of modern agriculture China attaches great importance to the construction of the Digital Water Project to promote the development of agricultural and rural information technology with water conservancy technology. The No. 1 Central Document for 2011, entitled Decision from the CPC Central Committee and the State Council on Accelerating Water Conservancy Reform and Development, put forward the requirement of promoting the construction of water information technology. We have to fully implement the Digital Water Project, accelerate the construction of the national flood and drought control command system and water resources management information system to improve water resources regulation and control, water conservancy and project operation at the information level, and finally achieve water modernization leading by water conservancy technology.[1]

(4) *Promoting agricultural and rural information technology in all areas*

Since the introduction of the strategy of integrating the development of industrialization, informatization, urbanization and agricultural modernization, China has made overall plans for coordinating development of industrialization, informatization, urbanization, and agricultural modernization. Since 2012, China has made many arrangements in the aspects of agricultural technology research and development, agricultural business patterns, and rural informatization education to comprehensively

---

[1] Decision from the CPC Central Committee and the State Council on Accelerating Water Conservancy Reform and Development, Chinese Central Government's Official Website, Dec. 31, 2010, http://www.gov.cn/gongbao/content/2011/content_1803158.htm.

promote informatization in agriculture and rural areas.

Promoting the research and innovation of agricultural technology continuously. In 2012, China has issued the idea of accelerating the research of frontier technologies that we should achieve a number of major independent innovations in agricultural biotechnology, information technology, new material technology, advanced manufacturing technology, precision agricultural technology. In 2013, the No. 1 Central Document entitled Several Opinions of the CPC Central Committee and the State Council on Accelerating the Development of Modern Agriculture and Further Strengthening the Vigorous Development of Rural Areas proposed that we should put our focus on developing technologies for information collection, precision operations, remote digitalization and visualization of rural areas, weather forecasting, and disaster warning. In 2014, China put forward the idea of solving major problems in agricultural science and technology, and promoting technology development for emerging industries with a focus on facility agriculture and further processing of agricultural products.

Focusing on the establishment of platforms for agricultural products sharing national and regional information, and improving agricultural information services through various means. China is deeply promoting the village-to-village projects such as promoting radio and television in rural areas, and accelerating the construction of rural information infrastructure and the popularization of broadband to make a great progress on information into villages and households. At the same time, China pays attention to informatization demonstration and guidance. It accelerates the implementation of rural informatization demonstration provinces, and focuses on strengthening the construction of grassroots agricultural informatization service stations and informatization demonstration villages. In 2013, the second phase of Golden Agriculture Project was initiated to promote the construction of the national rural informatization pilot province. In 2014, the project to improve the informatization of rural circulation facilities and agricultural products wholesale markets was launched. The government continues to support the construction of an e-commerce platform for agricultural products. In 2015, Several Opinions of the CPC Central Committee and the State Council on Intensifying Reform and Innovation to Accelerating Agricultural Modernization calls those officials at all levels should actively carry out the comprehensive demonstration of e-commerce into rural areas, mobilize all walks of life to improve the e-commerce platform, and support e-commerce, logistics, commerce, finance and other enterprises to participate in the construction of agriculture-related e-commerce platform.

(5) *Vigorously promote the development of "internet + modern agriculture" model*

Since the issue of Guiding Opinions of the State Council on Vigorously Advancing the "Internet Plus" Action in 2015, all walks of life have accelerated the deep integration of the internet and other fields and innovated development models. In agriculture, the "internet + modern agriculture" model strives to improve the level of agricultural development and realize agricultural modernization through measures such as building a new agricultural production and management system, developing precision production methods, improving networked service levels, and perfecting the quality and safety traceability system of agricultural and sideline products.

In 2016, Several Opinions of the CPC Central Committee and the State Council on the Implementation of New Concepts on the Development and the Acceleration of the Agricultural Modernization for the Realization of the Moderate Prosperity in All Respects explicitly request that we should use the Internet of Things, cloud computing, big data, mobile internet and other modern information technology, and vigorously promote "internet + modern agriculture" model, to promote agricultural industrial chain upgrade. The No. 1 Central Document for 2017, entitled Opinions of the CPC Central Committee and the State Council on Deepening Supply-side Structural Reform in Agriculture and Accelerating the Cultivation of New Growth Engines in Agriculture and Rural Areas proposed the idea of implementing intelligent agriculture project, promoting the agricultural IoT experimental demonstration and agricultural equipment intelligence, to accelerate the development of the "internet + modern agriculture". In the development of modern agriculture, China focuses on the construction of rural e-commerce service systems and the improvement of e-commerce platforms, and encourages the development of rural e-commerce industrial parks in order to improve the standard system for grading the quality of agricultural products and packaging and distribution.

5.2.1.2 Agricultural informatization has become a national development strategy

Agriculture is the foundation for completing the building of a moderately prosperous society in all respects and realizing modernization. The CPC Central Committee and the State Council have attached great importance to and actively guided the transformation of the agricultural development model, and made agricultural informatization a national strategy.

(1) *The CPC Central Committee continues to innovate agricultural development ways*

The issues of agriculture, rural areas, and rural people are related to the national economy and people's livelihood. The CPC has always made these issues the top priority in its work, constantly innovating its thinking on agricultural development, and building China into a strong modern agricultural country. The 17th and 18th CPC National Congress proposed that we should take the path of agricultural modernization with Chinese characteristics, to integrate the development of industrialization, informatization, urbanization and agricultural modernization. The 19th CPC National Congress requires the implementation of the rural revitalization strategy and the acceleration of agricultural and rural modernization.

The report to the 17th CPC National Congress calls for the path to agricultural modernization with Chinese characteristics by strengthening the basic position of agriculture. At the Third Plenary Session of the 17th Central Committee, the Decision of the Central Committee of the Communist Party of China on Promoting the Reform and Development of Rural Areas puts forward the development strategy of agricultural informatization in terms of agricultural equipment informatization, production and operation informatization, and service informatization, namely, accelerating scientific and technological innovation to promote production and operation informatization; accelerating the development of multi-functional, intelligent and economical agricultural equipment and facilities to promote the development of agricultural information service technology. The report to the 18th CPC National Congress put forward the requirement that we should realize the simultaneous development of industrialization, informatization, urbanization and agricultural modernization, drive agricultural development with industrial development, and promote agricultural modernization with informatization.

The rural revitalization strategy was put forward on the 19th CPC National Congress. In light of the characteristics of the new era of socialism with Chinese characteristics and the transformation of the principal challenge in society, the CPC Central Committee has proposed to actively build a modernized economic system under the guidance of the new concept of development. One of the tasks of constructing a modern economic system is the implementation of rural revitalization strategy. The CPC Central Committee requires governments at all levels to adhere to the priority development of agriculture and rural areas, build a modern agricultural industry system, production system and operation system, and improve the agricultural socialization service system in order to accelerate the modernization of agriculture and rural areas.

(2) *The construction of agricultural information technology plays an important role in the plan of national economic development*

Both the 12th Five-year Plan and the 13th Five-year Plan regard improving the level of agricultural informatization as the direction of agricultural development.

We must actively use the new generation of information technology, the internet and the IoT to realize the informatization of agricultural production, operation, management and services to develop precision agriculture and smart agriculture, as well as to accelerate the development of agricultural modernization.

In 12th Five-Year Plan for National Economic and Social Development of the People's Republic of China (2011-2015), the government issued the idea of providing agricultural informatization development guidance by strengthening the agricultural informatization foundation, speeding up the agricultural information technology research and development, promoting the industrialization of agricultural production and operation, promoting agricultural government management, strengthening the agricultural information service, to promote the healthy and rapid development of agricultural modernization. According to the Outline of the 13th Five-Year Plan for the National Economic and Social Development of the People's Republic of China (2016-2020), agricultural modernization is regarded as an important development strategy in the Plan. The outline also pointed out that the whole agricultural industry chain should be informatized, and that we should develop precision agriculture based on the IoT to improve information service capabilities supported by big data, and vigorously develop internet-based agricultural e-commerce. China has made overall plans to promote the integration of information technology with the management of agricultural production, operation and management, market circulation, resources and the environment. It also promotes the application of agricultural big data, enhances the comprehensive information service capacity of agriculture, and constantly improves the level of agricultural intelligence.

At the same time, the development direction and key measures of China's agricultural information construction in the new period are cleared in the Outline of the National Informatization Development Strategy, Outline of the 13th Five-Year Plan for the National Informatization, Opinions of the Ministry of Agriculture on Further Strengthening the Construction of Agricultural Informatization, National Framework for Agriculture and Rural Information Construction (2007-2015), National Agricultural Modernization Plan (2016-2020). The government proposed to make full use of the internet, agricultural IoT, to build a new agricultural production and management system. And also, we should establish agricultural information monitoring system, to improve the agricultural production of science and technology and refinement level and the network service level, so as to promote China's agriculture to networking internet based, intelligent, and refinement.

The Ministry of Agriculture has formulated a development plan specifically for agricultural and rural information construction. In 2011, the Ministry of Agriculture issued the 12th Five-Year Plan for the Development of National Agricultural and Rural Informatization, which is China's first Five-year Plan for the development of agricultural and rural informatization. In 2016, the Ministry of Agriculture issued the 13th Five-Year Plan National Agricultural and Rural Informatization Development Plan. The plan has mentioned that we need to strengthen the information technology and application of agricultural production, promote agriculture and rural areas to speed up the development of e-commerce, promote agricultural informatization gear upgrades, promoting agricultural rural information service is convenient to popularize and laying solid foundation support agricultural rural informatization development as "much starker choices-and graver consequences-in" during the main task of the agricultural informatization.

5.2.2　Major projects of agricultural informatization

In order to enhance the level of informatization in agricultural production, operation, management and services, China has taken the agricultural information technology innovation project, agricultural internet application demonstration project, agricultural e-commerce demonstration project, E-Agriculture project, and comprehensive information service platform project on agriculture, rural areas and rural people at 12316 platform as support and reliance, to promote the overall development of agricultural information technology.

5.2.2.1　Innovation project in agricultural information technology in agriculture

In terms of agricultural technology innovation, China has established an information technology exchange platform to improve its agricultural innovation capacity. Since the 10th Five-year Plan, China has launched the Special Research and Demonstration of Digital Agriculture Technology under the National High-tech R&D Program (863 Program), focusing on research and development of key digital agriculture technologies, building a digital agriculture technology platform, and initially building a digital agriculture technology framework. The Ministry of Agriculture is pooling resources from universities, research institutions, and enterprises to establish "Agricultural Information Technology Disciplines" and "Agricultural Remote Sensing Disciplines". The focus will be on research and scientific observation in areas such as agricultural information acquisition technology, agricultural information service technology, agricultural IoT system integration, and the integrated application of agricultural IoT technology.[1] During the 13th Five-year Plan period, China continued to implement the agricultural information technology innovation project, established key laboratories, and vigorously promoted the research and development of agricultural information technology. Ten new specialized key laboratories will be added, including the agricultural Internet of Things, big data, e-commerce, informatization standards, quality testing of agricultural information hardware and software products, agricultural spectral testing technology, systematic analysis and decision-making of crops, agricultural information traceability technology, animal husbandry information technology, and fishery information technology. Six new regional key laboratories have been set up in Northwest, Northeast, Huang-Huai-Hai (North China), South China, Southwest and tropical and subtropical regions.[2]

5.2.2.2 Demonstration project of the application of the IoT

China has launched demonstration projects and regional pilot projects for the application of the IoT in agriculture, giving full play to the advantages of the IoT and actively promoting the deepening application of it and other new generation information technologies in agricultural production. In order to implement the Smart Agriculture Project of the National Demonstration Project for the Application of the IoT, it is necessary to take the lead in supporting the promotion and application of it in Beijing, Inner Mongolia, Heilongjiang, Jiangsu and Xinjiang Production and Construction Corps. Since 2013, China has been implementing regional trial projects of agricultural IoT in Tianjin, Jilin, Shanghai, Jiangsu, Anhui and other provinces. Based on the agricultural IoT application demonstration project and the regional test project, the Ministry of Agriculture has selected 426 agricultural IoT technologies, software and hardware products and application models that are cost-saving and effective. Ministry of Agriculture gradually promoted them to the society to increase agricultural output rate, labor productivity, and resource utilization.[3]

5.2.2.3 Comprehensive demonstration project for introducing e-commerce into rural areas

In terms of agricultural operations, China has actively promoted comprehensive

---

[1] "Explanation of Issues Related to Smart Agriculture by Ministry of Agriculture", *Jilin Rural Daily*, Aug. 4, 2017.

[2] Ministry of Agriculture, 13th Five-Year National Agricultural and Rural Informatization Development Plan, Chinese Central Government's Official Website, Aug. 29, 2016, http: //www.moa.gov.cn/zwllm/ghjh/2016 09/t20160901_5260726.htm.

[3] "Explanation of Issues Related to Smart Agriculture by Ministry of Agriculture", *Jilin Rural Daily*, Aug. 4, 2017.

demonstration projects for introducing e-commerce into rural areas. In July 2014, the Ministry of Commerce and the Ministry of Finance jointly issued the Notice on the Comprehensive Demonstration of E-commerce in Rural Areas. The notice requires us to actively carry out the comprehensive demonstration work of e-commerce into rural areas, establish and improve the comprehensive service system of rural e-commerce, cultivate demonstration sites that can play a typical driving role in the country, and promote the development of rural e-commerce. China has coordinated demonstration projects with poverty alleviation and development work, and has given preference to poverty-stricken areas in various policies, with the focus on pilot e-commerce projects such as direct distribution of fresh agricultural products to communities, free access to agricultural means of production in the countryside, and online marketing of leisure agriculture. The scope of the pilot program has been extended to 56 counties in 8 provinces including Hebei, Henan, Hubei, and others, and 200 counties in central and western regions. Driven by the comprehensive demonstration project of e-commerce in rural areas, the public service system of rural e-commerce is becoming more and more mature. The e-commerce platform and the public service platform of e-commerce information provide effective services for the informatized management of new agricultural operators, distributors of agricultural products, state-owned farms and agricultural enterprises.[1]

5.2.2.4 Golden Agriculture project

In agricultural management, the state has promoted the implementation of the Golden Agriculture project, which has improved the quality and level of agricultural information services. Golden Agriculture project is an information application system project of integrated agricultural management and service, which was put forward at the third meeting of National Economic Informatization Joint Conference in December 1994.

The first phase of Golden Agriculture project has built 16 types of major business data collection systems and supervisory business systems, namely, comprehensive agricultural statistical information collection system, price monitoring information collection system, agricultural cost survey system, agricultural machinery accident reporting and analysis system, agricultural dispatch data management system of the Ministry of Agriculture, international agricultural product market information collection

---

[1] Ministry of Agriculture, 13th Five-Year National Agricultural and Rural Informatization Development Plan, the Chinese Central Government's Official Website, Aug. 29, 2016, http: //www.moa.gov.cn/zwllm/ghjh/201609/ t20160901_5260726. htm.

system, agricultural mechanization information statistical system, soil fertilizer information statistical system, flower information statistical system, plant protection information statistical system, agricultural business management survey system, foreign agricultural cooperation information system, pesticide supervision business system, agricultural machinery supervision business system, green food supervision business system and agricultural material counterfeit supervision business system.

During the 13th Five-year Plan period, the Chinese government will continue to promote and improve the implementation of the Golden Agriculture project and the construction of global agricultural data survey and analysis systems. At the same time, China also strengthens the construction of overseas agricultural data centers, accelerates the process of agricultural data collection, analysis and promulgate systems in major agricultural countries around the world, to continuously promote the upgrading of national agricultural data centers in the cloud.[1]

5.2.2.5 "12316" comprehensive information service platform project related to agriculture, rural areas and rural people

China continues to explore ways and means for all households in all villages to enjoy information services in order to improve the level of comprehensive services related to agriculture, rural areas and rural people. The Ministry of Agriculture has set up a nationwide public welfare "12316" comprehensive information service platform related to agriculture, rural areas and rural people (hereinafter referred to as "12316" platform) by coordinating the internet and other modern means of communication and taking the computer, TV and telephone "three in one" project as the driving force.

The "12316" platform is a multi-channel, multi-form, multimedia platform which has integrated "12316" hotline, website, TV programs, cell phone SMS, MMS, mobile client. It provides farmers with all-round instant information service such as policy, science and technology, fake and substandard agricultural complaints, agricultural market supply, and price. The country has continuously integrated resources to improve the service level of the platform. After the opening of the national unified public welfare hotline in 2006, the unified public welfare SMS was opened in 2009, and the Mobile News for Chinese Farmers was opened in 2011. Through these ways, the support capacity of the "12316" platform in information service has been effectively enhanced. The "12316" platform built the bridge between the government, enterprises, markets

---

[1] Ministry of Agriculture, 13th Five-Year National Agricultural and Rural Informatization Development Plan, Chinese Central Government's Official Website, Aug. 29, 2016, http: //www.moa.gov.cn/zwllm/ghjh/201609/ t20160901_5260726. htm.

and farmers to communicate. Farmers and enterprises can get timely and accurate information on agricultural weather warnings, pest control methods and other emergency information through the platform. Through the "12316" platform, new technologies and varieties can be promoted, and farmers can also get timely guidance on agricultural production to improve agricultural production efficiency and reduce economic losses.

In order to promote the smooth implementation of technological innovation projects, the government continues to improve the mechanism, increase financial support, improve financial support policies, and create a good policy environment for enterprises to play the main role in innovation. With the implementation of agricultural information technology innovation project and the IoT application demonstration project, China has initially established a set of "governments, industries, universities and research institutes" in one of the technological innovation systems. The system has provided a strong guarantee for the innovation and development of agricultural information technology, and the deep application of the IoT in agriculture. The Golden Agriculture project and the "12316" platform have set up a comprehensive service system for the development of agricultural informatization. This made a great effort for the establishment of a good communication mechanism for the cooperation between the government, enterprises, markets and farm households.

5.3　Main achievements of China's agricultural informatization

Under the leadership of the CPC Central Committee and the State Council, China's agricultural information construction has been steadily advancing and has achieved remarkable results. The infiltration of the internet, mobile internet, wireless induction technology, IoT, cloud computing and other modern information technology into all parts agricultural production, has realized the integration of information technology and traditional agriculture. From that, the informatization of agricultural production has taken an important step forward. With the continuous development and improvement of the e-commerce platform for agricultural products, the informatization of agricultural management develops rapidly. The application of information technologies such as the IoT and big data and internet thinking has realized the supervision and management of the whole process of agricultural production and sales, strengthened the safety supervision of the quality of agricultural products and means of production. Based on these, informatization of agricultural management has been advanced. The website of Ministry of Agriculture and the 12316 platform have formed a nationwide network of ministries and provinces to provide all-round services to farmers and agricultural production. And agricultural service informatization has been comprehensively enhanced.

5.3.1   Agricultural production informatization

5.3.1.1   Agricultural production information technology proceeds smoothly

Information technologies such as the internet, mobile internet, big data, IoT and artificial intelligence have been applied in agricultural production in different degrees. The use of information technology and the internet can help us to quickly grasp environmental information on agricultural production, monitor online and collect real-time information on natural resources that affect agricultural production to realize precise operations. Thus, we could reduce the risk and uncertainty of agricultural production. The Ministry of Agriculture in the 13th Five-Year National Agricultural and Rural Informatization Development Plan has made a comprehensive summary of China's agricultural production information achievements during the 12th Five-year Plan period—the application of information technology in field planting, facility agriculture, livestock and poultry breeding and aquaculture has been gradually enhanced, and the development of information technology has made significant achievements.

The application of agricultural remote sensing monitoring in agricultural production has been promoted. China has initially established monitoring systems for staple crops, agricultural resources and natural disasters. For field cultivation, remote sensing monitoring technology of agricultural conditions, remote diagnosis technology of pests and diseases, intelligent stratification technique of rice and soil formula fertilization technology have been applied on a large scale. And the level of automation, intelligence and precision of agricultural production has enhanced. Based on satellite remote sensing technology and geographic information system, China has established a national soil moisture monitoring system, water quality monitoring system, farmland climate monitoring station, national agricultural data center and other information systems, which have realized the monitoring and management of agricultural production environment. And also, the remote and real-time monitoring of crop growth conditions such as seedling situation, diseases and insect pests have been realized.

In terms of agricultural facilities, the automatic monitoring and control equipment for greenhouse environment based on the IoT have made progress. We now have the ability to monitor the humidity, light and other environmental information in the greenhouse in real time. In Beijing and Shanghai, remote control has enabled intelligent management of watering, fertilizing and medicating. In the field of livestock and poultry breeding, the monitoring of environment, rut and disease is widely used in a large-scale. With the help of intelligent monitoring technology, some of the larger feeding bases have achieved precision feeding. They personalize ingredient feeding according to the individual characteristics and growth and development of livestock. Automatic bait feeding, oxygenation, and milking technologies are also rapidly applied in some experimental areas. In the field of aquaculture, based on wireless intelligent technology, automatic monitoring of water environment, quality of feed, fish diseases, etc. is realized.

5.3.1.2 The IoT technology promotes the development of agricultural informatization

The government actively promotes the construction of the IoT application demonstration project, making full use of the superiority of the IoT to promote the development of agricultural information technology to a higher level. In 2011, the Ministry of Agriculture took three projects as the first batch of national intelligent agriculture project demonstrations namely, the demonstration of IoT application for large-field seeds in Heilongjiang Reclamation, the demonstration of IoT application for facility agriculture in Beijing, and the demonstration of IoT application for breeding in Wuxi, Jiangsu Province. It also took two national IoT application demonstration projects for large-field corn in Inner Mongolia and cotton in Xinjiang as the second construction projects to carry out the usage of IoT technology. Since then, Beijing, Heilongjiang, Jiangsu, Tianjin, Shanghai, Anhui, Inner Mongolia and Xinjiang Production and Construction Corps have carried out the National Demonstration Project for the Application of the IoT, a smart agriculture project and a regional pilot project for agricultural IoT. Nationwide, 426 items of IoT hardware and software products, technologies and models for agriculture that save costs and increase efficiency have been concluded and promoted.[1] Heilongjiang Province, as a large northern granary, has made great efforts to use the IoT technology in agricultural production. It adopted digital drainage and irrigation technology, established an expert consultation and information query system for soil testing and fertilization and an agricultural machinery management information system, and has achieved remarkable

---

[1] China Informatization Almanac Compilation Committee, *China Informatization Almanac 2015*, Beijing: Publishing House of Electronics Industry, 2016, p. 11.

results in the development of precision agriculture.

In 2013, the Ministry of Agriculture began to implement the agricultural internet of Things regional trial project, the development of the Work Program on Regional Trial Project of Agricultural Internet of Things[1] in Tianjin, Shanghai, Anhui to take the lead in carrying out pilot trials. With the establishment of the Tianjin facility agriculture and aquaculture IoT pilot area, Shanghai agricultural product quality and safety supervision pilot area, Anhui field production IoT, the goals of the penetrating IoT technology in the whole agricultural industry chain, exploring the application mode of agricultural IoT, and promoting the development of agricultural informatization and intelligence have been gradually achieved.

5.3.2   Agricultural operation informatization

5.3.2.1   Agricultural products e-commerce platform continues to develop and improve

With the development of information technology and the internet, e-commerce information platforms in many fields have emerged in China, such as agricultural production materials, leisure agriculture, and homestay tourism, and business information has developed rapidly. E-commerce platforms for agricultural products are developing and improving. The Ministry of Agriculture has actively promoted and built an e-commerce platform for agricultural product quality traceability, established a seed e-commerce platform company, and established the "Nongyi Net". Comprehensive demonstration work on rural e-commerce has been carried out in 56 counties in eight provinces including Hebei, Henan and Hubei and in 200 counties in the central and western regions, which has driven the development of e-commerce at the county level and promoted the development of agricultural management informatization.

The government strengthened top-level design and upgraded rural e-commerce development into a national strategy. The Several Opinions of the CPC Central Committee and the State Council on Intensifying Reform and Innovation and Accelerating the Construction of Agricultural Modernization, Opinions of the State Council on Vigorous Development of E-Commerce and Acceleration of Fostering of New Driving Forces for the Economy, and Guiding Opinions of General Office of the State Council on Promoting and Accelerating the Development of E-commerce in Rural Areas, and other policies were intensively introduced, proposing that the government

---

[1] Ministry of Agriculture, Work Program on Regional Trial Project of Agricultural Internet of Things, the Official Website of Ministry of Agriculture, Apr.23, 2013, http://www.gov.cn/govpublic/SCYJJXXS/201305/t20130506_ 3451467.htm.

should strengthen the construction of rural e-commerce platforms and carry out comprehensive pilot projects of e-commerce into rural areas. The government vigorously promotes and supports the rapid and standardized development of rural e-commerce from the aspects of policy support, infrastructure construction, personnel training, financial support and market regulation.

With the support of government policies, the rural information infrastructure is constantly improved, the rural logistics system is gradually growing, the quality of rural e-commerce talents is gradually improving, and the level of rural management talents is increasingly improving. And e-commerce of agricultural products has entered a stage of rapid growth. In 2014, the e-commerce transaction volume of agricultural products exceeded RMB80 billion. In 2015, the online retail transaction volume of agricultural products exceeded RMB150 billion, which was more than double the growth from 2013. The number of producers selling agricultural products online has increased significantly, and the types of transactions have become more and more.[1] E-commerce of fresh agricultural products has developed rapidly, reaching RMB26 billion in 2014. Compared to last year, it has increased 100%.

5.3.2.2 Significant results have been achieved in the quality traceability of agricultural products

With the development of the IoT technology, China has made remarkable achievements in the quality traceability of agricultural products. We realized the whole-process information perception, transmission, integration and processing of agricultural products, and realizing the whole-process traceability of agricultural products "from farm to table". Using barcode and RFID technologies, the collection, tracking, monitoring, and integrated control of product data information have been achieved. At present, a meat quality and safety traceability system and a vegetable quality and safety traceability system have been established in China. An influential agricultural product traceability information platform has also been built, such as the Shanghai Edible Agricultural and Sideline Products Quality and Safety Information Inquiry System, Shiji Agricultural Food Safety Traceability Management System, and China Beef Cattle Quality and Safety Traceability System.[2]

---

[1] Ministry of Agriculture, 13th Five-Year National Agricultural and Rural Informatization Development Plan, the Official Website of the Ministry of Agriculture, Aug. 30, 2016, http: //www.moa.gov.cn/zwllm/ghjh/201609/t20160901_5260726.htm.

[2] Kong Fantao, Zhang Jianhua and Wu Jianzhai et al., *Research on the Development of Agriculture Whole Process Informatization*, Beijing: Science Press, 2015, p. 19.

Jiangsu Province officially launched the "digital food" project in 2012. It has promoted the application of information technology such as the IoT in the field of grain distribution. China has now built more than 40 "digital grain depots". And the coverage of the IoT in large-scale agricultural facilities has reached 11.5%.[1] Jiangsu Province is fully implementing the "1210" project in grain circulation, which is 1 data center, 2 management platforms and 10 informatization sub-systems. Its aim is to build a modern grain logistics system based on the Internet of Things, develop a grain e-commerce platform and promote the establishment of a food quality traceability system.

5.3.3   Informatization in agricultural management

5.3.3.1   Agricultural affairs informatization made a significant progress

The level of application of information technology in agricultural government has been improving, and the effectiveness of agricultural management information technology is remarkable. On June 19, 2014, the first phase of the Golden Agriculture project was completed and successfully accepted. China has built a national agricultural data center, a national agricultural science and technology data sub-center and 32 provincial agricultural data centers. It realizes the integration, consolidation and processing of the country's agricultural data resources and shares them with the society, providing critical and reliable information for agricultural monitoring and early warning and production decision-making. The completed databases include the database of agricultural economic statistics, the database of Chinese crop resources, database of scientific and technological achievements in agriculture, animal husbandry and fishery, as well as the integrated database of animal husbandry, document database of Chinese agriculture and forestry, database of phytosanitary diseases and pests. All these have greatly improved the scientific nature of agricultural production management. At present, China has opened a number of application systems covering agricultural industry statistics monitoring, regulatory assessment, information management, early warning prevention and control, command and dispatch, administrative law enforcement, administrative office and other businesses.[2] Agricultural-related administrative approval has achieved the combination of online and offline processing methods to improve

---

[1] The Ministry of Agriculture Information Center Research Group, *Agricultural Information Research Report 2016*, Beijing: China Agriculture Press, 2017, p. 12.

[2] Ministry of Agriculture, 13th Five-Year National Agricultural and Rural Informatization Development Plan, the Official Website of Ministry of Agriculture, Aug. 30, 2016, http: //www.moa.gov.cn/zwllm/ghjh/201609/t2016 0901_5260726.htm.

efficiency. The website of the Ministry of Agriculture has opened an online service function that farmers can do online consultation, online application, online inquiry, online complaint and other functions through the functional module.

5.3.3.2 The level of market supervision of agricultural products and agricultural materials has improved

Some provinces in China have used information technology such as the Internet of Things and big data technology to realize the supervision and management of the entire process of agricultural production, transportation and sales. They also used internet thinking to strengthen the supervision of the quality and safety of agricultural products and production materials. The development of agricultural product quality and agricultural material safety supervision in Zhejiang Province is relatively mature, and a complete traceability system has been formed. In 2011, Zhejiang Province began to establish a traceability system for the quality and safety of agricultural production materials. In 2014, Zhejiang Provincial Department of Agriculture completed the construction of a provincial-level agricultural product quality and safety traceability platform. Fujian Province has established a quality and safety supervision system for agricultural products based on the whole process of traceability based on the unified traceability code identification system. Guangdong Province has established a basic resource database and information platform for agricultural materials supervision, and a ledger accounting system to record the use of agricultural means of production in all aspects.

5.3.4 Agricultural service informatization

5.3.4.1 The ministerial-level collaborative service network has achieved full coverage of the service scope

The Ministry of Agriculture has built a group of agricultural portals covering the ministry, provinces, prefectures and counties, which can release timely and accurate information on policies and regulations, industry dynamics, agricultural supervision, agricultural science and education to farmers. They have become the most authoritative and popular comprehensive agricultural portals for farmers.

The "12316" platform has established a ministry-province collaborative service network, and its service scope has covered the whole country. The website receives more than 20 million consultation calls a year. The "12316" data sharing platform based on search engine has been built, too. Provinces and cities combined with their own conditions, and constantly innovate and improve the "12316" service mechanism to effectively meet the information needs of the majority of farmers. Liaoning Province promotes the integration and application of government resources and market resources through the purchase of services. It also provides comprehensive services, and the cumulative number of services provided by "12316" hotline has exceeded 12 million cases. Fujian Province has integrated the service resources of 48 offices of the Department of Agriculture and 13 agriculture-related bureaus to build a unified "12316" platform at the province-level. It also established "12316" civilized service windows in all cities and counties to provide open services to the community. In terms of improving information services, Heilongjiang Province has used the "internet +" to build an information platform and set up 16 information collection points in Heilongjiang that have expanded the access to information. Heilongjiang Province also uses an advanced information collection, processing and dissemination platform to carry out monitoring and early warning of grain production and agricultural markets.[1]

5.3.4.2   The project of information into the villages and households gives help to improve the overall level of agricultural information services

Since 2014, based on the experience of "12316" agricultural information service practices, the Ministry of Agriculture actively promoted the implementation of the project of information into the villages and households, to improve the overall level of agricultural information services. The pilot project information into the villages and households was first launched from Beijing, Jiangsu, Zhejiang, Hunan and other provinces. And now the area of pilot has covered 116 counties in 26 provinces, and a total of 7,940 agricultural information units have been built and operated. Through the cross-field service of "12316" hotline, service platform, information station and information officers, the project of information into the villages provides farmers and agricultural production with a full range of information on the production, market and national policies and subsidies, taking information as the link and village level agricultural information station as the base point. That has improved the efficiency of agricultural production. Agricultural public welfare services, convenience services, e-commerce and training and experience services have been introduced into villages and households through the information-to-home project. It has improved the overall level of agricultural services and provided basic information guarantee for the transformation of agricultural production methods as well as for farmers to increase their income.

---

[1] The Ministry of Agriculture Information Center Research Group, *Agricultural Information Research 2016 Report,* Beijing: China Agriculture Press, 2017, pp. 56-57.

5.4 Key factors in the steady progress of agricultural information technology

Since the 21st century, under the overall planning and unified deployment of the CPC Central Committee and the State Council, China's agricultural informatization construction has achieved remarkable results, and the informatization of the whole process of agricultural production, operation, management and service has been steadily promoted. With the guideline of informatization integrating the development of industrialization, IT application, urbanization and agricultural modernization of the CPC Central Committee, China's agricultural modernization has come out of a characteristic and efficient path of information development. The guidance of the "internet +" strategy, the innovation of agricultural IT, the improvement of agricultural information infrastructure construction, and the coordinated development of agricultural informatization and national targeted poverty alleviation projects have become key factors in the steady advancement of agricultural informatization in China.

5.4.1 "Internet +" provides power for agricultural informatization

In 2015, China put forward the "internet +" modern agricultural development strategy to cultivate a new model of networked, intelligent and refined modern agriculture, so as to realize the informatization of the agricultural operation system, the agricultural management system based on networking internet and the intellectualization of the agricultural service system.

The thing that internet runs through the whole industry chain of agricultural production and management services has provided inexhaustible power for the development of agricultural information technology and the realization of agricultural modernization. The internet provides support for various aspects, such as the top-level design of agricultural development strategies, the research and development of agricultural information technology, the establishment of the center of agricultural big data and the agricultural information service platform. In terms of top-level design of agricultural informatization development, national policy-making department uses big data and cloud computing to summarize, organize, filter and analyze the basic data of agricultural development in various regions of the country as well as in various periods, and finally formulates agricultural development strategies and plans that meet the economic development conditions of China.

The popularization and application of the internet in agriculture and rural areas is helpful for integrating various types of information, data and resources, providing a good innovation environment for the development of agricultural information technology. And also, it can promote the integrated application of technologies such as the IoT, satellite remote sensing, intelligent terminals and geographic information systems in agriculture. With the help of the internet, China has realized the sharing and common use of agricultural big data. The government, enterprises and farmers can use the database of our arable land, water resources, agricultural equipment and financial capital for data discovery, analysis and decision making in order to improve the science of agricultural development. Through the use of "internet +", China has developed and improved its public opinion monitoring system and information feedback collection platform, and established an agricultural monitoring and early warning system finally. Through the information platform, government management departments can receive the latest information on the whole industrial chain of agricultural products, accurately grasp the latest market situation of agricultural products, and make agricultural and trade policies based on accurate data. The internet is widely used in the agricultural business process. As a new type of product distribution, agricultural e-commerce on resources and products has combined producers and consumers to reduce distribution costs and improve operational efficiency.

In the process of the whole industrial chain of agricultural products, China vigorously implements the strategy of network strengthening agriculture. Based on the internet, we promote the deep integration of information technology and agricultural modernization to advance the comprehensive application of internet technology and thinking in agricultural development. The collection, discovery, sharing and application of agricultural database information driven by the internet in agricultural development can continuously improve market supervision and agricultural information services, and promote the development of precision agriculture. With the increase of rural internet popularity, the development potential of rural e-commerce will be gradually released. So, we can say that the application of "internet +" provides inexhaustible power for the sustainable development of agricultural modernization.

5.4.2   Innovation in agricultural information technology can accelerate the process of agricultural informatization

The infiltration of modern information technology such as the IoT and cloud computing has improved the development of intelligent agriculture. The innovation and development of agricultural information technology is the key to the success of agricultural information construction. And it is also the accelerator of agricultural modernization. The key technology of IT adoption in agriculture mainly includes agricultural big data, cloud computing, IoT, agricultural precision equipment, monitoring and early warning, remote sensing technology, geographic information system, global position system and agricultural information analysis.[1] Among them, agricultural IoT and agricultural precision equipment play a key role in agricultural informatization.

5.4.2.1 Agricultural IoT

The IoT is the third wave of information revolution after computer and internet. Agricultural IoT is an important means to promote the accelerated realization of agricultural informatization and modernization. The Ministry of Agriculture Information Center Research Group precisely defined the agricultural IoT from two perspectives in 2016. That is, for the agricultural IoT, from the technical perspective, it refers to the application of radio frequency identification, sensing, network communication and other technologies to sense internal and external signals involved in the process of agricultural production and management. It connects the internet to achieve intelligent identification of agricultural information and efficient management of agricultural efficient management of production. From the management point of view, it refers to the social complex that anyone and anything, at any time and any place can implement information interconnection through various types of information sensing devices and technical systems, for intelligent production, life and management in a large agricultural system, in accordance with the protocol of authorization.[2] As an emerging agricultural information technology, the IoT can finely manage and control the agricultural production process and the storage and transportation process of agricultural products, and realize quality and safety traceability of agricultural products and agricultural production materials. It realizes the reliable transmission of agricultural data and promotes the development of precision agriculture.

Due to the importance of supporting the development of agricultural IoT, China has made agricultural IoT a major special development plan. In 2011, the Ministry of Agriculture promulgated the 12th Five-Year Plan for the Development of National Agricultural and Rural Informatization, which proposed to strengthen the application of

---

[1] Kong Fantao, Zhang Jianhua and Wu Jianzhai et al., *Research on the Development of Agriculture Whole Process Informatization*, Beijing: Science Press, 2015, p. 27.

[2] The Ministry of Agriculture Information Center Research Group, *Agricultural Information Research Report 2016*, Beijing: China Agriculture Press, 2017, p. 249.

modern information technology such as the IoT and sensor networks in agricultural and rural informatization. In 2015, the Guiding Opinions of the State Council on Vigorously Advancing the "Internet +" Action was promulgated. It requires us to promote the application of the IoT in intelligent water-saving irrigation, formula fertilization by soil testing, positioning farming by agricultural machinery, accurate feed delivery, automatic diagnosis of disease, automatic waste recycling, etc., to promote mature and replicable application model for agricultural IoT, and developing refined production methods. The combination of agricultural internet of things and cloud computing has promoted efficient agricultural data processing, scientific agricultural decision-making and precise agricultural management.

Since 2013, China has launched a regional trial project of agricultural IoT to promote the application and development of agricultural IoT in China. The role of agricultural IoT in agricultural informatization is mainly reflected in the following aspects.

First, the use of IoT technology can realize the fine monitoring of agricultural resources and agricultural production environment and the fine management of agricultural production process. In agricultural production, the use of radio frequency technology, sensor technology, "3S" technology (remote sensing technology, geographic information system, global position system) and information systems can obtain and analyze agricultural resource information such as resources on climate, biology, water, etc., and monitor and dispatch agricultural resources and agricultural production materials involved in the production process in a comprehensive manner. The application of IoT technology in field planting and facility vegetable production enables farmers to grasp the growth environment, growth situation, pest and disease status of crops and vegetables in a timely manner. Thus, we could improve the accuracy of production decision and management. We have realized real-time monitoring of the shed environment and aquatic environment through the application of IoT technology in the breeding of livestock and aquatic organisms. So that we could enable timely regulation of temperature, humidity, lighting and other conditions according to the growth of livestock and fish. In the process of agricultural production, the use of IoT technology can achieve intelligent analysis, expert guidance and precise regulation on agricultural water, agricultural fertilization, livestock feeding and aquaculture environment. These advantages can help us promote efficient agricultural production, reduce costs and losses, and achieve the desire to increase production and income.

Second, the use of IoT technology can achieve quality and safety supervision of agricultural products, traceability and tracking of product quality. The use of wireless radio frequency technology, sensing technology, electronic tags, bar codes and the internet can realize the quality monitoring and traceability of agricultural products from raw material collection, production and processing, transportation and storage, wholesale and retail, and other parts of production, to improve the quality of supervision and traceability efficiency. At present, consumers can obtain agricultural production data by scanning electronic tags such as QR codes and bar codes to realize the traceability of products. Agricultural IoT technology improves the transparency of the whole process of agricultural production and guarantees the quality and safety of products.

Third, the use of IoT technology can realize the monitoring of agricultural warehousing and logistics, to achieve intelligent storage management and logistics distribution, and improve circulation efficiency. The configuration of sensors and intelligent identification terminals in the agricultural products storage can realize remote monitoring and management, access to the incoming and outgoing situation of the warehouse in time, and improve the efficiency of storage management. In the logistics distribution of agricultural products, we can collect and track information and provide real-time feedback in the process of agricultural products circulation by using radio frequency technology and bar code. At the same time, we can use GIS to optimize distribution routes and improve the efficiency according to the time and location of agricultural products distribution.

5.4.2.2 Agricultural precision equipment

From 2004 to now, with the rapid development of agricultural machinery and equipment, China's industrial scale came into a steady growth phase, and its average annual growth rate of the main business income of large-scale enterprises maintain at about 20%. According to the China Association of Agricultural Machinery Manufacturers, in 2014, the main business income of large-scale agricultural machinery and equipment enterprises in China reached RMB398.89 billion, and in 2015 reached RMB428.37 billion which has exceeded the limitation of RMB400 billion. During the 12th Five-year Plan period, the scientific, technologic and informative level of China's agricultural machinery and equipment continues to improve. China has made major breakthroughs in the research and development of key equipment such as power-shifting tractor, precision sowing and efficient medication, and has successfully overcome key core technologies of heavy-duty wheeled tractors such as continuously variable transmission system and intelligent control system. At present, China is actively promoting the development of high precision navigation operations, yield measurement, loss monitoring, operating conditions measurement and control and other intelligent control technology and systems as the development priorities for large combine harvester.[1]

In order to promote the development of precision agriculture, China has accelerated the integrated development of information technology and agricultural equipment, and has improved the intelligent level and precision decision-making ability of agricultural machinery and equipment. The application of agricultural equipment sensing, intelligent control, navigation, and communication technology continues to improve the ability to collect information and transmission capabilities. The application of the IoT, radio frequency and two-dimensional code and other information technologies in agricultural machinery and equipment has achieved product traceability.

5.4.3   The improvement of agricultural information infrastructure is the basic guarantee of agricultural informatization

The improvement of agricultural information infrastructure is the basic guarantee of agricultural informatization and modernization. Now, China's support capacity on agricultural information technology infrastructure has been significantly enhanced. The research system of agricultural information technology was formed preliminarily. A large number of scientific research institutes, colleges and universities and IT enterprises have established agricultural information technology research and development institutions one by one. Comprehensive key laboratories of agricultural information technology and scientific observation experiment stations of the Ministry of Agriculture have been used. The continuous development and improvement of agricultural infrastructure for IT has provided a guarantee for agricultural technology research and development and promoted the rapid development of agricultural informatization in China.

At the same time, China has developed a number of comprehensive information service projects to provide basic support for agricultural informatization. In 2004, Ministry of Industry and Information Technology (MIIT) carried out the nationwide "project of connecting every village with telephones" —a communication project that can facilitate the popularization of communication services in rural areas. The three major basic telecom operators—China Telecom, China Unicom and China Mobile, have provided financial and technical support for the "project of connecting every village with telephones". In the process of implementing the "project of connecting every village with telephones", China adheres to the "triple three-step strategies". First,

---

[1] National Manufacturing Strategy Advisory Committee, *2016 Blue Book on Made in China 2025*, Beijing: Publishing House of Electronics Industry, 2016, pp. 162-164.

in terms of network coverage, according to the distance from the telecom trunk line, we cover the township firstly, then the administrative village, and finally the natural village from near to far. Second, in terms of service capacity, we open the telephone firstly, then the internet, and finally the broadband according to the actual needs of rural areas from low to high, to achieve a step-by-step upgrading of technology. Third, in the process of information technology, according to the order of building first and using second, we build the communication infrastructure firstly, then build the information service platform, and finally promote services that are suitable for agriculture.[1] By the end of the 11th Five-year Plan, China had achieved the 100% telephone coverage in administrative villages and 100% internet coverage in townships.

In 2005, the Ministry of Agriculture selected 6 prefecture-level and 50 county-level agricultural departments with a certain foundation to launch the project of "Convergence of Three Appliances (computer, television, telephone)", which comprehensively use television, telephone, computer and other information carriers to carry out information services, improve the coverage and usage of information in households, and improve information coverage in rural areas. In 2006, the Ministry of Agriculture opened the hotline "12316" for agricultural information service and established a comprehensive information service platform related to agriculture, rural areas and rural people. In the same year, the Ministry of Commerce opened a new rural business network to provide public information services for farmers and post information timely on agricultural-related policies and the circulation of agricultural and sideline products. In 2007, the Ministry of Agriculture launched the Golden Agriculture project, and in 2014, the Ministry of Agriculture launched the project of information entering villages and households. The continuous improvement of agricultural and rural information infrastructure provides the basic guarantee for the development of agricultural information technology.

5.5 Promoting agricultural informatization in targeted poverty alleviation

Since the 18th CPC National Congress, the CPC Central Committee with Xi Jinping as

---

[1] "The 11th Five-Year Plan Summary and the 12th Five-Year Plan Launch Conference of National Village Access Project: An Important Speech of Xi Guohua, Vice Minister of Industry and Information Technology", *Digital Communication World*, 2011(5), pp. 12-13.

its core, has attached great importance to the work of targeted poverty alleviation. They have continued to innovate new approaches to poverty alleviation to promote agricultural development and improve people's living standards in impoverished rural areas. The CPC Central Committee and the State Council attach great importance to the role of information technology and information networks in the work of targeted poverty alleviation. We can promote the application of internet in the work of poverty alleviation and development, and also agricultural and rural informatization in the process of targeted poverty alleviation.

5.5.1　Accelerating the development of network infrastructure construction in impoverished rural areas

China's continuous acceleration of the network infrastructure construction in impoverished rural areas to provide basic support for agricultural and rural informatization. In the process of targeted poverty alleviation, the government has intensively promulgated policies to promote the construction of information infrastructure in impoverished rural areas. Based on this, the basic guarantee for agricultural and rural informatization was provided.

Policies for poverty alleviation help rural information infrastructure to be developed continuously. China has put forward the requirement to accelerate the construction of information network infrastructure in impoverished rural areas in poverty alleviation documents. The Outline for Development-Oriented Poverty Reduction for China's Rural Areas (2011-2020) issued in 2011 clearly states that we should popularize information services and give priority to the popularization of cable TV, telephone and internet in key counties. The Opinions on Innovating New Mechanism to Firmly Promote the Work of Poverty Aid Development in Rural Areas issued by the General Office of the CPC Central Committee and the State Council in 2014 called for accelerating the process of accessing internet that meets national standards in incorporated villages in poor areas, eliminating the gap caused by the "digital divide", integrating and opening up all kinds of information resources, and providing information services for farmers. In April 2014, the Ministry of Industry and Information Technology, the Ministry of Agriculture, the Ministry of Science and Technology, the Ministry of Education and the State Council Leading Group Office of Poverty Alleviation five departments jointly issued the Implementation Plan for Informatization in Impoverished Villages. It states, by 2020, villages have basically achieved full broadband coverage. The Decision of the CPC Central Committee and the

State Council on Winning the Tough Battle against Poverty, issued in 2015, clearly stated that the process of covering broadband networks in impoverished villages should be accelerated. The Guiding Opinions on Strengthening Poverty Alleviation Efforts to Support the Development and Construction of Old Revolutionary Base Areas released in 2016 proposed that we should give support to accelerate the implementation of the "Broadband China" strategy in old revolutionary base areas. In 2016, the Office of Central Cyberspace Affairs Commission, the National Development and Reform Commission and the State Council Leading Group Office of Poverty Alleviation jointly issued the Action Plan for Network Poverty Alleviation, which clearly states that we should launch the five projects of "network coverage, rural e-commerce, intelligent network, information services and network public welfare" to accelerate the pace of internet construction and application in poor areas. And also, we should accelerate the popularization of universal pilots of telecommunications services, promote the development of broadband in rural and remote areas, and narrow the digital divide between urban and rural areas. At the same time, it is also necessary to increase the policy and funding for poor counties, giving priority to supporting network coverage projects in ethnic areas, border areas, old revolutionary areas and poor areas, and driving economic and social development and information technology upgrading in rural and remote areas.[1]

5.5.2 The "Internet + e-commerce" poverty alleviation

Against poverty through the promotion of e-commerce and network has become an important way to alleviate poverty in China. In 2016, the Office of Central Cyberspace Affairs Commission, the National Development and Reform Commission and the State Council Leading Group Office of Poverty Alleviation jointly issued the Action Plan for Network Poverty Alleviation, which clearly states that we need to accelerate the construction of improved logistics service networks and facilities in poor areas, encourage the construction of e-commerce platforms to open poverty alleviation channels for poor areas, lower the threshold for cooperation between e-commerce platforms and poor areas, open online sales platforms for special agricultural products, promote the development of online industrial action project of "One Brand in One Village" (every impoverished village is encouraged to develop one special product of its

---

[1] The Office of Central Cyberspace Affairs Commission, the National Development and Reform Commission, the State Council Leading Group Office of Poverty Alleviation, "The Action Plan for Network Poverty Alleviation", The Office of Central Cyberspace Affairs Commission Website, Oct. 27, 2016, http://www.cac.gov.cn/2016- 10/27/c1119801364.htm.

own), and support the development of e-commerce in impoverished areas. "One Brand in One Village" industrial action project gives supports to the development of e-commerce in impoverished areas. In November 2016, the State Council issued the 13th Five-Year Plan for Poverty Alleviation to further clarify the importance of rural e-commerce as a vehicle for precise poverty alleviation. The "internet + e-commerce" poverty alleviation model promotes the informatization on the operation and circulation of agricultural products continuously.

In the process of poverty alleviation through e-commerce, the government formulates incentive policies in order to give full play to the leading role of new agricultural business entities such as large breeders, family farms, cooperatives and leading agricultural industrialized enterprises in impoverished rural areas, and to use internet thinking and information technology to transform the way of operation, circulation and management. The government actively promotes the cooperation between new agricultural business entities and e-commerce platforms to achieve effective results, and drives the informatization of the whole industrial chain of agricultural products with informatization on business, while providing various service information for the production, sales and circulation of agricultural products. For example, Tongren City, Guizhou Province, vigorously develops e-commerce in poverty alleviation, establishes e-commerce incubation center, agricultural products testing center and data guarantee center to provide various guarantees for online sales of agricultural products, and promotes the development of informatization on agricultural business. In the process of e-commerce poverty alleviation, the government has formulated measures to build a logistics and distribution system in impoverished rural areas, such as the establishment of a perfect three-level logistics and distribution infrastructure in counties, townships and villages to promote the development of e-commerce for agricultural products. E-commerce poverty alleviation introduces internet thinking to impoverished rural areas. And it has facilitated the transformation of poor farmers' production and lifestyles. Through education and training, resource investment, and policy support, China promotes farmers to carry on e-commerce transactions of agricultural products, boosts the online conversion rate of agricultural products, and promotes the informatization on agricultural operations. E-commerce for agricultural products optimizes the supply chain, reduces distribution steps, and improves distribution efficiency. Thus, it improves agricultural operations. The informatization of agricultural business with e-commerce as a breakthrough has led to the informatization on agricultural production and management.

5.5.3 "Internet + rural entrepreneurship and innovation"

"Internet + rural entrepreneurship and innovation" provides the driving force for agricultural and rural informatization. The government makes full use of modern information technology and internet thinking, formulates incentives and safeguard policies to promote mass entrepreneurship and innovation in the vast rural areas to build a platform for agricultural and rural informatization. Ministry of Agriculture issued the Poverty Alleviation Through Development Plan for the Agricultural Industry (2011-2020), proposes that it is necessary to accelerate the construction of comprehensive agricultural information service platforms in impoverished rural areas, make full use of modern media means, strengthen the guidance of production and marketing information, and provide timely and effective information services for farmers. In the process of entrepreneurship and innovation in impoverished rural areas, the government firstly improves the network infrastructure in impoverished rural areas and extensively promotes the full coverage of wireless network in urban and rural areas to solve the problem of so-called "last mile". Secondly, it provides various training and lectures on entrepreneurship and innovation for new rural business subjects, and invites technical experts to provide technical guidance and services through network connection and data sharing to guide investment institutions, experts and scholars to support entrepreneurship and innovation of new agricultural business entities, so as to put practice into the concept of helping the poor before helping the wise and improve the innovation and entrepreneurship ability of farmers. At the same time, the government also supports entrepreneurs to establish the e-commerce platforms with independent intellectual property rights.

5.6 Development practice of agricultural informatization

The information technology in new generation such as big data and the IoT deeply integrated and widely applicated in the process of agricultural production, operation, management and service has improved the efficiency of agricultural production. It has promoted the transformation and upgrading of China's agriculture type from traditional to modern. Based on information technology and information networks, numerous new development models have emerged in the whole country. Smart agriculture, precision agriculture, ecological agriculture and efficient agriculture have become the trend of agriculture development.

5.6.1   Application of IoT in agricultural production: fresh peaches planting in Shandong Linqu by using IoT[1]

Linqu County, in Shandong Province, is located in the middle of Shandong Peninsula, at the northern foot of Yishan Mountain and the upper reaches of the Mi River. It is a large agricultural county with a large proportion of the income coming from planting fruit products. The county has an area of 3,333 hectares of peach trees, with larger planting areas in Songshan, Longshan, Jiushan, Shanwang and Dongcheng. Among them, 667 hectares of greenhouse peaches have an annual output value of RMB500 million. In the development of recent years, Linqu County has made great efforts to develop ecological recycling agriculture in accordance with local conditions and combined with local efficient agricultural infrastructure. Due to this, its economic benefits have been significantly improved. In 2017, Linqu County was awarded the first batch of provincial ecological recycling agriculture demonstration units in Shandong Province. Linqu County seizes the opportunity of the information revolution. It actively introduces modern information technology such as the IoT to promote the agricultural informatization, build the mode of intelligent agriculture and improve agricultural production efficiency.

In the process of agricultural modernization, with the implementation of the brand-driven strategy, Linqu County vigorously promotes the development of brand agriculture with the goal of "high-yield, high-quality, high-efficiency, ecological and safe" agricultural products. At present, Linqu County has 173 "Sanpin Yibiao" (pollution-free agricultural products, green food, organic agricultural products and geographical indications of products) within the validity period, 5 national geographical indication products and 17 Chinese geographical indication certification trademarks. Linqu County has built the Songshan Fruit (Peach) Garden with National Standard, Wang Laowu Family Farm Standard Garden and Zhenyue Cherry Professional Garden with Cooperative Standard. The government of Linqu County continuously strengthens the standardized management of the park. It improves the management system for the use of agricultural inputs, product testing and quality tracing, and establishes sound management files for production records, planting information, quality testing, product sales and the use of agricultural inputs to ensure the standardization and traceability of the park's production and provide comprehensive and efficient services and guarantees for agricultural modernization and the development strategy of agricultural brands. The

---

[1] Liu Mingzhi, Lyu Bingbing, "Linqu County: Growing Peaches Through Internet of Things", *Farmers' Daily*, Aug. 17, 2017.

brand of peach products represented by Songshan peach has driven the development of the peach industry in the county.

In the cultivation and operation of fresh peaches, Linqu County introduces advanced information technology such as the IoT and vigorously develops intelligent production and intelligent operation to improve the quality and efficiency of production and management. During the production of peaches, integrated irrigation systems of water and fertilizer are all applied. They install "automatic controller of humidity" in the soil and IoT control system in the smart terminal of cell phone. The IoT enables an intelligent connection between the producer and the soil. Once the soil moisture falls below a set minimum value, the system will automatically irrigate the field. By using the integrated system of irrigation and fertilization, the intelligent terminal provides water and nutrients directly to the crop in proportion, which saves water and fertilizer and improves yield at the same time.

In the operation and management of peaches, intelligent operation has been achieved. Linqu uses the internet, IoT and modern information technology to innovate its operation methods, allowing fresh peaches to reach consumers directly. They have developed a peach tree custom adoption system in cooperation with McShell.com. By scanning the QR code, customers can enter the adoption interface and choose their favorite peach trees for adoption. Customers can monitor the whole process of fertilization, watering and bagging of peach trees through the intelligent terminal. Planters can use various types of organic fertilizers such as soybean cake fermented fertilizer and farmyard manure to customize their own healthy fruits according to different needs of customers. The application of the IoT in agricultural production practices truly realize personalized production with intelligence and efficiency.

5.6.2 Service platform of agricultural informatization: mobile client of "Yinongbao for Plowing" in Jilin Province

In the development of agricultural informatization, Jilin Province strives to be a pioneer in the demonstration. On April 14, 2016, the Leading Group of Agricultural Modernization of Jilin Province took the lead in formulating the Implementation Opinions on Achieving Agricultural Modernization in 2016. The opinions put forward the requirement of vigorously promoting the supply-side structural reform of agriculture. It emphasis that we should establish a sound agricultural information service platform to provide quality services for agricultural information technology, and vigorously develop the "internet + modern agriculture" to find an intensive, efficient, safe modern agriculture development path with sustainable scale and efficiency.[1] In the opinions, Jilin Province proposed the requirement of continuously strengthening the construction of comprehensive information infrastructure, establishing the system of information data resources sharing and exchange, and actively providing farmers with information-based vocational education and training to improve the level of agricultural information services.

The first is upgrading and renovating the system of 12316 platform, strengthening the construction of the internet App, WeChat public platform, and fully promoting the application of cell phone service system for soil testing and fertilization, "Yinongbao" cell phone client, "farmers' wallet" and so on, to improve the four-level agricultural and rural information management and service network in cities, counties, townships, and villages. At the same time, we must also actively build a data resource sharing and exchange system with the provincial water resources department, the meteorological department and other agriculture-related departments, and strengthen the construction of e-commerce and rural logistics systems. The second is innovating "internet + training" model. We can accelerate the cultivation of new professional farmers by means of information technology through education and training in the form of scenario-based simulated teaching, online policy consultation and expert lectures.

The cell phone client "Yinongbao" has played an important role in the construction of the agricultural information service platform in Jilin Province. In 2013, based on 12582 voice SMS and MMS services, the Jilin Provincial Agriculture Committee and Jilin Mobile jointly created a cell phone client product of professional service for farmers— "Yinongbao for Plowing", to provide farmers with timely, targeted agricultural information services. "Yinongbao" has set up four modules for farmers—easy production, easy life, easy trading and easy business. The function of easy production can provide classified services such as agricultural disease pest and weed, expert guidance, soil testing and fertilization, and remote control. The function of Easy Life can provide guidance for farmers' work and employment. The function of easy trading can easily realize the balance of supply and demand for agricultural products, and provide farmers with trade services through the KaiLi Mall. The function of easy business can provide farmers with timely information services such as the status of loan processing and benefiting-farmers policy.

In the soil measurement and fertilization service, "Yinongbao" has combined

---

[1] "Implementation Opinions of the Leading Group of Jilin Province on Achieving Agricultural Modernization in 2016", *Agriculture of Jilin*, 2016 (10).

positioning system of mobile base station with agricultural soil measurement data platform. Users can get expert guidance of formula fertilization only standing in their own field by selecting crop varieties and ground strength level. At the same time, due to the combination of software and agricultural e-commerce, users can directly purchase customized formula fertilizer. In the expert guidance service, experts provide users with professional answers and handling measures for problems related to planting and breeding in agricultural production. At present, in Jilin province, there are more than 300 authoritative experts from the fields of planting, breeding, agricultural machinery, policy, law, meteorology, etc., which can provide users with timely and reliable all-round answers. In the remote video diagnosis and treatment service, village information service stations and township veterinary pharmacies are the main service places, and the 12582 platform is its core support. Users can interact with experts online with voice, text and other demands, realizing face-to-face communication between farmers and experts. Through the function of Easy Business, users can accurately manage the workflow, search for national laws and regulations, conduct legal consultation, and keep themselves informed of the latest policies issued by governments at all levels for the benefit of agriculture. With the development of information technology and the diversification of farmers' needs, "Yinongbao" has been upgraded and improved. In July 2015, the new version 3.0 of "Yinongbao" App was officially launched. As of April 2017, there are more than 440,000 registered users, and the weekly clicks of users are more than 350,000 times since the opening.[1]

5.6.3 "Internet + agriculture" development practice: "123 + N" model for intelligent agriculture in Jiangxi Province

5.6.3.1 Actively strengthening the top-level design to promote the development of smart agriculture

Jiangxi Province actively formulates policies to strengthen the top-level design of agricultural information technology. The CPC Jiangxi provincial Committee and the People's Government of Jiangxi Province attached great importance to the construction of modern agriculture. In 2015, they formulated the Opinions of the CPC Jiangxi Provincial Committee and the People's Government of Jiangxi Province on Accelerating the Transformation of Agricultural Development and Building a Strong Modern

---

[1] Yan Hongyu, "The App 'Yinongbao' of Jilin Province Registered Users More than 440,000 for Online Two Years", *Farmers' Daily*, May 16, 2017.

Agricultural Province, followed by the Department of Agriculture of Jiangxi Province, which formulated the Opinions on Implementing the Internet + Agriculture Action Plan to Accelerate the Construction of Intelligent Agriculture in Jiangxi Province. In 2016, the Department of Agriculture of Jiangxi Province also developed the Technical Regulations for IoT Network, Technical Construction and Agriculture Production Site of Jiangxi Province and Guidance on the Construction of Jiangxi Province Intelligent Agriculture in Cities and Counties. Jiangxi Province made an overall plan and unified layout of agricultural modernization and development, and actively promoted the internet, IoT and other modern information technology in the development of agriculture, to promote the development of intelligent agriculture.

5.6.3.2   "123 + N" model for the development of intelligent agriculture[1]

Jiangxi Province is actively integrating the internet in the development of modern agriculture. It has created the model of "internet + agriculture" and deploying the use of "123 + N" model for the development of intelligent agriculture which has promoted the comprehensive integration of mobile internet, cloud computing, big data, the IoT and other new-generation information technology with agricultural production, operation, management and services to accelerate the transformation of agricultural production methods. The development mode of intelligent agriculture realizes the four goals of intelligent agricultural production, e-commerce operation, efficient management and convenient service, as well as the four functions of good planting, proper management, more sales and good service.

The construction path to promote intelligent agriculture in Jiangxi Province is the "123 + N". "1" refers to the agricultural data cloud; "2" refers to two centers—the agricultural command and dispatch center and 12316 information service center; "3" refers to 3 platforms—the platform of agricultural IoT, the platform of quality and safety supervision and traceability for agriculture, and the agricultural e-commerce platform; "N" refers to multiple subsystems involving agricultural production, project management, fund supervision, comprehensive law enforcement, administrative approval, market information, agricultural technology services and government affairs.

(1) *An agricultural cloud can support the storage and computing of the province's intelligent agricultural system*

Jiangxi's Agricultural Data Cloud includes two fundamental platforms—Jiangxi Agricultural Cloud Platform and Jiangxi Agricultural Data Center. Jiangxi Agricultural

---

[1] Platform for Intelligent Agriculture of Jiangxi Province, http://zhny.jxagri.gov.cn/.

Cloud Platform provides centralized and unified computing resources to support the operation of all kinds of agricultural information systems. It is the basis for building Jiangxi's smart agriculture. At present, the cloud platform mainly relies on 20 cloud hosts and cloud server clusters with more than 1,000T storage capacity to guarantee computing capacity of trillion times and 10,000 trillion export bandwidths. It maximizes the integration of existing computing and storage resources to provide powerful cloud service support for the efficient operation of various agricultural information systems for intelligent agriculture. The main work of the Jiangxi Agricultural Data Center is bringing together basic agricultural data, pictures, images, and other data resources from various places and departments, in order to realize the collection of big data, analysis and prognosis of modeling, and interconnectivity and sharing of information. At the end of 2015, Jiangxi Province had completed the construction of agricultural data cloud infrastructure, which was operated in 2016.

(2) *Creating a province-wide agricultural science and IT service system by two centers*

The two centers refer to "12316" information service center and agricultural command and dispatch center, which can provide scientific guidance and perfect services for agricultural production. "12316" information service center is an integrated agricultural information service platform established by Jiangxi Province with great efforts. It can provide policy, regulation, agricultural technology, market and other information consultation and expert remote video diagnosis services for agricultural production, operation and management through "12316" hotline, SMS, MMS, "12316" live agricultural radio program, remote expert diagnosis system, mobile App, WeChat public number and other services, to build a service system of agricultural science and technology information that covers the production and management entities of the whole Jiangxi province including its cities, counties, townships and villages. The Agricultural Command and Dispatch Center has been completed and put into use in 2015. Through this center, we can realize real-time monitoring of major animal and plant diseases and epidemics, emergency treatment of major natural disasters, and emergency disposal of agricultural quality and safety events. So that we can improve the command and management level of the agricultural sector.

(3) *Developing application of information technology in agricultural development by three platforms*

The three platforms are agricultural internet of Things platform, platform for quality and safety supervision and traceability of agricultural products, and e-commerce platform of agricultural products.

Jiangxi agricultural IoT cloud platform is a "total switch" of the province's agricultural IoT construction. It provides data collection and analysis, precision control, decision-making guidance and other services for the province's agricultural IoT project to achieve precision production and remote control. The data collected through the sensors will be connected to the IoT cloud platform. And then, the platform will analyze and process it and unify the operating instructions later to achieve whole-process intelligent production.

Jiangxi Province has established a unified province-wide platform for quality and safety supervision and traceability of agricultural products by the use of radio frequency identification (RFID), QR code and other technologies. This platform focuses on monitoring agricultural enterprises, cooperatives, family farms and other agricultural products as well as information on agricultural production materials, and the establishment of the province's unified system for information publishing and inquiry according to industries and regions.

Agricultural products e-commerce platform to take the departmental cooperation to build a mature agricultural products e-commerce "Jiangxi model". "Ganongbao" is an authoritative e-commerce platform for agricultural products that Jiangxi Province strives to build. It has built a new e-commerce marketing system for Jiangxi agricultural products by bringing together the province's "Sanpin Yibiao" and special agricultural products, realizing one-stop presentation and one-stop procurement. Due to the integration of O2O, crowd-funding, adoption, private customization and other new circulation modes, Ganongbao realizes the functions of agricultural products quality and safety inquiry, IoT planting environment, and production index online view.

(4) *The "N" systems to promote the development of information technology throughout agriculture*

The "N" systems in Jiangxi's smart agriculture involve 47 subsystems such as planting, farming and OA paperless office, comprehensive agricultural law enforcement and agricultural technology services, which can be shared by provinces, cities and counties. While sharing, cities and counties can also develop localized systems with their needs, which can not only improve efficiency but also save costs. Platforms and systems such as OA paperless office system, fishery administration and dispatching system, quarantine of livestock and poultry online, formula fertilization by soil testing have been put in use over whole province.

Chapter 6
The Development Path of China's
E-Commerce Innovation

With the rapid development and penertration of the new generation of information technologies such as the IoT, cloud computing and mobile internet, more and more enterprises carry out business activities at home and abroad using the internet. Featured as openness, sharing, transcendence of time and space, and high efficiency of the internet, e-commerce emerged in the mid-1990s and gradually boomed. As a new business model, e-commerce has become an important means to drive the transformation and upgrading of the traditional service industry and promote the modern operation of enterprises. Besides, it will boost the change of enterprise production mode, promote the innovation of the production service industry, and bring new sources of economic growth for enterprises.

6.1 E-commerce development mode

6.1.1 Relevant concepts of e-commerce

6.1.1.1 E-commerce

E-commerce is a commercial activity centered on commodity exchange by means of information network technology, and is also a new business transaction mode based on information technology and the internet. "In the opening internet environment and based on the browser and server applications, buyers and sellers carry out all kinds of commercial activities without meeting each other, realizing online shopping of consumers, online transactions among merchants, online electronic payment and various business activities, trading activities, financial activities as well as related comprehensive service activities."[1]

---

[1] China International E-commerce Network: E-commerce Encyclopedia.

As the pioneer of e-commerce, IBM believes that e-commerce is a commercial activity generated in line with the combination of the internet and information technology, and all participants like buyers, sellers, financial institutions and governments should jointly engage in the commercial or social electronic application in the integrated environment of the internet, local Intranet, and extranet, rather than only in trading activities.

According to the Organization for Economic Co-operation and Development (OECD), "E-commerce is the business activity of products or services among enterprises, households, individuals, governments, and other public or private institutions through computer-mediated networks. The transaction is done online, and the payment and final delivery of the product or service can be done both online and offline."[1]

According to the United Nations Statistics Division, "E-commerce refers to business activities that are conducted by business units when receiving orders and selling their goods and services through different means like telephone, fax, television, electronic data interchange, mini-tel, and the internet."[2]

International organizations have defined e-commerce from different perspectives, and its connotation and denotation are different. However, in the current application of e-commerce, the trading medium is mainly the internet, while telephone and TV are applied in a smaller range. According to the definition of e-commerce by the OECD, we can divide it into complete e-commerce and non-complete e-commerce. The whole transaction process of e-commerce can be divided into the business flow, information flow, capital flow, logistics, and other different links. The complete e-commerce means that the whole process of the transaction, such as the transaction agreement, payment and product or service delivery, is completed through the internet, and the business flow, information flow, capital flow and logistics are integrated through the internet. The non-complete e-commerce refers to the mode that the transaction is completed through the internet and the payment, after-sale service, product delivery and other related auxiliary links are carried out offline.

Therefore, e-commerce activities include not only business transactions but also a general scope of consultation, finance, insurance, logistics, and other related activities carried out by all participants around transactions. Buyers and sellers are the initiators and main participants of e-commerce activities, and the government, financial and insurance institutions, logistics enterprises and other participants provide various

---

[1] OECD, Information Technology Outlook 2002, 2002.

[2] Zhou Hongren, *On Information Technology Application*, Beijing: People's Publishing House, 2008, p. 544.

support and assistance for business transactions.

6.1.1.2 Electronic data interchange

An early form of e-commerce can be traced back to electronic data interchange (EDI), a widely applied online transaction among enterprises. In the specific operation, buyers and sellers transfer standard economic information through communication networks in accordance with a unified prescribed common standard format for data exchange and automatic processing between the electronic computer systems of trading partners.

EDI has pioneered paperless transactions and realized convenient trade and data sharing among enterprises based on the internet and information technology. The whole process of EDI is automatically completed through standard formats, which improves the efficiency of enterprise's transactions and reduces costs. EDI is mainly applied to large enterprises, which can integrate raw material purchasing and manufacturing, ordering and inventory, market demand and sales, and other businesses like finance, insurance, transportation and customs in an organic way. By combining advanced technology and scientific management, it greatly improves the working efficiency.

6.1.1.3 Technical means of e-commerce

The development and improvement of e-commerce must be supported by a strong IT infrastructure, i.e., e-commerce technology means. Zhou Hongren (2008) believes that the current infrastructure of e-commerce mainly includes e-mail, internet, LAN, extranet, EDI, electronic funds transfer, and call center.[1] With the development of e-commerce, more and more information technologies have been applied in e-commerce activities, such as big data, cloud computing, AI, the IoT and other new generations of information technology as well as bar code, RFID, GIS and GPS.

6.1.1.4 Mobile e-commerce

Mobile e-commerce is a new e-commerce model, which is the result of development and extension of e-commerce in the mobile field and a necessary supplement to traditional e-commerce. "It perfectly combines the internet, mobile communication technology, short-range communication technology and other information processing technology, enabling people to carry out all kinds of commercial activities at any time or any place and conduct online shopping and trading, online electronic payments, various trading activities, business activities, financial activities and related comprehensive service activities."[2] Mobile e-commerce has expanded the scope of supply chain management

---

[1] Zhou Hongren, *On Information Technology Application*, Beijing: People's Publishing House, 2008, p. 532.

[2] China International E-commerce Network: E-commerce Encyclopedia.

and reduced its cost, with an increasingly wider application.

At present, the mobile e-commerce facilitates the transaction of enterprises, and plays an important role in warehousing, sales terminals, after-sales service and other aspects of enterprises. Mobile terminal equipment enables sellers to obtain product sale information accurately and quickly, which is beneficial to promote precise marketing and improve the quality and efficiency of after-sales service.

6.1.2   Traditional model of e-commerce

With the development of the information revolution, modern information technology, the next generation of information technology and the internet have been integrated and promoted, making e-commerce models increasingly diverse. According to the application of e-commerce in different industries, it can be divided into industrial e-commerce, agricultural e-commerce, service e-commerce and e-government. In terms of different participants in e-commerce activities, it can also be divided into three different models of business-to-business (B2B), business-to-consumer (B2C), and consumer-to-consumer (C2C). B2B refers to business-to-business procurement and wholesale, which is the mainstream of e-commerce, B2C is the online sales of businesses to consumers, and C2C is an exchange and sales platform based on individual auctions. Among them, B2B and B2C have a large transaction volume and a wider application, marking the main part of e-commerce business.

6.1.2.1   Business-to-business (B2B)

B2B e-commerce, also known as eB2B, refers to the business transactions through the internet or private network by networking and electronic means. According to the difference of business relationship between transaction subjects, eB2B can be divided into the vertical B2B between enterprises and supply chain members and the horizontal B2B for intermediate trading markets. In terms of the vertical B2B, enterprises and upstream suppliers or downstream sellers carry out business activities such as raw material and component procurement as well as product marketing through the network. Haier Mall is a typical representative of B2B e-commerce platform between enterprises and supply chain members. As for the horizontal B2B, e-commerce platforms bring together buyers and suppliers and provide trading opportunities and platform for both sides. For example, Alibaba e-commerce platform allows enterprises of different fields and types to conduct transactions on it. The eB2B model is the main part of e-commerce, with the largest trading volume, accounting for more than 90% of the total trading volume of e-commerce.

In the eB2B model, the transaction objects are extensive, with raw materials, components, semi-finished products and final products all traded through the e-commerce platform. The eB2B model overcomes the problems of high search costs and low transaction efficiency of traditional business activities. Buyers and sellers use information technology and internet to improve the efficiency of enterprise communication, reduce the transaction cost between enterprises, and reduce the inventory of enterprises, thus shortening the production cycle of enterprises and improving economic benefits.

The eB2B model has gone through two phases: the information interaction phase and the online transaction phase. In the rise of e-commerce around 2000, B2B was mainly based on interactive information. Enterprises obtained supply and demand information through e-commerce platforms, while the real transaction docking and marketing services were conducted offline, making this stage incomplete e-commerce. Interactive information-based eB2B platforms can be divided into integrated platform and vertical platform according to the different service contents. Alibaba, HC360.COM, and Global Resources are all integrated platforms, which provide integrated information across industries and products and have a wide range of business, while ChemNet, Viku Electronics Network, Global Hardware Network and other platforms are vertical platforms, which mainly offer supply and demand information of a specific industry with strong professional capability. With the breakthrough of modern information technologies like big data, cloud computing, IoT, as well as the internet, eB2B platform has developed to a stage focused on integrated online transactions. E-commerce platform can provide buyers and sellers with comprehensive services such as transaction services, data services, financial services and logistics services, and integrate information flow, order flow, logistics and capital flow through the internet.

6.1.2.2 Business-to-consumer (B2C)

B2C is an e-commerce activity in which enterprises and consumers transact through the internet, and it is an electronic retail mode in which enterprises directly sell products and services to consumers through the information network. According to the different transaction content and business model, B2C e-commerce platform can be divided into integrated platform and vertical platform. The integrated eB2C platform operates a complete range of goods for all types of consumers, while the vertical eB2C platform operates specialized products for only a single type of subdivided groups. Based on the service objects of e-commerce platforms, eB2C platform can be divided into independent operated platform and third-party platform. At present, the mature

B2C platforms mainly include portal websites, electronic retailers, content providers, and trading brokers.

Portal websites mainly provide consumers with integrated comprehensive services and content about search, news, shopping, entertainment, and other services. In terms of consumers, portal websites are divided into horizontal and vertical types. Horizontal portal website faces all internet users with a wide range of audience, while vertical portals mainly target specific groups and provide them with content or services on specific topics.

Electronic retailers refer to online retail stores, providing online retail services for online consumers, and they can be divided into B2C retailers operating offline stores and virtual B2C retailers without offline stores. Some enterprises operate offline stores, with online retail as a marking channel for them to expand the market, while some enterprises operate virtual B2C retail business, with online sales being their only way to operate.

Content providers are media and information providers in the network, offering consumers with information, entertainment services and digital products. Trading brokers are online transaction processors and act as intermediaries between enterprises and consumers, mainly serving consumers with employment opportunities, financial services and travel services as well as providing information dissemination, information transmission and contract conclusion services necessary for the trading parties to conclude online trading contracts.

6.1.3   New eC2B model[1]

With the development of modern information technology, the innovation of the internet and the influence of modern consumption concept, new e-commerce models such as C2B, A2A, P2P, ASP, X2X, ESP, ITM and O2O continue to emerge and get applied and developed.

C2B (customer-to-business) is a new consumer-centered and consumer-driven e-commerce model. With the deepening application of information technology and internet, this new business model has gradually developed and brought about great growth points of interest. Consumers can buy their favorite products through the Meituan App at a group price, young consumer groups with individual, fashionable and simple lifestyles can customize home appliances on the leader platform, and Tmall can realize the pre-sale of products and put them into production after gathering orders. Besides, tourists can find tickets and hotels consistent with their own needs through Ctrip, and

---

[1] Zhu Yan, "Research on the Operational Efficiency of New C2B E-Commerce Model and Its Impact on Social Welfare", *Journal of Commercial Economics*, 2015 (28), pp. 66-67.

individuals can publish their creative designs through Toidea for subscription by merchants. The above are all the typical applications of C2B model in the "internet +" era.

6.1.3.1 Main types of eC2B model

The core of eC2B model is to aggregate a large number of scattered consumer groups with the help of network platform, form a powerful purchasing group, and change the weak position of consumers in the B2C model, thus realizing personalized production and on-demand customization. With the development of emerging e-commerce, C2B has been applied more and more widely, with five common models of aggregated consumer demand model, personalized customization model, consumer bidding model, business subscription and service claim model.

(1) *Aggregated consumer demand model*

The eC2B platform gains huge consumer groups by gathering small markets, and consumers have more initiative in the transaction process, typically represented by group buying and merchandise pre-sale.

(i) Group buying. C2B mainly focuses on group buying, with third-party commerce platforms forming a huge number of purchase orders by aggregating consumers, such as Juhuasuan, Nuomi, Meituan, etc. The platforms gather a large number of consumers with the same demand in groups to enjoy a preferential price, that is, group customized price. With the improvement of living standards, consumers pay more attention to the quality of goods, thus giving rise to group customized products.

(ii) Pre-sale mode. Enterprises release product information through the C2B platform, gather consumer orders through the pre-sale product tool, and provide products to consumers at the appointed time. This mode gathers target orders first, and then enterprises integrate the front-end supply chain and organize procurement, production and fast delivery within a short period of time. In other words, there are orders first and then production. The on-demand production of enterprises makes zero inventory, reduces the occupancy of capital and warehousing costs, enabling consumers to enjoy lower prices. Therefore, consumers are trading "time" for "price".

(2) *Personalized customization mode*

Consumers customize products according to their own personalized demands, and enterprises make customized production. Consumers make personalized demands for styles and functions of products, or participate in product design, so the products reflect their personalized demands. Enterprises change the original standardized production process, adjust production links, and increase production costs, thus requiring consumers to pay a premium for personalized elements.

Haier Group adheres to the brand concept of "You Design, We Make" and takes a function-based concept in product design and manufacturing, creating a customized home appliance brand "Leader". It catches the users' personalized needs through the official website of Leader Electric Appliances and meets users' needs offline in a timely manner. Consumers can customize personalized books, stamps, household articles through www.uudiy.com, and design their rooms in the Homekoo platform.

(3) *Consumer bidding mode*

This mode is also known as the offer mode, in which the positions of enterprises and consumers are exchanged. Consumers release the commodities they demand and prices they offer on the platform, then the e-commerce platform passes the consumer information to the supplier, and the enterprises have a final say whether to accept the offer or not. If the enterprises accept the offer, then the deal will be reached. However, if multiple suppliers bid, the consumer will rebid or make higher demands for the products. Since consumers have different demands and payment capacities, the highest prices they are willing to pay will be distinct. Therefore, by eventually creating differential pricing through the offer mode, enterprises can maximize revenue on differentiated customers respectively. This model is widely used in tourism, hotels, tickets, financial payment and other fields. For instance, as a personal broker, Ctrip can match consumers with hotels, tickets and travel agencies for their needs.

(4) *Merchant subscription and service claim mode*

The e-commerce platform encourages individuals to show their original designs, photographic works, animations, videos and other things on the website, and enterprises will purchase according to the demand and price, which is the merchant subscription mode. This mode provides a great platform for art college students and home office workers (SOHO). In addition, enterprises with creative needs can also release their demand on the platform, and consumers can claim them personally, that is, the service claim mode.

The zbj.com and Toidea are platforms to realize the two-way docking between enterprises and consumers. They trade in various industries, such as creative design, website construction, online marketing, copywriting, and life services. The ideas and skills are traded between clients and creators, creating business value from them.

6.1.3.2   Supply chain analysis of the C2B model

Michael Porter, an American strategic scholar, put forward the value chain model, dividing the value-added activities inside and outside the enterprise into five forces and the value chain and the four corners model. The traditional value chain is a push strategy dominated by enterprises, which are at the source of the value chain. The upstream supply chain conducts raw materials procurement, the enterprises then produce products, the downstream distributes the products, and finally the consumers can acquire the standardized products and services. The traditional mode pursues "large-scale procurement+large-scale production+wide distribution+large-scale logistics+large-scale retail". and the intermediate links between producers and consumers are complicated with low efficiency. Consumers are at the end of the value chain, excluded from the design of products, and unable to enjoy personalized products and services. In the C2B mode, consumers put forward their personalized demands on the e-commerce platform, and service providers connect with users through the e-commerce platform to complete the integration of the upstream supply chain according to consumers' demands, so as to form a reverse supply chain. C2B commodity dominance and first-mover rights are transferred from the seller to the buyer. Driven by consumers, the operation mode of the industrial chain is changed through front-end customization, and the backward transmission is carried out every link in the business chain "starting from consumer demand" (see Figure 6-1).

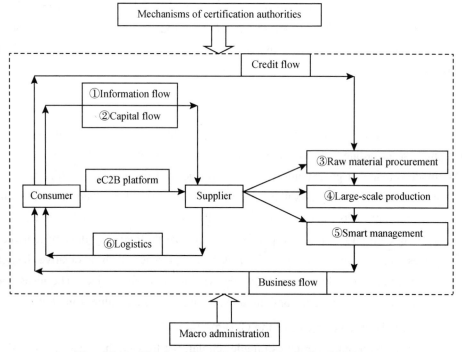

Figure 6-1　The flow of backward supply chain of C2B mode

C2B takes the differentiated demands of consumers as the starting point, and the information flow is the reverse process from consumers to merchants, with the information being more transparent. The enterprise can directly carry out mass production according to consumers' preferences and needs, thus eliminating intermediaries, optimizing the value chain, realizing flat management, reducing inventory costs, and improving the operational efficiency of the whole chain. In the C2B mode, consumers directly drive the supply chain according to their demands, thereby greatly enhancing the precision of enterprise products. At the same time, with the shortening of the supply chain, the efficiencies of production and product flow of enterprises have been greatly improved.

In the era of "internet +" where personalized needs of consumers are gradually emerging, the development of C2B is highly praised by differentiated consumers, who can customize personalized products and bargain collectively to obtain higher consumer surplus. For enterprises, through the eC2B platform, they can gather orders in a short time, make mass production, generate economies of scale, shorten and integrate the supply chain, improve operation efficiency, and realize the optimization of social welfare. Therefore, the development of the new C2B mode is a win-win result for both buyers and sellers. Driven by the interests of both sides and the e-commerce platform, the eC2B mode will gradually be perfect and mature, and become the mainstream mode of e-commerce operation.

6.2   Key measures for the development of e-commerce in China

The concept of e-commerce was first introduced into China in 1993. It was not until 1998 that Alibaba, the first online trading platform, was established in China. Since then, e-commerce has been widely applied. Since the 21st century, China's e-commerce has entered a prime time of development and rapid growth with the support of the national policies. China's e-commerce has constantly developed in the process of exploration and now has become the largest online retail market in the world, making great contributions to the world economic growth and becoming an important force leading the growth of national economy. High-speed railway, Alipay, shared-bikes and online shopping have been called China's four great inventions in the new era. The rapid growth of e-commerce in China benefits from the environment of favorable national policy, the promotion of e-commerce demonstration projects, the implementation of the national strategy of "mass entrepreneurship and innovation", and the coordinated development strategy of targeted poverty alleviation and e-commerce. At present, rural e-commerce, cross-border e-commerce, and mobile e-commerce in China are playing an increasingly important role in economic growth.

6.2.1 Numerous policies issued to strengthen the top-level design of the e-commerce development in China

The development of e-commerce is an important measure to drive industrialization by information technology and take a new road of industrialization. The government has strengthened top-level design and issued a series of policies, regulations and guidelines to vigorously promote the development of e-commerce.

At the beginning of the 21st century, China's e-commerce was in the initial stage of development. In order to create a favorable environment for the development of e-commerce, the CPC Central Committee and the State Council issued policies to strengthen the guarantee from the aspects of system construction, laws and regulations construction. In 2005, the Opinions of the General Office of the State Council on Accelerating the Development of E-commerce, which is one of the earliest documents put forward in China to improve the policy and legal environment for the development of e-commerce. The opinions proposed to give full play to the main role of enterprises, constantly improve the e-commerce technology and services, better the policy and regulatory environment through fiscal and tax policies, laws and regulations, and investment and financing mechanisms, and accelerate the construction of credit, certification, standards, payment and modern logistics, so as to form a supporting system conducive to the development of e-commerce.

The National Informatization Development Strategy (2006-2020) released in 2006 takes the e-commerce as the strategic action plan for informatization development in China, putting forward to build a complete e-commerce value chain led by large key enterprises and actively participated by SMEs through supply chain and customer relationship management, and to explore multi-level and diversified ways of developing e-commerce.

Since the 18th CPC National Congress, e-commerce has entered a period of rapid development. The CPC Central Committee and the State Council issued many policies to provide a sound environment for the healthy and orderly development of e-commerce and promote the development of e-commerce to a higher level.

In 2015, the Guiding Opinions of the General Office of the State Council on Promoting the Sound and Rapid Development of Cross-border E-commerce was released, to promote the healthy, orderly and rapid development of "internet + foreign trade". This guiding opinion proposed to improve the supporting customs control measures, improve inspection and quarantine supervision policies and measures, strength e-commerce payment and settlement management, provide active fiscal and financial support, and build comprehensive service systems, so as to support the development of Chinese enterprises' cross-border e-commerce and upgrading of the open economy.

In 2015, the Guiding Opinions of the General Office of the State Council on Promoting and Accelerating the Development of E-commerce in Rural Areas was released, pointing out that China should promote the full integration of rural e-commerce and rural tertiary industry through introducing policies, cultivating e-commerce talents, improving the rural logistics system, accelerating the construction of rural infrastructure, and increasing financial support measures.

In April 2016, the Opinions of the General Office of the State Council on Deepening Implementation of the "internet + circulation" Action Plan, calling for promoting the development of e-commerce through informatization in the circulation field.

The Ministry of Commerce, the Office of Central Cyberspace Affairs Commission, and the National Development and Reform Commission issued the E-Commerce Development During the 11th Five-Year Plan, E-Commerce Development During the 12th Five-Year Plan, E-Commerce Development During the 13th Five-Year Plan in 2007, 2012 and 2016, respectively, providing a specific development plans and guidance for different periods of the e-commerce development.

6.2.2   Promoting a wider application of e-commerce through demonstration projects

Under the support and guidance of national policies, the central and local governments at all levels have supported a batch of e-commerce pilot enterprises to promote the cross-border e-commerce comprehensive experimental zone, cross-border e-commerce integrated pilot cities, e-commerce demonstration cities, e-commerce demonstration bases, e-commerce demonstration enterprises, rural comprehensive demonstration county and other major projects. China has taken e-commerce demonstration to promote economic transformation and upgrading and foster new driving forces for economic growth, and it has facilitated the transformation and upgrading of traditional service industries, advanced the development of rural e-commerce and cross-border e-commerce, widely applied the e-commerce on the basis of summarizing experience, and promoted its dissemination and application.

In September 2009, National Development and Reform Commission and the Ministry of Commerce officially approved Shenzhen as the first national e-commerce demonstration city, embarking on the path of exploring the development of e-commerce with Chinese characteristics. Beijing, Tianjin, Shanghai, Chongqing and other 23 cities became the first batch of national e-commerce demonstration cities in November 2011; the second batch of national e-commerce demonstration cities were established in 30 cities, including Dongguan, Yiwu and Quanzhou in March 2014; and the third batch of national e-commerce demonstration cities were set in 17 cities, including Dalian, Baotou, Haikou and Xining in January 2017. The demonstration cities have taken the opportunity of developing themselves as national e-commerce demonstration cities to build e-commerce infrastructure and transaction supporting measures, improve the business environment and policy system for e-commerce, and ensure the rapid growth of e-commerce. Moreover, they have taken the establishment of national e-commerce demonstration city as a new way to enhance their public services and competitiveness, so as to promote the transformation and upgrading of traditional service industry through e-commerce.

The first batch of pilot projects to introduce e-commerce into rural demonstration counties were launched in 2014, involving 56 counties in China. The number of demonstration counties increased to 100 in 2015, 240 in 2016, and 260 in 2017, which has driven the development of rural e-commerce throughout the country.

In 2012, the Ministry of Commerce listed 34 business bases, including Beijing Tongzhou Business Park, as the first batch of national e-commerce demonstration bases, and then listed 66 bases, including Zhongguancun Software Park, Haidian District, Beijing, as the second batch of national e-commerce demonstration bases in 2015. National demonstration projects, such as national e-commerce demonstration enterprises and smart logistics distribution demonstration units, have driven and supported the dissemination and application of e-commerce across all industries.

6.2.3 Mass entrepreneurship and innovation: a significant push for the e-commerce development

With the implementation of mass entrepreneurship and innovation strategy in China, e-commerce has become a popular and first choice for its participants, with both mutually reinforcing in coordinated development. The mass entrepreneurship and innovation development strategy has boosted the development of e-commerce, and e-commerce has also driven entrepreneurship and innovation. In 2016, e-commerce has directly and indirectly created 37 million jobs, becoming a business form to promote employment and to stabilize the society.

China has put forward specific policies and measures to promote the development of the "crowd innovation, crowdsourcing, crowd support and crowdfunding" supporting platform from four aspects, including creating a favorable development environment, consolidating the foundation for healthy development, establishing a self-disciplined development mechanism, and building a sustainable development environment. In 2015, the Guiding Opinions of the State Council on Accelerating the Building of Supporting Platforms for Mass Entrepreneurship and Innovation proposed to give full play to the national comprehensive advantages in internet application and innovation, fully stimulate the entrepreneurial and innovative vitality of the broad masses of the people and market entities, and vigorously develop crowd innovation, crowdsourcing, crowd support, and crowdfunding. China provides a favorable environment for e-commerce entrepreneurship and innovation activities through the support of fiscal and financial policies, taxation and system reform, so as to stimulate the enthusiasm for e-commerce entrepreneurship.

Mass entrepreneurship and innovation refers to gather all kinds of innovation resources and integrate various wisdoms to make innovation through the entrepreneurship and innovation service platform. The Chinese government encourages and promotes mass innovation on online platforms: large internet enterprises and industry leaders are encouraged to share resources such as technology, development, marketing and promotion to various types of entrepreneurial and innovative subjects through online platforms, and various e-commerce platforms are encouraged to provide support for SMEs and entrepreneurs. Crowdsourcing uses the "internet +" to divide the tasks traditionally performed by specific enterprises and institutions among all enterprises and individuals who voluntarily participate, so as to mobilize all efforts to increase employment. The Chinese government encourages enterprises and R&D institutions to connect supply and demand through online platforms and communities, so as to form a new model of gathering and sharing the wisdom of the masses. Crowd support is to help SMEs and entrepreneurs grow by means of government and public welfare support, business assistance and individual mutual support, so as to integrate all strength to entrepreneurship. The Chinese government encourages the support of mass entrepreneurship and employment through online platforms. Crowdfunding raises funds from the society through the internet platform to meet the financing needs of product research and development, enterprise growth and individual entrepreneurship, so as to gather social capital to promote development. The Chinese government encourages internet enterprises to set up online lending platforms in accordance with law and regulations to provide investment and financing parties with lending information exchange, matching, credit assessment and other services.[1]

At present, e-commerce entrepreneurship has become a hot issue nationwide, and the coast cities in the east of China including Guangzhou, Jinhua and Shenzhen rank the top three cities with the most active e-commerce entrepreneurship. In order to provide a favorable environment for e-commerce entrepreneurship, China has vigorously constructed a platform for innovation and entrepreneurship, actively promoted the public service platform construction, constructed business cloud platform of public service, carried out tracking all process of circulation of commodities and query service, facilitated the building of public service platform of SMEs network, and built information exchange and interagency collaboration platform, so as to promote the development of e-commerce through mass entrepreneurship and innovation in an all-round way. By the end of 2016, 247 platforms for mass entrepreneurship and innovation were set up by central enterprises, 159 national-level and local technological innovation strategic alliances were established, and the largest industrial products e-commerce platform—"www.epec.com" were built by Sinopec, China. At the same time, governments at all levels vigorously promote the establishment of e-commerce industrial parks, maker spaces, business incubators and other platforms, so as to establish and improve the e-commerce entrepreneurship service system.

6.2.4 New forces in the e-commerce market: rural e-commerce, cross-border e-commerce and mobile e-commerce

China has increased the support for issues related to agriculture, rural areas and rural people through various preferential policies, and rural e-commerce has become a popular part for enterprises to invest, serving as a new market for the development of e-commerce in China. Thanks to the continuous improvement of rural information infrastructure and the continuous expansion of the population of rural netizens, e-commerce of agricultural products and agricultural supplies has developed rapidly, with more and more websites of agricultural products and agricultural supplies and

---

[1] The State Council, Guiding Opinions of the State Council on Accelerating the Building of Supporting Platforms for Mass Entrepreneurship and Innovation, Chinese Central Government's Official Website, http://www.govcn/xinwen/2015-09/26/content_2939239htm.

year-on-year growth of the transaction volume of e-commerce. Rural e-commerce has become a significant force to promote the agricultural informatization and agricultural modernization. At present, the community complex of rural e-commerce integrating wholesale, logistics, finance, tourism, entrepreneurship and other services has been established in rural areas of China, and rural e-commerce has entered the stage of branding. With the support of the internet and modern information technology, an e-commerce ecosystem covering the whole industrial chain of agricultural pre-production, in-production and after-production has been established, and a full integration covering farmers, processing enterprises, logistics enterprises, e-commerce service centers, financial and insurance institutions has been constructed with efficient operation through e-commerce.

Cross-border e-commerce has been included in the Belt and Road Initiative, becoming an important engine to drive the growth of foreign trade and economic cooperation in the new era. With the support of national policies and the establishment of the comprehensive experimental zone for cross-border e-commerce, China has constantly innovated its industry chain of the cross-border e-commerce and deepened the development in terms of policies and regulations, supervision models, administrative services and other aspects.

With the increasing number of mobile netizens, China's mobile e-commerce has become a new market and the main force in the development of e-commerce. According to the E-commerce in China 2016 released by Ministry of Commerce, the number of mobile netizens in China reached 467 million by the end of 2016, accounting for 95% of the country's total internet users, and mobile phone has become the main way for residents to surf the internet. Supported by the huge number of mobile netizens, the users doing mobile online shopping in China reached 441 million in 2016, accounting for 94% of the total online shopping users. Mobile shopping has been becoming the mainstream of online shopping. In 2016, mobile shopping accounted for 70.7% of the total online shopping transactions in China.[1]

6.3   Informatization in logistics to develop the e-commerce

A better logistics system is an important support for the development of e-commerce.

---

[1] Ministry of Commerce, E-commerce in China 2016, Ministry of Commerce, Website of the Ministry of Commerce, Jun. 14, 2017, http://dzsws.mofcom.gov.cn/article/ztxx/ndbg/201706/20170602591881shtml.

The modern logistics supported by information technology is the trend of logistics development. Some Proposals Concerning Quickening the Development of Modern Material Flow of China defines modern logistics as "the modern material flow generally refers to the whole process through which raw materials, products, finished products and the relevant information effectively flow from the starting point to the end point. It forms a complete service chain, combining altogether effectively and efficiently such aspects as transportation, storage, loading and unloading, processing, clearing up, arranged delivery and information, to provide users with multifunctional and integrative services."[1] Therefore, the modern logistics with Chinese characteristics provides comprehensive logistics services by information technology, which has achieved the full integration of supply chain through information technology. The development of logistics has experienced the stages of enterprise self-managed logistics, third party logistics and fourth party logistics. With the rapid growth of e-commerce in China, logistics enterprises have gradually increased their investment to realize the IT application such as the IoT, bar code and electronic data interchange (EDI) in the logistics supply chain. At present, China's logistics has gradually entered the stage of the fourth party logistics, and the modern logistics system supported by information technology has gradually developed and improved, becoming an important support for the rapid growth of e-commerce.

6.3.1 The rise of the fourth party logistics

Modern logistics includes not only basic logistics services such as transportation, warehousing, distribution, loading and unloading, packaging, and logistics information processing, but also value-added services provided according to customers' personalized demands. Modern logistics industry is producer service industry, which provides high added-value service for various production activities of enterprises. The third party logistics, fourth party logistics, and logistics parks are all new forms of business in the development of modern logistics industry. With the transformation of development pattern and the pursuit of efficiency, enterprises have gradually given up the self-managed logistics mode and outsourced the growing logistics business to professional third-party logistics and fourth-party logistics service providers.

Third party logistics (3PL or TPL), also known as contract logistics, refers to

---

[1] State Economic and Trade Commission, etc., Some Proposals Concerning Quickening the Development of Modern Material Flow of China, Chinese Central Government's Official Website, Mar. 1, 2001, http://www.gov.cn/gongbao/content/2002/content-61945htm.

entrusting the logistics business of productive enterprises to professional logistics companies in the form of contract and realize the management and control of the logistics process through the information system. By outsourcing logistics business, enterprises can streamline departments and reduce inventories, so as to concentrate on developing core businesses and improve their competitiveness. With the development of enterprise business, their requirements are becoming increasingly diversified, and enterprise customers want more personalized value-added services such as order processing, inventory management, and supervision of the supply chain. However, TPL enterprises cannot meet the special needs of heterogeneous enterprises due to the lack of relevant technologies and management capabilities for integrating the supply chain. Under this background, the new organization form of the modern supply chain, the fourth party logistics, has gradually emerged with stronger material resources, information resources integration and management. The innovation of information technology and communication technology and the prosperity of e-commerce have also boosted the emergence and development of the fourth party logistics.

The concept of fourth party logistics (4PL or FPL) was first put forward and registered as a trademark by Arthur Andersen Consulting Company (later renamed Accenture) in the United States. The company believes that "they (the FPL) handle an organization's entire supply chain management by acting as an integrator — they curate, evaluate and handle resources, processes and technologies required by an organization to manage their supply chain operations."[1]

With the innovation and wide application of cloud computing, IoT, AI and other new generations of information technologies, the modern logistics industry represented by the FPL has grown rapidly, becoming an important means for enterprises to reduce costs, improve efficiency, and enhance international competitiveness. The FPL is also the third source of profit for enterprise development. The FPL emerged along with the development of information technology. It uses the information technology and information network to establish collaborative information sharing service platform, provides customers with systematic supply chain solutions and value-added services, and integrates and improves the supply chain to reduce the circulation costs, promote transformation and upgrading of structures, and improve overall operating efficiency of enterprises.

As a new pattern of logistics outsourcing, the FPL integrated and upgraded the TPL

---

[1] John Gattorna, *Strategic Supply Chain Alignment: Best Practice in Supply Chain Management,* Aldershot: Gower Publishing Company, 1998.

enterprise, information technology providers, management consultancy, e-commerce service providers, and value-added service providers through the FPL platform. Meanwhile, it provides comprehensive supply chain solutions, realize the sharing of resources and information, so as to reduce the cost of every link of supply chain, shorten logistics cycle time and improve the whole supply chain structure. The FPL provider not only integrates various service capabilities, but also helps customers design the optimal solution of the whole logistics process, and provides high efficiency, low cost and humanized one-stop integrated service for the logistics, business flow, capital flow and information flow on the enterprise supply chain, forming the supply chain cooperation alliance. The FPL platform mainly provides a systematic and integrated services such as logistics route design, storage center design, information system planning, distribution scheme optimization, financial and legal services, supply chain cost management, selection of TPL suppliers and other services. The FPL has changed the traditional transportation process by helping enterprises establish new business models.

6.3.2 The operation mode of the FPL

The FPL is a supply chain integrator with information, technology and management as its core, and develops on the basis of full integration of information and comprehensive technological innovation. The FPL platform has integrated multiple service providers and enterprise customers by establishing an information resource network platform through modern information technologies such as computers and the internet. With the increasing number of various service providers on the platform, complex information has formed a huge database. Cloud computing can select the best logistics service provider for enterprise customers through processing and analyzing the database. Cloud computing technology has improved the information processing capacity of the FPL network platform. In the implementation process of specific logistics business, the IoT technology strengthens the management and supervision of the logistics implementation process by the FPL provider, providing a support for the standardization and safe operation of logistics.

Computer and information networks are the basic information facilities to realize resource sharing, while the application of new generations of information technologies, such as cloud computing and the IoT, has greatly improved the transmission speed and logistics efficiency of information resources and pushed the development of modern logistics industry forward informatization, automation, intellectualization, and integration.

The FPL platform can integrate and share the resources of all links of the supply chain.

Based on cloud computing and IoT, the FPL provides enterprise customers with integrated supply chain solutions through information sharing platform, and the specific operation modes mainly include collaborative operation mode, solution integrator mode, industry innovator mode and dynamic alliance mode.[1] The former three modes are respectively applied to the primary, intermediate and mature stages of the development of the FPL, while the latter one is a temporary form of business alliance as a market complement.

6.3.2.1 Collaborative operation mode

Collaborative operation mode is also known as the strong alliance mode. This mode combined the TPL with strong logistics distribution capacity and the FPL with the best supply chain solutions. It provides the best comprehensive services through signing commercial contracts or forming strategic alliances, integrates superior resources, and jointly develops the logistics market. In this mode, the FPL does not emerge in an independent form, but works in the internal of the TPL enterprises, providing supply chain solution services including supply chain strategy, business process design, project management, technical support and other services. The FPL does not contact customers directly, but provides customers with logistics supply chain solutions through the TPL service providers. Through the strategic alliance, the logistics distribution capabilities of the TPL and the supply chain solutions of the FPL have achieved tight junction, with the former providing various information and consulting services and the latter taking specific logistics business. The two parties give play to their respective expertise, so as to improve the overall logistics efficiency. In this mode, the TPL has a more obvious dominant position and serves the hub of the whole supply chain, while the FPL provides more support services.

6.3.2.2 Solution integrator mode

In this mode, the FPL is a comprehensive solution integrator that integrates the resources and technologies of the TPL and other service providers, providing a comprehensive and integrated supply chain solution for a major customer. The FPL, as the hub and core of the supply chain, integrates the resources and capabilities of multiple service providers related to the logistics supply chain according to the personalized needs of customers, so as to provide customers with optimal logistics services. The FPL targets a major customer, and provides personalized supply chain solutions through the

---

[1] Compilation Committee of Knowledge Training Series on the Deep Integration of Informatization and Industrialization, *Reader for Knowledge on Innovation and Development of Producer Service Industry*, Beijing: Publishing House of Electronics Industry, 2012, p. 131.

integration of resources, technologies and capabilities.

6.3.2.3 Industry innovator mode

The major difference between the industry innovator mode and the solution integrator mode is that the former provides service and supply chain solutions for multiple customers in multiple industries instead of serving one major customer. The FPL integrates the TPL suppliers, information technology service providers, consulting and management service providers and value-added service providers in various industries through the logistics information platform and designing logistics solutions for customers in multiple industries. In this strategic alliance, it is the leader and organizer that makes a targeted docking through gathering the demanders of logistics business and all kinds of suppliers from the network information platform. The FPL is the hub of all kinds of service providers and multi-industry customer groups. As a result, it must have strong multi-industry information integration competence and cross-industry management experience to provide services for multiple industries and enterprises.

6.3.2.4 Dynamic alliance mode

Dynamic alliance model is a manifestation of virtualized organization, which means that some relatively independent service providers, such as the TPL, consulting organizations, production enterprises and technology providers, form temporary business alliances to provide logistics services through information and management technology when there is market demand. Each member of the alliance takes the completion of a certain business process as the main line, sharing benefits and risks, and the alliance will be dissolved when the project is completed. This kind of logistics mode appears as a market complement, and is a market-oriented dynamic alliance, playing a significant role in capturing the demand information. Therefore, there must be a strong information technology platform and information network between dynamic alliances to make sure that the rapid and smooth transmission of information.

6.3.3 The dynamic supply chain of the FPL

The FPL has reintegrated the logistics supply chain through different operation modes, and thus formed the dynamic supply chain centered on personalized needs of enterprise customers, led by the information platform of the FPL, and integrating logistics, information flow, capital flow, and business flow.

The supply chain is a functional network connecting producers and consumers, and it realizes the management of the whole process from raw material procurement to finished product sales by controlling the logistics, information flow, capital flow, and business flow. High-quality supply chain is centered on the final demand of consumers, and coordinates and integrates all participants in the supply chain to achieve seamless connection of each activity.

The FPL carries out logistics activities based on the enterprise customers' demand, and the final supply chain solution is to meet the enterprise's personalized needs for logistics services. Therefore, the FPL provides a personalized supply chain centered on enterprise customers. Based on an information-based network platform, the FPL integrates information resources and shares them with information technologies such as computers, internet, big data and cloud computing, and the demander and supplier of logistics realize docking and matching through the network platform. Therefore, the FPL provides an information-based supply chain. The informatization on supply chain has also improved the velocity and safety of capital flow such as capital settlement and financial insurance. Through the IoT and other technologies, it has realized the supervision of the logistics execution process, so as to monitor and share the business capability and reputation of each logistics service provider to the FPL information platform. Therefore, the information on the platform is dynamically updated. According to the changed information, the FPL provider will reselect the supplier for the demand side and redesign the supply chain solution by using big data and cloud computing. Therefore, the FPL provides a dynamic supply chain. Dynamic information-based supply chain integrates the information flow, logistics, capital flow and business flow, among which information flow is a fundamental element, and the completion of capital flow, logistics and business flow is based on information sharing (see Figure 6-2).

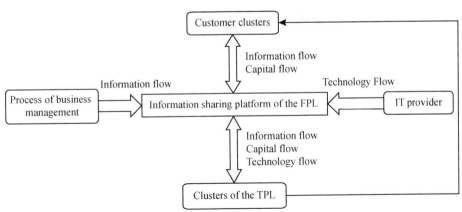

Figure 6–2　Integrated supply chain solutions for the FPL

6.3.4 Rapid development of China's FPL

The FPL is a new trend of the development of modern logistics industry and the result of informatization in logistics. With its advantages gradually emerging, the FPL is becoming an important strategic pillar industry in the development of national economy, as well as the new driving force and profit source of economic growth. To vigorously support the development of this new business form, the Chinese government has issued documents such as Opinions on Promoting the Development of Modern Logistics Industry in China, Adjustment and Revitalization Plan for the Logistics Industry, Logistics Informatization Development Plan, Opinions of the General Office of the State Council on the Policies and Measures for Promoting the Sound Development of the Logistics Industry, and Medium- and Long-Term General Plan for the Development of the Logistics Industry (2014-2020) and other documents, proposing to accelerate the construction of logistics informatization, boost the development of new modern logistics industry by perfecting the standardized logistics system, developing logistics technology and building the public information platform of logistics, promoting the industrial restructure, and improving the competitiveness of national economy.

6.3.4.1 The strengthened R&D capabilities of logistics technology

China has proposed to vigorously develop logistics informatization with the support of emerging information technologies such as the IoT, RFID, GIS and GPS. China has continued to strengthen the independent R&D of logistics technologies, increase the investment, focus on the key technologies such as cargo tracking and positioning, RFID, logistics information platform, intelligent transportation, logistics management software, and mobile logistics information service, so as to promote the innovation and application of logistics technologies. On November 5, 2017, China's BeiDou-3 Navigation Satellite System has made a successful launch from Xichang Satellite Launch Center, showing that the BeiDou Navigation Satellite System has entered a new era of global networking. The BeiDou Navigation Satellite System can provide highly precise and reliable positioning services for all kinds of users around the world, and offer important technical support for logistics informatization.

6.3.4.2 A modern logistics system has taken shape

Modern logistics industry is an important medium that connects the upstream and downstream supply chains of enterprises and the domestic and international markets. The Chinese government has issued a number of policies to strengthen the application of advanced information technologies in logistics such as BeiDou Navigation Satellite

System, IoT, cloud computing, big data and mobile internet, so as to promote the development of public information platforms for logistics and the improvement of the modern logistics industrial system. As early as 2004, the National Development and Reform Commission and other nine ministries and commissions jointly issued the Opinions on Promoting the Development of Modern Logistics Industry in China, putting forward to establish a multi-level logistics information platform and logistics service network system among the national, regional, urban, enterprise to improve the comprehensive service capability. In the development of logistics information technology in China, the construction of logistics information supervision and the standard information system of logistics were regarded as the key content. The Guiding Opinions of Ministy of Industry and Information Technology on Promoting Logistics Informatization issued in 2013 proposed that China should enhance the informatization level in logistics service and supervision of government departments, establish a cross-sector supervision platform, and strengthen the collaborative service and supervision. At the same time, the state has taken the standards system of informatization, laws and regulations system and safety system as the main task, so as to establish a sound logistics information service and supervision system.

6.3.4.3 The reform of the logistics system

The establishment of China's modern logistics is an important guarantee for enterprises to reduce operating costs, which can not only reduce the inventory and transportation costs of enterprises, but also eliminate the institutional costs. Traditional logistic supply chain has complex links and involves a large number of logistics related departments and government management agencies, so that the logistics efficiency was affected by industry's high institutional costs. Especially for SMEs, high logistics costs are a key limitation for the development of enterprises. The Opinions of the General Office of the State Council on Promoting the Sound Development of Distribution in Domestic Trade issued in 2014, put forward that the state should strengthen the reform of administrative examination and approval system, enhance administrative supervision, vigorously reduce the institutional costs of logistics, and improve the environment of logistics industry. The reform of the national administrative system and the improvement of the policy system have provided new impetus for logistics informatization for many SMEs relying on the new generation of information technology.

At present, equipped with the IoT, big data system, industrial robots, AI, unmanned vehicles, and unmanned aerial vehicles (UAV), the super intelligent hub warehouse has realized automatic sorting and packing, and the construction of China's intelligent logistics system represented by the FPL has taken the lead in the world. With the development of economic globalization and the promotion of the Belt and Road Initiative, the demand for the FPL and other intelligent logistics will be increasingly raised. Thanks to the support of national policies and the drive of market demand, the FPL has grown rapidly in China, constantly driving the development of e-commerce, the transformation and upgrading of enterprises, and the construction of informatization. The logistics informatization has promoted the development of supply chain to integration, realized the optimal allocation of resources, reduced all kinds of costs in the circulation link, facilitated the structural adjustment and transformation and upgrading of enterprises, and further advanced the process of the new type of industrialization of China. However, the problems such as the shortage of high-quality logistics technicians, logistics managers and the national imperfect logistics standardization system are still hindering the development of modern logistics. Therefore, the construction of logistics informatization in China has a long way to go. The Chinese government needs to break new ground in policies, strengthen system reform, and enhance research and development investment and talent cultivation, so as to create a sound environment for logistics informatization.

6.4   E-commerce and China's poverty alleviation

On the guidance of "internet +" action strategy and the decision on winning the battle against poverty, the CPC Central Committee, the State Council and local departments at all levels have actively carried out the approach of "internet + poverty alleviation", deeply integrated the internet and the poverty alleviation work, continuously innovated new form for poverty reduction, and transformed the e-commerce into an important platform for targeted poverty alleviation. Poverty alleviation through the promotion of e-commerce has become a new mode of poverty alleviation under the "internet +" era. The impoverished rural areas have seized the development opportunity of "Mass Entrepreneurship and Innovation", combined local advantageous resources with e-commerce, and promoted the transformation of offline real economy through online business, thus facilitating the transformation and upgrading of agriculture and increasing farmers' income. E-commerce has provided a new development philosophy for rural poverty alleviation work.

6.4.1 Multiple measures to promote e-commerce in poverty alleviation

The CPC Central Committee and the State Council have issued a number of policies to facilitate e-commerce to support poverty alleviation work. China has successively issued policies and documents, such as the Outline for Development-Oriented Poverty Reduction for China's Rural Areas (2011-2020), the Opinions on Innovating New Mechanisms to Firmly Promote the Work of Poverty Aid Development in Rural Areas, the Decision of the CPC Central Committee and the State Council on Winning the Tough Battle against Poverty, the Guiding Opinions on Strengthening Poverty Alleviation Efforts to Support the Development and Construction of Old Revolutionary Base Areas, the Guiding Opinions of the General Office of the State Council on Promoting and Accelerating the Development of E-commerce in Rural Areas, and the Guidance on the Promotion of Targeted Poverty Alleviation through E-Commerce, requiring to accelerate the construction of information infrastructure in rural areas, implement the project of providing cable TV, telephone and internet access to every village, speed up the coverage of broadband network in poor villages, and promote the implementation of targeted poverty alleviation by e-commerce.

Poverty alleviation through e-commerce is one of the ten national targeted poverty alleviation projects, which was included into the national mainstream poverty alleviation policy system in the National Poverty Alleviation Work Conference in 2014. The Decision of the CPC Central Committee and the State Council on Winning the Tough Battle against Poverty issued in 2015 proposed to vigorously alleviate poverty through the "internet +" and carry out poverty alleviation through e-commerce. The Guidance on the Promotion of Targeted Poverty Alleviation through E-Commerce issued by the Poverty Alleviation Office of the State Council in 2016 put forward to promote targeted poverty alleviation through e-commerce. Through a full range of measures, China has standardized the poverty alleviation behavior of e-commerce, strengthened e-commerce legislation and supervision by improving the service support system. Meanwhile, China actively develops and improves the information education system of farmers and strengthens the cultivation of poverty alleviation talents of e-commerce, so as to effectively play the leading role of e-commerce.

The National Poverty Alleviation Information Network System established by the State Council Leading Group Office of Poverty Alleviation facilitates the implementation of the "internet +" poverty alleviation program. The State Council Leading Group Office of Poverty Alleviation, together with Suning Appliances Group and other enterprises, has explored a poverty alleviation model of "farmers working with companies and bases to promote e-commerce" and jointly promoted the "Double Hundred Demonstration Project of E-commerce Poverty Alleviation". China has advanced industrial poverty alleviation through e-commerce, employed e-commerce services into the whole process of industrial production and operation, and promoted the transformation of traditional industries in impoverished rural areas. It has continuously provided technical support and fiscal tax incentives for the development of e-commerce in impoverished areas, strengthened skill training and policy guidance for farmers through 12316 platform, and enhanced the supporting capability of comprehensive information service for poverty alleviation work. The implementation of the project of e-commerce into rural comprehensive demonstration county has effectively promoted the development of county economy.

6.4.2　Making full use of the spillover effects of rural e-commerce to facilitate poverty alleviation

E-commerce has brought great vitality to rural poverty alleviation and development work, playing a significant role in poverty alleviation in rural areas. Online sales of agricultural products have become the breakthrough point for e-commerce poverty alleviation. The Chinese government helps impoverished areas to establish e-commerce platforms through policy support, education and training, and provision of services, so as to promote the online sales of agricultural products with impoverished areas' conditions and expand the market. E-commerce in poverty alleviation provides opportunities for the poor households, making them improve their ability of independent management and get rid of poverty. The development of e-commerce promotes the scale and branding of agricultural production, helps farmers adjust the industrial structure, gives play to the leading role of new agricultural operating entities such as large family farming businesses in impoverished areas, establishes an e-commerce agricultural industry chain, and drives all poor households to get rid of poverty. The development of rural e-commerce has not only created more methods for farmers to increase their income and provided more jobs for farmers, but also improved the capability of poor farmers to become rich.

With the support of national policies, the internet is deeply integrated with poverty alleviation and development, and the poverty alleviation model of e-commerce keeps innovating, showing a trend of diversified development. The "nongcuntaobao", "Longnan Model", "Shaji Model", "M-Online" (Mother E-commerce) and other typical poverty alleviation e-commerce models play a leading and exemplary role in rural e-commerce. With the coverage and penetration of the internet to rural areas, rural e-commerce has rapidly emerged, and "nongcuntaobao" has become a typical model for impoverished rural areas to get rid of poverty. Longnan City of Gansu Province has developed e-commerce agricultural products to support poverty alleviation and development, and has tentatively explored the "Longnan Model" to achieve poverty alleviation and prosperity through rural e-commerce. In 2015, Longnan, as the only pilot city of e-commerce for poverty alleviation in China, carried out poverty reduction by e-commerce supported by the government. According to local environments and conditions, the government has transferred the local agricultural products to the outside world through e-commerce. Longnan has created the mechanism of "one shop driving one village and multiple households" in the process of development, using the e-commerce's spillover effects of agricultural products to drive the development of poor households and help poor farmers to entrepreneurial and find jobs at home. "Longnan Model" has become an example of e-commerce increasing farmers' income and promoting rural economic development. Shaji Town of Suining County, Jiangsu Province has explored a "Shaji Model" of "famers plus network plus enterprise" to promote the development of rural e-commerce to alleviate poverty.[1] Farmers connect with the market directly by internet, and achieve the online sales of products through the public e-commerce trading network. Oriented to the market, farmers promote the processing and manufacturing of products through online sales, and improve the development and expansion of enterprises of their own independently, thus establishing a market-oriented sound industrial chain. Through the internet and e-commerce, "Shaji Model" has promoted the processing and manufacturing of agricultural products, optimized the e-commerce poverty alleviation mechanism, and realized the increase of income of farmers. Tongren City of Guizhou Province has explored a poverty alleviation and development model of "M-Online",[2] which promotes the e-commerce of agricultural products and provides jobs for women through internet thinking.

With the penetration of the internet in rural areas and the increasing demand of consumers, the rural e-commerce is matching forward to the direction of integration. Rural e-commerce industrial parkshave been emerging, becoming a new model of poverty alleviation by e-commerce. As the carrier and core, the rural e-commerce

---

[1] Wang Xiangdong, Zhang Caiming, "New Ideas on Rural Poverty Alleviation of China in the Internet Era: Inspiration of Shaji Model", *Informatization Construction*, 2011(2).

[2] Zhou Yulin, "Tongren, Guizhou: 'Mother E-Commerce' Will Create a New Model of Entrepreneurship for Poverty Alleviation", *China Women's News*, Dec. 18, 2015.

network platform has gathered the scattered individual online agricultural products retailers on a platform, and integrated the R&D and design, management, logistics, finance and other services to build an integrated and complete industrial chain, thus achieving scale operation. The comprehensive and integrated e-commerce industrial parks have realized the rapid and accurate connection between farmers and the market, thus effectively providing information infrastructure of the "last mile" service related to agriculture, rural areas and rural people.

6.5　Achievements in China's e-commerce development

Since the beginning of the 21st century, global e-commerce has maintained a strong momentum of development. Under the protection of a sound policy environment, e-commerce in China has grown rapidly and become an important growth area under the new normal of economy. The scale of e-commerce transactions has grown by leaps and bounds, and the industrial chains of rural e-commerce and cross-border e-commerce have been constantly improved. With the deepening application of information technology and internet, enterprises have integrated internal business processes and external transactions by applying e-commerce platform, established a complete e-commerce supply chain from suppliers to enterprises and then to consumers, and thus realized e-commerce in the whole process.

6.5.1　E-commerce: a new area of China's economic growth

Global e-commerce has entered a period of rapid growth. According to the data reported by the United Nations Conference on Trade and Development, the scale of global e-commerce reached US$25 trillion in 2015, and the global online retail transaction volume was US$1.915 trillion in 2016. From the regional distribution, the Asia-Pacific region is the region with the highest online retail sales, with an average annual growth rate of more than 20%, faster than the global average. According to the E-commerce in China 2016 released by the Ministry of Commerce, China's online retail transaction volume accounted for 39.2% of the global e-commerce retail market in 2016. China has been the largest online retail market in the world for many years and has become an important part of growth in promoting world economic recover.[1] The data of E-commerce Development in China (2016-2017) released by China Electronic

---

[1] Ministry of Commerce, E-commerce in China 2016, Ministry of Commerce, Website of the Ministry of Commerce, Jun. 14, 2017, http://dzsws.mofcom.gov.cn/article/ztxx/ndbg/201706/20170602591881shtml.

Commerce Association shows that in 2016, the total e-commerce transaction volume of China reached RMB26.1 trillion, among which the online retail sales reached RMB5,155.6 billion, with a year-on-year growth of 26.2%.

Driven by the internet and the new generation of information technology, China's e-commerce has developed rapidly, and the information technology and traditional economy have continuously integrated, providing a new force for the upgrading of China's economic industrial structure and sustainable economic development and becoming a new engine for economic growth. The CPC Central Committee and the State Council have fully recognized the strategic meaning of e-commerce development and then constantly strengthened the top-level design of e-commerce development to provide strategic guidance for the diversified development of e-commerce in China. In recent years, the development of e-commerce in China has been characterized by diversification, service and globalization, and new models and new business models have emerged. With continuous growth in transaction scale, the growing number of online shoppers, and the increasing proportion of mobile shopping year by year, the rapid development of rural e-commerce and cross-border e-commerce has become a new source of growth for economic development under the new normal.

6.5.2　The steady expansion of the scale of online retail transactions

With the dissemination and application of the internet and the rapidly growing number of netizens, China's online retail market share is gradually increasing, and the development potential is constantly released. From the scale of online shopping, e-commerce transaction volume and other indicators, China has become the world's largest e-commerce market. According to statistics from the China Internet Network Information Center, at the end of December 2015, China's online shopping consumers reached 413 million, with a growth rate of 14.3%, higher than that of 6.1% of netizens. At the end of December 2016, there were 731 million netizens in China, 467 million online shopping consumers, and 441 million mobile internet shopping consumers.

Data from the National Bureau of Statistics of China shows that with the support of a large number of netizens and online shopping consumers, the e-commerce transaction volume, which was only RMB930 billion in 2004, grew rapidly to RMB26.1 trillion in 2016, and it has maintained rapid growth for more than a decade, with a year-on-year growth rate of 57.62% in 2014. In 2016, the total amount of online retail transactions reached RMB5.16 trillion, while in 2011, the figure was only RMB780 billion, achieving a rapid growth in the years from 2011 to 2016 (see Table 6-1). In 2016, the transaction volume of B2C and C2C in online retail was RMB2.82 trillion and RMB2.34 trillion respectively. According to iResearch's 2016 Annual Data Release Collection Report, the scale of mobile online shopping in China continues to grow and has become the main way of online shopping. In 2016, the scale of mobile online shopping accounted for 70.7% of the overall online shopping.[1]

Table 6-1   Total transaction volumes and growth rate of e-commerce transactions in China from 2004 to 2016

Year	Total transaction volumes of e-commerce (RMB trillion)	Growth rate (%)	Total transaction volumes of network retail transmission (RMB trillion)	Growth rate (%)
2004	0.93	—	—	—
2005	1.30	39.80	—	—
2006	1.55	19.26	—	—
2007	2.17	40.11	—	—
2008	3.14	44.76	—	—
2009	3.67	16.87	—	—
2010	4.55	23.88	—	—
2011	6.09	33.80	0.78	53.70
2012	8.11	33.20	1.31	67.25
2013	10.40	28.23	1.86	42.20
2014	16.39	57.62	2.91	56.10
2015	21.79	32.95	4.09	40.40
2016	26.10	19.78	5.16	26.20

Source: National Bureau of Statistics and Ministry of Commerce, E-commerce in China.

The online retail market is also developing centrally with the increasing scale of online retail in China. The comprehensive B2C online retail market of Tmall, JD.COM and Suning.com rank the top three in China, with the transaction volume accounting for more than half of the total market share. The market share of vertical B2C oriented to a single market segment is also gradually increasing, but the overall share is lower than that of comprehensive e-commerce platforms. With the expansion of the scale of B2C online retail market, the trade coverage through the e-commerce platform is getting

---

[1] iResearch, 2016 Annual Data Release Collection Report, iResearch Website, Jan. 19, 2017, http://www.iresearch.com.cn/report/2889.html.

wider and wider, and the product categories are getting more various. Increasingly offline entities have established e-commerce platforms, realizing the integrated online and offline development. One of the important reasons for the expansion of China's online retail market is that many vertical B2C e-commerce platforms are developing towards a comprehensive platform, thus expanding the scale of consumers. China's B2C e-commerce is matching forward to a path of comprehensive, diversified and service-oriented since the increase of consumption demand.

6.5.3   A prime period for B2B e-commerce

At present, B2B e-commerce is still the main force and backbone of China's e-commerce, occupying the largest market transaction volume. In the period of China's supply-side structural reform, innovation-driven e-commerce has developed rapidly. The dissemination and application of the internet and modern information technology are growing rapidly. The new generation of information technologies, such as big data and the IoT, are continuously developing and driving the improvement of e-commerce platforms. B2B e-commerce represented by iron and steel, petroleum, coal, chemical industry, building materials, agriculture, logistics and other fields has entered a golden period of development. B2B e-commerce platform business has developed profoundly, starting from online transactions, gradually expanding its scale to logistics distribution, supply chain management, supply chain finance and other services. B2B e-commerce platform gives full play to the function of efficient internet connection and helps the efficient docking between upstream and downstream enterprises in the supply chain. The platform integrates raw material suppliers and purchasers through the network, thus shortening trading links, improving trading efficiency and reducing search costs.

The Annual Analysis Briefing of B2B E-commerce Market in China[1] released by China E-commerce Association shows that in 2016, the transaction scale of China's B2B e-commerce market reached RMB15.26 trillion, with a year-on-year growth of 25.6%. In recent years, the revenue scale of China's B2B market has grown rapidly, rising from RMB19.84 billion in 2012 to RMB172.09 billion in 2016. The revenues were RMB19.84 billion, RMB22.38 billion and RMB26.75 billion respectively in 2012, 2013 and 2014. With the dissemination and application of the new generation of information technology, the business scope of B2B e-commerce expands and greatly grows. In 2015, the revenue scale jumped to RMB138.57 billion, and grew to RMB172.09

---

[1] China Electronic Commerce Association, Annual Analysis Briefing of B2B E-commerce Market in China, Website of China Electronic Commerce Association, http://www.ec.org.cn/? info – 1047.html.

billion in 2016. Taking Alibaba, the leading e-commerce enterprise in China, as an example, its business has gradually become comprehensive, developing from the initial information release platform, marketing platform and procurement trading platform to the current global trade ecosystem, and the business scope has expanded to core e-commerce, cloud services, digital media, entertainment and other equity investments. The number of Alibaba's active buyers increased to 0.443 billion in 2016, and the number of its online trading customers reached to 20,705, with more than 100,000 brands trading through its platforms. The expansion of the scale has promoted the continuous growth of enterprise's net profits. In 2016, Alibaba's net profit of B2B e-commerce reached to RMB36.688 billion.

6.5.4　Rapid growth of rural e-commerce in China

Through various sound policies, China has continuously strengthened the information infrastructure in rural areas, carried out the project to extend the internet access to every village and direct broadcast satellite communication project to every household, accelerated the full coverage of broadband network in rural areas, made great efforts to narrow the digital divide, and promoted the continuous development of information technology in rural areas. The "Broadband China" 2015 special action launched by the Ministry of Industry and Information strategy clearly requires that the upgrading in urban areas and universal services in rural areas be promoted simultaneously, so as to achieve coordinated development of urban and rural network infrastructure. With the wide application of information technologies such as the integration of three networks, the IoT, big data and cloud computing, China's e-commerce environment in agriculture has been improved gradually. The improvement of rural information infrastructure has provided support and foundation for the development of rural e-commerce, and the construction of agricultural e-commerce platform has been further strengthened. The Ministry of Agriculture has continuously strengthened the construction of the agricultural product quality traceability system and actively promoted the establishment of an e-commerce platform for the quality traceability on land reclamation and agricultural product. Guangdong, Shanghai, Heilongjiang and other reclamation areas have established independent e-commerce platform with the promotion of the Ministry of Agriculture. The Ministry of Commerce promotes the establishment of a national public service platform for agricultural product business information, and cooperates with the Ministry of Finance to jointly promote the comprehensive demonstration of rural e-commerce, thus boosting the development of e-commerce at the county level.

Demonstration of rural e-commerce in 56 counties in eight provinces, including Hebei, Henan and Hubei, and in 200 counties in the central and western regions has achieved remarkable results. The improvement of rural information infrastructure and the development of agricultural e-commerce platforms provide a sound environment for the rapid growth of rural e-commerce in China.

Today, China's rural e-commerce market system and network system have been gradually improved, including agricultural-related online futures trading, bulk commodities electronic trading, B2B e-commerce trading platform, and B2C e-commerce trading platform. According to statistics from the Ministry of Commerce, the scale of rural online shopping market reached RMB353 billion in 2015, with a year-on-year increase of 96%. E-commerce in China 2016[1] released by the Ministry of Commerce shows that the transaction volume of China's rural online retail market in 2016 reached RMB894.54 billion, accounting for 17.4% of the national online retail sales. From the regional perspective, the eastern region has a relatively high level of rural e-commerce development, with online retail sales reaching RMB566.08 billion, accounting for 63.3% of the country's total volumes, while the central and western regions have a relatively low level of e-commerce development. Rural e-tailing is dominated by physical commodities and agricultural products, with a share of 64.8%, while the share of service-oriented e-tailing is only 35.2%. In recent years, the number of online traders of agricultural products has grown rapidly, and the transaction volume of e-commerce in agricultural products has grown rapidly. In 2014, the e-commerce trading volume of agricultural products exceeded RMB80 billion, and the e-commerce trading volume of fresh products reached RMB26 billion. In 2015, there were 402 agricultural commodity trading markets in China, and the e-commerce trading volume related to agriculture exceeded RMB20 trillion, among which the online trading volume of fresh agricultural products reached RMB54.4 billion. Online retail sales of agricultural products reached RMB158.87 billion in 2016.

The development of e-commerce in agricultural supplies is relatively backward, but it boasts huge potential. The e-commerce development modes of agricultural supplies enterprises mainly include the third-party e-commerce platform mode and the self-supporting mode of agricultural enterprises. In 2016, China international e-commerce center issued the China Rural E-commerce Development Report (2015-2016), pointing out that with the implementation of the strategy of "internet +", enterprises such as Alibaba,

---

[1] Ministry of Commerce, E-commerce in China 2016, Website of the Ministry of Commerce, Jun. 14, 2017, http://dzsws.mofcom.gov.cn/article/ztxx/ndbg/201706/20170602591881shtml.

Jingdong, Noposion, Kingenta, and ync365 vigorously developed the e-commerce of agricultural supplies, and that national agricultural e-commerce transactions volumes reached more than RMB15 billion in 2015, a fivefold increase from 2014.[1] The Nongyi Net is an e-commerce platform to provide professional service for agricultural retailers and growers. It has created a unique operation mode of "platform working with county workstation and purchasing agent", organized enterprises to transform the traditional sales methods through informatization methods, and promoted the e-commerce of agricultural supplies trading. At the same time, the website continues to expand the scope of business operation, and it has now developed into an integrated e-commerce platform combined a set of warehousing, technical services, product promotion, and distribution together.

6.5.5 The improvement of cross-border e-commerce industry chain

Under the support and guidance of national policies, cross-border e-commerce has developed rapidly, and the comprehensive experimental zone of cross-border e-commerce has achieved remarkable results. On March 7, 2015, the Chinese government set up the China (Hangzhou) Cross-border E-commerce Comprehensive Pilot Area, which took the lead in technical standards, business processes, regulatory models, and informatization in cross-border e-commerce of payment, logistics, customs clearance, tax refund, and foreign exchange settlement. China (Hangzhou) Cross-border E-commerce Comprehensive Pilot Area has built six systems including the system of information sharing, financial service, intelligent logistics, electric business credit, statistical monitoring, and risk prevention and control, as well as two platforms like online single-window platform and offline comprehensive park platform, through the innovation of system, management, service, and collaboration, so as to build a complete cross-border e-commerce industrial chain and ecological chain and facilitate the convenient and standard development of cross-border e-commerce. Based on some basic experience of Hangzhou cross-border e-commerce, the State Council issued the Official Approval of the Establishment of Comprehensive Cross-border E-commerce Pilot Area in 12 Cities Including Tianjin, stipulating to establish 12 cities of comprehensive pilot areas in Ningbo, Tianjin, Shanghai, Chongqing, Hefei, Zhengzhou, Guangzhou, Chengdu, Dalian, Qingdao, Shenzhen, and Suzhou. By promoting the relevant experience of policy system and

---

[1] China International Electronic Commerce Center, China Rural E-commerce Development Report (2015-2016), Website of China International Electronic Commerce Center, Oct. 26, 2016, http://www.ec.com.cn/article/nsfzdh/nsfzxwzx/201610/12477_1.html.

management system that initially explored in Hangzhou to a larger scope, China would boost the development of China's cross-border e-commerce, and advance the diversification of China's international trade forms.

Thanks to the preferential policies and the experience of many cross-border e-commerce comprehensive pilot areas established before, China has maintained a sound momentum of development in both cross-border e-commerce market scale and growth, with the trading partners of cross-border e-commerce covering 220 countries and regions around the world. The number of online shopping consumers of cross-border e-commerce in China is gradually expanding, and the regional distribution is also gradually shifting from first-tier cities to second-tier and third-tier cities. E-commerce in China 2016[1] shows that in 2016, cross-border e-commerce transaction volume in China was about RMB5.85 trillion, with a year-on-year growth of 28.2%. The B2B export of China's cross-border e-commerce grew rapidly in Europe and the United States. In North America and Canada, the growth rate of the IT-based Chinese cross-border e-commerce transaction volume was more than 50%, and the annual growth rate of cross-border e-commerce transaction volume towards Spain, Germany, France, the Netherlands and other countries reached more than 30%. The support system of China's cross-border e-commerce service has been promoted in all aspects, and the industrial chain of cross-border e-commerce, including information exchange platforms, online trading platforms, and cross-border e-commerce service platforms has also been improved. With the advancement of the Belt and Road Initiative (BRI), the international trade scale between China and the other BRI countries has increased significantly. The demand for economic cooperation has provided development opportunities for cross-border e-commerce.

---

[1] Ministry of Commerce, E-commerce in China 2016, Website of the Ministry of Commerce, Jun. 14, 2017. http://dzsws.mofcom.gov.cn/article/ztxx/ndbg/201706/20170602591881.shtml.

Chapter 7
Practice and Exploration of
E-Government in China

The efficient management and effective services of the government are indispensable to the informatization of the national economy, and the governments of all levels use information technology to improve administrative efficiency and public services. In short, e-government underpins the informatization of the national economy.

Now, e-government has emerged as a crucial part of national information system in China. President Xi Jinping once pointed out, "China must have a deep understanding of the role of the internet in national management and social governance. We should focus on promoting e-government and building new smart cities, and use data concentration and sharing as the means to build a national integrated big data center, thus promoting information integration in technology, business and data to achieve cross-level, cross-regional, cross-system, cross-department, cross-business collaborative management and services."[1] On May 25, 2016, when attending the China Big Data Industry Summit & China E-commerce Innovation and Development Summit in Guiyang, then Premier Li Keqiang remarked that government should connect up the information islands and information silos to promote government information sharing and improve the government efficiency, thus facilitating enterprises and the general public to handle personal affairs and entrepreneurship. E-government can promote the capability of social management and the level of public service of the government, advance the construction of a service-oriented government, and provide a support for the development of economic modernization in China.

---

[1] The 36th Group Study Session of the Political Bureau of the CPC Central Committee on the Implementation of the National Cyber Development Strategy, The State Council of the People's Republic of China, Oct. 9, 2016, http://www.gov.cn/xinwen/2016-10/09/content_511644.htm.

7.1   Connotation and modes of e-government

7.1.1   Connotation of e-government

E-government refers to a process in which the government uses modern information technology and the internet to assist government departments at all levels to accomplish their administrative affairs, thereby establishing a more efficient government, providing better services to the public, and continuously improving its administration. The continuous innovation of information technology has brought constant changes to the practice and definition of e-government. Among its definitions, the more authoritative ones are the summaries by the United Nations Economic and Social Council (ECOSOC) and the World Bank.

The ECOSOC defines e-government as that: "E-government is the public sector's use of information and communication technologies with the aim of improving information and service delivery, encouraging citizen participation in the decision-making process and making government more accountable, transparent and effective. E-government involves new styles of leadership, new ways of debating and deciding policy and investment, new ways of accessing education, new ways of listening to citizens and newways of organizing and delivering information and services."[1]

According to the World Bank, "E-government refers to the use by government agencies of information technologies (such as Wide Area Networks, the internet, and mobile computing) that have the ability to transform relations with citizens, businesses, and other arms of government. These technologies can serve a variety of different ends: better delivery of government services to citizens, improved interactions with business and industry, citizen empowerment through access to information, or more efficient government management. The resulting benefits can be less corruption, increased transparency, greater convenience, revenue growth, and/or cost reductions."[2]

Therefore, e-government is a full combination of information technology and government management functions. Building an information-based public service system through information technology and the internet is beneficial to promote the transformation of government functions, improve social management, and enhance the government's capability to provide public services. The improvement of government public services marks the progress of a country's e-government development.

---

[1] [2] Fujian Information Association, "Report on the Scientific Development of E-government in Fujian Province", *Straits Science*, 2011(1), pp. 162-169.

The specific functions of e-government are embodied in four aspects: first, it can establish an internet-based e-government public service system that combines multiple technical means, so as to improve public services; second, it can set up a comprehensive and efficient social management information network, thus strengthening social management and comprehensive social governance capabilities; third, it can deepen the construction of related business systems, promote business collaboration among departments, and improve government supervision capabilities; fourth, it can upgrade economic operation information system and enhance macro-control capabilities.

7.1.2 Modes of e-government

According to different service targets, e-government can be divided into four basic modes of government to government (G2G), government to business (G2B), government to citizen (G2C), and government to employees (G2E).

The G2G refers to the e-government activities among governments of all levels and government departments. Governments and departments at all levels use management information systems such as electronic official document systems, financial management systems, personnel and salary management systems, and corporate basic information exchange systems to carry out administrative activities, so as to achieve the collaboration among departments and improve efficiency of administrative work. The information systems among government departments mainly include the internal governmental network office system, electronic regulation and policy system, electronic official document system, electronic judicial file system, electronic financial management system, electronic training system, vertical network management system, horizontal network coordination management system, network performance evaluation system, urban network management system, and other information network systems.

The G2B means that various government departments conduct electronic procurement and bidding through network information systems, and provide enterprises with various online services, including electronic tax filing, processing and approval of electronic licenses, the release of related policies, and provision of consulting services. Through the information network systems, the business-related departments of the governments can efficiently provide various kinds of information services for enterprises on the basis of resource sharing, simplify procedures, streamline work processes and improve efficiency through online services, thus creating a quality environment for enterprises.

The G2C refers to the government providing citizens with various services through the information network system, and receiving feedback and opinions from the public in a timely manner. Its main applications include public information services, electronic identity authentication, electronic taxation, electronic social security services, electronic democratic management, medical and health services, social insurance services, labor and employment services, digital libraries, electronic education and training services, electronic traffic management, etc. Through the G2C platform, a good interactive channel has been established between the government and the public to achieve the two-way communication.

The G2E means that the government agencies set up a government intranet through network technology to realize internal electronic management and establish an effective administration and employee management system, thus improving the government efficiency and the management capabilities of civil servants.

Therefore, in the G2G mode, the government departments of different levels in the internal structure of the government achieve information sharing and business collaboration through the information network and information system. In the G2B and G2C modes, government, enterprises and citizens achieve the disclosure, dissemination and feedback of government information and realize the online processing of business through the information networks and service platforms. As for G2E, government agencies employ information technology and networks to achieve office and management automation, thus improving administrative efficiency.

7.2   Evolution of e-government in China

The e-government in China arose in the 1980s when government departments used information technology to achieve office automation. Some scholars divided the development of e-government in China into four stages, including the initial stage, the stage of electronic business management, the online government stage, and the all-round development stage.[1] However, other scholars classified it into three stages, including the office automation of the offline application stage, the stage of overall promotion of online government and capacity building, and the application-led stage.[2] Looking at the evolution of e-government in China, the author divides it into three stages of the office automation stage, the government online stage, and the comprehensive application and development stage.

---

[1] Zou Sheng, *Ten Lectures on IT Application*, Beijing: Publishing House of Electronics Industry, 2009, p. 98.
[2] Wang Xiangdong, "The Progress, Present Situation and Development Trend of E-Government in China", *E-Government*, 2009(7), pp. 44-68.

7.2.1 Office automation stage (1980s to 1999)

In the 1980s, e-government was in its initial stage, and the development of e-government was marked by the office automation of government departments, which introduced computers for file management in the office-related process. In this period, the level of IT application was relatively low, only in the stage of offline application and decentralized development. However, some government departments began to actively prepare and establish information agencies, develop information systems, and establish national-level government information systems in the fields of economy, finance, railway, electric power, civil aviation, statistics, finance and taxation, customs, meteorology, and disaster prevention.

In 1989, the first-generation national data communication network formed by the General Office of the State Council was launched. By October 1990, the First-Generation Email System had been applied between the State Council and all provincial governments across the country.[1] In March 1993, then Premier Zhu Rongji proposed to build the E-Custom Project, and in December 1993, China officially launched the first step of IT application in national economy. Marked by the 3E projects, namely the e-expressway, the e-customs, and the e-money, the State Council departments concerned have built a number of business systems one after another. China's 3E projects were in full swing and actively promoted.

7.2.2 Online government stage (1999-2001)

In January 1999, the Government Online Project was officially launched, and the official website www.gov.cn was put into operation. At the same time, government departments at all levels began to establish websites on the internet, marking that China's e-government entered the stage of the internet application. The year 1999 was known as the Year of Government Online. According to the China Internet Network Information Center, the number of registered domain names with "GOV." in China was only 561 as of June 1998, but it then surged to 4,615 in December 2000 and further grew to 5,864 in December 2001. The launch of the Government Online Project has promoted the establishment of online government by various government departments in China and ticked off a new stage of e-government.

During this period, the State Council formulated a number of policies to promote the large-scale construction of information infrastructure, furthering the online application of government affairs and the construction of information infrastructure in government

---

[1] Wang Xiangdong, "Progress, Status and Development Trend of E-Government in China", *E-Government*, 2009(7), pp. 44-68.

system. In 2000 and 2001, the General Office of the State Council issued the Notice on Further Promoting the Construction and Application of Office Automation in the National Government System and the Outline of the 2001-2005 Plan for the Construction of Government Informatization in the National Government System respectively, putting forward the task of building three networks and one database (intranet, private network, internet and information resource database).

7.2.3   Comprehensive application and development stage (2001 to present)

7.2.3.1   Proposition of the strategy of government-led informatization development

In August 2001, the new National Informatization Leading Group was established with Premier Zhu Rongji as its leader. It held its first meeting in December of the same year and proposed the strategy of government-led informatization. In August 2002, the General Office of the CPC Central Committee and the General Office of the State Council jointly forwarded the Guideline of the National Informalization Leading Group on the Construction of E-Government in China, the first document for the e-government construction in China. The National Informatization Leading Group decided to take e-government construction as the focus of China's information work in the coming period and make government lead the informatization of national economy and social development. Since then, China's e-government has entered a new stage of orderly development. The informatization in government public services has driven the full application of information technologies in economy and other social domains and provided security and support for national informatization.

The Guideline of the National Informalization Leading Group on the Construction of E-Government in China proposed that the e-government in China should be promoted through "two networks, one website, four databases and twelve e-projects". The main tasks of e-government construction are to build a unified e-government network, shape and improve key business systems, plan and develop important government information resources, actively promote public services, establish an e-government network and information security system, improve a standard e-government system, strengthen training and assessment for civil servants in information technology, and speed up the construction of law-based e-government.

The portal of the Chinese Central Government's Official Website was launched on October 1, 2005 on a trial basis and officially operated on January 1, 2006. The functions of China's government websites are gradually expanding, transforming from simple information release to comprehensive applications of information disclosure, public participation and online affairs dealing, and the government portal system has initially taken shape.

7.2.3.2　Taking the IT application as the focus of e-government

Since the beginning of the 21st century, the CPC Central Committee and the State Council have issued many policies to foster a sound environment for the e-government development in China. China has constantly emphasized the applicability of e-government to promote the continuous improvement of the government's social management capability and public services through e-government. In 2006, the National Informatization Leading Group issued the Overall Framework of the National E-Government, proposing to establish information sharing and business collaboration mechanisms to promote the administrative and institutional reform and drive informatization with greater emphasis on the level of its application and the tapping and utilization of government information resources. By doing this, we are able to take the path of e-government development with Chinese characteristics. In October 2007, the Report to the 17th CPC National Congress proposed to improve the public service system, implement e-government, and strengthen social management and public services.

The relevant departments have actively studied and promoted the application mode of cloud computing in e-government, and innovatively put forward the "cloud computing service first" model. In December 2011, Ministry of Industry and Information Technology issued the 12th Five-Year Plan on the National E-Government, proposing to strengthen the top-level design of e-government public platforms based on cloud computing, encourage e-government to apply cloud computing, and vigorously promote government departments to improve the competence and level of performing their duties. The plan determined the development direction and application focus of China's e-government during the 12th Five-year Plan period, including accelerating the development of important government affairs applications, speeding up the protection and improvement of people's livelihood applications, advancing innovation in social management, strengthening the development and utilization of government information resources, building and improving e-government public platforms, and increasing the information security assurance capabilities of government information systems.

In 2014, the Office of Central Cyberspace Affairs Commission issued the Notice on Strengthening the Safety Management of Websites of the Party and Government Organs, and the General Office of the State Council issued the Guiding Opinions on Promoting Coordinated Development of E-Government. In 2015, National Development and Reform Commission unveiled the Opinions on Carrying out the Performance Assessment for National E-Government Projects and Programs. The CPC Central Committee and the State Council have strengthened website security management through different aspects and actively carried out performance evaluation work to continuously improve the comprehensive development level of e-government.

7.2.3.3   Actively promoting the model of "internet + government services"

China has constantly made fresh innovations of the model of e-government. In 2015, then Premier Li Keqiang proposed at the first executive meeting of the State Council to actively promote online administrative approval, and "internet + government services" model has become the key area of China's e-government development after 2016.

In March 2016, Li Keqiang proposed in the Report on the Work of the Government that "we will carry out the 'internet + government services' model and promote better information sharing between government departments, so that the public and businesses need to make fewer visits to government departments to get things done, find procedures simpler, and find the service satisfactory." In April of the same year, the National Development and Reform Commission and other departments formulated the Promotion of the Internet Plus Government Services Initiative and the Implementation Plan of the Pilot Information Application Program for the Benefit of the People, which stipulates to actively push forward the "internet + government services", step up information sharing between departments, deepen the streamlining of administration and decentralization, improve regulation, optimize services, and achieve the goal of "one number, one window, one network" in the pilot areas to improve the government's public service capabilities. One number application means that the citizen's ID number is used as a unique identifier, with a unified data sharing and exchange platform, to realize the "one application" for people to handle their affairs. One window for matter processing is to process matters at a single window, and build a unified data sharing and exchanging platform and an information system for government services. One website platform for processing all matters refers that the online unified identity authentication system is built to promote the masses to conduct online business with "one authentication and multiple interconnections" and realize the handling of affairs through a network of multi-channel services.[1] The State Council unveiled Guiding Opinions on Accelerating

---

[1] Notice of General Office of the State Council on Forwarding the Promotion of the "internet + government Services" Initiative and the Implementation Plan of the Pilot Information Application Program for the Benefit of the People, The State Council of the People's Republic of China, Apr. 14, 2016, http://www.gov.cn/zhengce/content/2016-04/26/content_5068058.htm.

the Promotion of the "internet + government services" Work and Construction Guidelines for "internet + government services" Technical System, aiming at higher-level development of the "internet + government services".

7.3 Key e-government projects of China

With the guidance of the strategy of the government-led development of information technology, the e-commerce in China has entered a period of rapid development since the year of 2002. The development of e-government starts with the construction of information infrastructure and the system of the government for core business. The CPC Central Committee and the State Council have vigorously carried out major information system projects to provide basic support for information application in government affairs as well as in the national economy.

7.3.1 One government website, two government networks, four databases and twelve administrative information systems

Since the Guidance of the National Informalization Leading Group on the Construction of E-Government issued in 2002, "One government website, two government networks, four databases and twelve administrative information systems" have become the focus of the e-government construction, marking China's entering a comprehensive application stage in e-government building.

"Two networks" refer to the government intranet and e-government internet. The government intranet is the office network of government departments at the sub-provincial level or above, while the e-government internet is the government's service network, mainly for the professional services of government departments for the society and businesses that do not need to run on the intranet. "One website" refers to the government portal website. "Four Databases" are four basic databases, including National Population Basic Information Database, Corporation Basic Information Database, National Natural Resources and Geospatial Basic Information Database, and China Macro Economy Database. "Twelve administrative information systems" are twelve e-projects of government services, which are divided into four categories according to their contents. The projects that offer support for macro decision-making are the office business resource system and macroeconomics system; the projects that enhance fiscal and financial supervision include China taxation administration information system, e-customs project, government fiscal management information system, e-money project and government audit information system; the projects that consolidate the foundations for national economic and social development cover e-agriculture project, water resources information system and e-administration of quality supervision system; the projects that are related to social order are the information protection system and social security information system.[1]

7.3.2   Further development of the "one government website, two government networks, four databases and twelve administrative information systems"

In May 2012, the National Development and Reform Commission issued the Planning for the National Government Affairs Informationization Construction During the 12th Five-Year Plan Period, which outlined four key tasks for the central government informatization project: building the national electronic network for government affairs, deepening the development and utilization of national basic information resources, improving the national network and information security infrastructure, and advancing the construction of national important information systems. These four key tasks are essentially the deepening development of the "one government website, two government networks, four databases and twelve administrative information systems" initiative. Firstly, China should build the national e-government network. It should develop and improve the national e-government intranet platform and the internet platform, and integrate and upgrade ready-made administrative networks.

Secondly, China should deepen the development and utilization of national basic information resources. The national basic information database mainly includes the basic information database and administrative information database. The cultural information resource database is added to the original "four databases" and then we get "five databases".

Thirdly, China should upgrade the national network and information security infrastructure. It includes the development and improvement of network and information security infrastructure and important information system security facilities. The development of national information technology insists on promoting development and ensuring security as the main work to accelerate the development of security facilities and improve the security of basic information networks and important information systems.

Fourthly, China should boost the building of the national major information systems, which is the expansion of the "twelve e-projects". The state proposed to promote the e-customs project, government fiscal management information system, China taxation

---

[1] The Guidance of the National Informalization Leading Group on the Development of E-Government, Ministry of Industry and Information Technology, Aug. 6, 2002, http://www.cac.gov.cn/2002-08/06/c_1112139134.htm.

administration system, government audit information system and computerized agriculture project. China also focuses on the building of the major information systems that enhance people's livelihood, ensure economic and social security, and step up the governance capability. The specific extensions include the IT application projects in terms of national health protection, national housing protection, national social security, drug safety supervision, food safety supervision, safety production supervision, market price supervision, financial supervision, energy security, credit system construction, ecological environmental protection, emergency stability protection, administrative law enforcement supervision, legal system construction, and governance capacity building.[1]

The "one government website, two government networks, four databases and twelve administrative information systems" have played an important role in strengthening social management, public services, macro-control and overall supervision, and have raised the level of the government's abilities to social management and public services. Thanks to the e-projects, the e-government in China has been progressing constantly.

7.3.3 An integrated data platform for government affairs

E-government has entered a new stage of big platform sharing and smart governance with the development of the new generation technologies such as big data. In 2017, the National Development and Reform Commission unveiled the 13th Five-Year Plan for Construction of National Government Service Informatization Project, a guiding document for the building of e-government, which made systematic designs for the goal. In accordance with the integration and innovation trend of digitalization, cloud computing, internet and intelligent terminals and the need for intensive construction of e-government, the construction of an integrated government data platform has become a key project of the China's e-government initiative during the 13th Five-year Plan period.

The integrated government data platform proposed in the 13th Five-Year Plan for Construction of National Government Service Informatization Project is an intensive and comprehensive public infrastructure platform. The main contents of its construction include building a unified national e-government network to realize the integration, transfer and integration of various government special networks, a national government

---

[1] Notice of the National Development and Reform Commission on the Issuance of the 12th Five-Year National Government Informatization Project Construction Plan, Chinese Central Government's Official Website, May 16, 2012, http://www.gov.cn/gzdt/ 2012-05/16/content_2138308.htm.

data center integrating data center and cloud computing to support government business collaboration and data sharing and aggregation, a unified national data sharing and exchange hub to form a national government information sharing system, and an open public data website to ensure the effective use of public data. The state uses large platforms to share information facilities and promote the coordinated development of the national e-government networks, the national government data center, the national data sharing and exchange project, and the national open public data website, thereby connecting up the "information island" and facilitating the integration of government information systems.

7.4   The new trend of e-government development in China

In the process of evolution, China's e-government has gradually changed from e-government capacity building to full application stage, from decentralized construction to the system integrating all government information resources, and from government internal business to public services. The openness of government data continued to increase, integration was deepening, and various innovative applications continued to spring up. The public service capabilities of government websites have been greatly improved, and a basic public service system that benefits all people has taken shape.

7.4.1   Integration of e-government

Although being a latecomer in the development of e-government, China has scored significant breakthroughs in online public services and government administrative application with the support of national policies and information technology infrastructure through the rapid development of e-government in the period of 10th Five-year Plan to 12th Five-year Plan. The Guidance of the National Informalization Leading Group on the Construction of E-Government in China proposed that the development of e-government should be promoted based on "one government website, two government networks, four databases and twelve administrative information systems". The Overall Framework of the National E-Government put forward that the development should focus on the improvement of the application. The Guiding Opinions of the State Council on Accelerating the Promotion of the "Internet + Government Service" Work called for the strategy of developing "internet + government services" and the integration of online administrative deliberation and approval by the CPC Central Committee and the State Council. According to the development trend of the times and the needs of economic and social development, a number of policies have been promulgated to provide a good environment for the e-government development in China. The basic policy on e-government has also shifted from promoting office automation in government departments and ensuring internet access for the government to performing public service functions, and building a service-oriented government in an all-round way.

With the development of the internet, the national network infrastructure has been continuously improved, the construction of the national e-government intranet has been steadily advanced, and the improvement of the network infrastructure has promoted the enhancement of the level of e-government applications. The nationwide e-government internet access and coverage rates have gradually increased. As of May 2015, the national e-government internet has reached 100%, 94.3%, 83.5%, and 33.6% at the four levels of province, city, county, and township respectively.[1] With the increase in the coverage of government websites, government services have gradually developed in the direction of integration, and citizens can handle the administrative approval items of all relevant departments through a single window. Guangdong, Zhejiang and other provinces have established an integrated online service hall, building a unified, efficient and integrated e-government cloud platform. The Ministry of Industry and Information Technology of the People's Republic of China actively promotes the construction of government cloud and the widespread application of cloud computing in the field of e-government. Some provinces, such as Guangdong and Beijing, have set up a unified, efficient and integrated e-government cloud platform, greatly reducing the construction and operation costs of government infrastructure and improving the efficiency of government services. In 2017, China deployed a reform pilot for the integrated online data processing of road traffic accident damage disputes, which has promoted the development of the integrated government services.

7.4.2 A stream of innovative applications of e-government

The government website has become the main channel for the government to release information, provide online services, and communicate and interact between the government and the people. Currently, 100% of the State Council's departments and provincial governments, 99.1% of governments at the prefecture level, and more than 85% of county governments have established and opened government websites, and the feasibility of all-year-round access to homepage links has gradually improved

---

[1] China Electronic Information Industry Development Research Institute, *The Blue Book on the Development of Informatization in China (2015-2016)*, Beijing: People's Publishing House, 2016, p. 99.

throughout the year. The new generation of information technologies such as big data, cloud computing, and the IoT have penetrated into the field of government affairs, and new models of "internet + e-government" have continuously emerged, promoting the in-depth development of digitalization and networking internet based social management and public services.

First of all, the Weibo accounts, WeChat accounts, and mobile App have become important means for governments at all levels to promote e-government. According to the Report on the Overall Influence of Government Affairs New Media released by the Xinhuanet, as of late 2014, the authenticated government Weibo accounts (including Sina Weibo and Tencent Weibo) had reached 277,000, covering a total of 4.39 billion people. According to The 2015 WeChat White Paper on Government Affairs and People's Livelihood, as of the end of August 2015, there had been more than 83,000 official government WeChat accounts in the country, with the proportion of authenticated accounts reaching 62.6%, and the ownership of official WeChat accounts of ministries and commissions exceeding 40%. Hospitals, government offices, and neighborhood communities had been the top 3 in terms of the number of official WeChat accounts.[1] The government Apps are developing steadily, and Beijing, Zhejiang and other provinces have launched government Apps covering transportation, education, medical care, government services, tourism, employment, etc. The "Beijing E-Service" App and the "Zhejiang E-Government" App have provided intelligent, convenient and mobile services to their citizens.

Moreover, the integration of online and offline government has improved the efficiency of public services. In recent years, the O2O e-government model has been popularized and applied, especially in the fields of civil affairs and public security. Applications for passport, visa, ID card and other businesses can be done online after appointments, thus simplifying the work processes and shortening the waiting time of the public and improving work efficiency.

7.4.3 The rapid expansion of mobile government services

China's huge scale of mobile broadband users and mobile phone netizens have accelerated the development of e-government, and provided the basis for the development of China's e-government to catch up with and surpass the countries that are most advanced in this field. According data to from the China Internet Network Information

---

[1] Tencent Research Institute, The 2015 WeChat White Paper on Government Affairs and People's Livelihood, Website of Tencent Research Institute, Dec. 2015, http: //www. tisi.org/ Article/lists/id/4357.html.

Center, China's mobile broadband users totaled 674 million, and the number of mobile internet users reached 620 million, accounting for 90.1% of all internet users in 2015. As of June 2017, the number of mobile internet users in China has reached 724 million, and the proportion of mobile phone users in internet users has increased from 95.1% at the end of 2016 to 96.3%, with the proportion of mobile internet users being constantly increasing. The large number of mobile internet users have provided a foundation for the development of China's mobile e-government applications, and promoted the expansion of its scope and the improvement of processing capabilities. At present, the administrative scope of mobile government apps has been extended to water and electricity payment, medical registration, transportation, court filing, the renewal of Exit-Entry Permit for Travelling to and from Hong Kong and Macao, etc.

Chapter 8
Conclusion: Experience, Challenges and Prospects of Informatization Path with Chinese Characteristics

After the founding of the People's Republic of China in 1949, especially since the beginning of the reform and opening up, the CPC Central Committee and the State Council have led the Chinese people of all ethnic groups to carry out construction of informatization, implement the national big data strategy and promote an internet power and a digital China. Great achievements have been made as follows. Firstly, the number of internet users, the volume of online retail transactions, and the scale of electronic information product manufacturing rank first in the world, with a relatively sophisticated industry system of information being established. Secondly, with the continuous deepening of the IT application, "internet +" has been widely applied in the various fields of the economic society. Thirdly, information technology has fully integrated with industrialization, informatization, and agricultural informatization has developed fast, and e-commerce has been a new source of economic growth. E-government has greatly improved the government's capacities in social management and public services, and information technology has played an increasingly prominent leading role in the whole process of modern construction. With the arduous explorations during the several decades, China has embarked on a development path of informatization with Chinese characteristics guided by the vision of innovative, coordinated, green, open and inclusive development.

8.1 Experience of informatization with Chinese characteristics

8.1.1 China taking informatization as a national development strategy

8.1.1.1 Chinese leaders seizing up the developmental opportunities of information revolution in a timely and appropriate manner

The CPC Central Committee and the State Council have attached great importance to information application, and regard it as the strategic measure for China's modernization. Based on the basic national situation during the primary stage of socialism, China has taken active part in global information revolution, strengthened the top-level design and institutional improvement according to the trend of the times, and made overall planning and coordinated development, so as to the informatization in China.

After the founding of New China, Chinese leaders seized up the opportunities of information revolution in a timely and appropriate manner. In 1956, the Long-term Plan for Development of Science and Technology (1956-1967), which was formulated under the auspices of Premier Zhou Enlai, included computer, semiconductor and electronics as key projects of science and technology. Since the reform and opening up, all successive Chinese leaders have attached great importance to the information application. In 1984, Deng Xiaoping proposed to "develop information resources and serve the four modernizations."[1] In 1991, Jiang Zemin pointed out that "the four modernizations cannot be separated from information technology."[2] In 2000, Hu Jintao stated in his speech at the Fourth Plenary Session of the 14th Central Committee of the Communist Youth League that "how to utilize high technology to narrow the gap with developed countries has become an urgent issue common to the majority of developing countries, including China."[3] In 2001, Zhu Rongji proposed that "informatization is the global trend of economic and social development, and is also a key link in the industrial optimization and upgrading and the realization of industrialization and modernization in China."[4] In 2014, Xi Jinping pointed out at the first meeting of the Central Leading Group on Cybersecurity and Informatization: "Without ensuring cyber security, we cannot safeguard national security; without promoting informatization, we cannot realize modernization."[5] In line with the political and economic situation and the growing trends of informatization at home and abroad, all Chinese leaders take information application as an integrated part of modernization, and also consider national economy and information technology in all fields as strategic measures during the whole modernization process.

---

[1] Party Literature Research Center, CPC Central Committee, *Chronicles of Deng Xiaoping (1975-1997)* (Vol. III), Beijing: Central Party Literature Press, 2004, p. 994.

[2] [4] *Selected Works of Important Documents Since the 15th National Congress of the Communist Party of China* (Vol. III), Beijing: Central Party Literature Press, 2003, p. 361.

[3] Speech of Hu Jintao at the Fourth Plenary Session of the 14th Central Committee of the Communist Youth League, The CPC News, Dec. 20, 2000, http://cpc.people.com.cn/GB/64162/124333/124349/17730336.html.

[5] Shen Yi, "Promoting the Building of a Network Power", *Guangming Daily*, Apr. 18, 2017.

8.1.1.2　The efforts of the Chinese government to support the informatization in China

The close attention of Chinese leaders serves as the significant driving force for the comprehensive and rapid advancement of information technology. With the support of the CPC Central Committee, China has successively set up the Electronic Rejuvenation Leading Group Office of the State Council in 1983, the Joint Conference on National Economic Informatization in 1993, the Informatization Leading Group of the State Council in 1996, the National Informationization Work Conference to deploy the national informationization development in 1997, and the National Informatization Leading Group in 2001. Besides, it also held the National Informatization Work Conference to deploy the construction of national informatization. In the early 1990s, the Central Committee and the State Council launched the major information technology projects, such as E-Custom Project, E-Money Project and E-Taxation Project. The Fifth Plenary Session of the 15th CPC Central Committee elevated information technology as a national strategy, and the 16th CPC National Congress made a strategic plan to take a new road of industrialization—using the information technology to promote industrialization and letting industrialization support the development of the information technology.

The information technology is a sophisticated project, which not only involves penetration and application of information technology in the fields of politics, economy, society, culture and military, but also the reforms of system and management. It is a major project involved by all people, and requires the participation and integration of governments at all levels, various types of enterprises, and people of the whole society. Therefore, the information technology can only be carried out smoothly under the leadership of the CPC and the overall planning of the government. The efforts of the Chinese government is a necessary condition and important support for the success of the information technology in China

8.1.2　Government's overall planning and market's positive role in informatization

On the National Informatization Work Conference in 1997, China proposed guideline for construction of informatization, that is, "overall planning, government guidance, unified standard, joint construction, nationwide connectivity and shared resources." According to the 2006-2020 National Informatization Development Strategy, the information application in China must be conducted based on the strategic policy of "unified planning and resource sharing, in-depth application and solid progress, market-oriented and innovation-based development, and civil-military integration and security." The Outline for the National Informatization Development Strategy released in 2016 adjusted the basic principle of informatization to "overall planning, innovation-oriented, development-driven and benefits to the people's livelihood," which shows that overall planning and overall promotion are the fundamental strategic guidelines for information technology in China. The informatization is momentous force for driving economic and social revolution, concerning the long-term sustainable development of national economic society, long-term political stability and the general public's welfare. Hence, the CPC and Chinese government are supposed to coordinate the relationship between the central and local governments, the stage and long-term goals, the role of government and market, the coherent development of urban and rural informatization, and the regional balance among the eastern, central and western regions, so as to facilitate the comprehensive, harmonious and sustainable advancement of informatization in China.

8.1.2.1 Overall planning and unified deployment

In order to maintain the continuity and coordination of informatization, the CPC Central Committee and the State Council are committed to making coordinated plans for both and implement them in a unified way. Informatization has been an important strategic means of national modernization and an urgent requirement for building a well-off society and an innovative country. On the condition that China is transforming from an agricultural country to an industrial society, the national informatization will confront lots of challenges during the process. Faced with complex situations at home and abroad, the CPC and Chinese government must conduct overall planning and formulate the developing targets and construction priorities in the areas of politics, economy, military, science and technology, culture and society with the strategic perspective and scientific planning. At the same time, the informatization cannot flourish without the safeguard of institution and system, the support of fiscal and monetary policies, and the legal norms and restraints. Therefore, the government and other departments should jointly conduct unified planning and improve measures for its development, covering formulating and perfecting policies and system, deepening structural reform, improving investment and financing policies, and promoting the legal system construction. The strategic plans, including the 2006-2020 National Informatization Development Strategy, Key Special Plan of Informatization in the 10th Five-Year Plan of National Economic and Social Development, Several Opinions on Vigorously Promoting Informatization Development and Effectively Safeguarding Information Security, the Outline of 13th Five-Year Plan for the National Informatization, the 13th Five-Year Informatization Standard Work Guide, and Outline of the National Informatization Development Strategy, define the direction, specify the principle and provide institutional support for the development of national informatization.

8.1.2.2 Application-led, market-oriented, open and fair competition

While making overall planning to promote coordinated development, China insists on being market-oriented and application-led in practice. Besides, China also fully plays the role of enterprises as the key participants in innovation and research, speeds up the establishment of technological innovation system that is enterprise-led, market-oriented and IUR (Industry-University-Research collaboration between industries, universities and research institutes)-integrated, boosts the innovation of informatization standard in technology, system, application and management, and carries forward its innovative achievements. The Outline of the 10th Five-Year Plan for the National Economic and Social Development pointed out a new thought of the national information technology: "application-led, market-oriented, internet co-construction, resource sharing, technological innovation, and open and fair competition." [1] The innovation and application of information technology must be market-oriented and take market demand as the starting point and enterprises as the main body, so as to fully release the potential of innovation.

Information infrastructure construction is a huge basic project for the development of information technology and requires a large amount of resource investment. The state extensively polls social resources while spending public money and gives full play to the role of market mechanism to optimize the allocation of resources. Therefore, the market has made great contributions to the achievements of the informatization in China. The idea of "application-led, market-oriented, open and fair competition" provides innovative impetus for the continuous development of IT industry and promotes the information technology in China to make breakthroughs. In short, the driving role of government and market has jointly developed the information technology in China.

8.1.3 Government pioneering the informatization

In 2001, the National Informatization Leading Group led by Zhu Rongji was set up to enhance the leadership of China's informatization. In December, 2001, the group held the first meeting and proposed the strategy of "government taking the lead to drive the information industry," that is, the information application of the government motivates the economic and social development.

The informatization in China covers the politics, economy, society, culture and military affairs, which is inseparable from government management and public services.

---

[1] Outline of the 10th Five-Year Plan for the National Economic and Social Development, *People's Daily*, Mar. 18, 2001.

The IT application of the government rapidly improves the capabilities of management and services so as to better serve the economic society. Although the e-government in China started late, the CPC Central Committee and the State Council attached great importance to it. They formulated the e-government development plan, intensively issued policies to strengthen the construction of national information infrastructure, promoted the e-government construction, improved government's abilities of macroeconomic regulation, social management, market supervision and public services, and enhanced government's role in supporting economic and social development.

Informatization in the economic and social fields requires the support and guarantee of hardware, software and systems. In terms of hardware, the information infrastructure has been constantly improved through the efforts of government, with the various world-class facilities emerging. In terms of software, the government has launched the construction projects of national major information system since 1990s, and the projects, such as "two networks, one website, four databases and twelve e-projects", have provided the systematic support for the informatization in macroeconomic management, quality supervision, banking, finance, agriculture and water conservancy projects. In terms of supporting conditions, the government has vigorously promoted the institutional reform, formulated fundamental standard, improved national information education system, conducted national training on information skills, and built cross-sector business system and application engineering for information sharing. The government takes the lead to put information application into practice and vigorously popularizes e-government mode, so as to enhance its service capacity in every field of economy and society and drive the coordinated development of national economy and social informatization.

8.1.4　The path of integration of informatization, industrialization and agricultural modernization

Western countries began to implement informatization after the completion of industrialization, while China started informatization before completion of industrialization and modernization in agriculture. China is still in the primary stage of socialism and will remain so for a long time to come, and the basic national context requires the synchronous development of informatization, industrialization, agricultural modernization and new urbanization during the process of its modernization. Under the leadership of the CPC, China has innovated a coordinated development path of these works.

The CPC and Chinese government have innovated the focus of development to promote industrialization with the help of information technology and follow a new path of industrialization, thus facilitating the integrated development of information technology and industrialization. Agriculture is the foundation of national economy. In order to consolidate the basic position of agriculture, promote the stable development of agriculture and increase the sustainable income of farmers, China is committed to cultivating agricultural information technology as a new power for modern agriculture and propelling harmonious development of informatization and modern agriculture. The Fifth Plenary Session of the 15th CPC Central Committee proposed that "vigorously promoting the national economy and social informatization is the strategic initiative in light of the overall interests of the modernization. China will use information technology to stimulate industrialization, give full play to its late-mover advantages and achieve leapfrog development of social productivity."[1] The 16th CPC National Congress proposed that "information technology is essential to China's industrialization and modernization. China will take a new road of industrialization—using the information technology to promote industrialization and letting industrialization support the development of the information technology, opening a new road to industrialization featuring high sci-tech content, good economic returns, low resources consumption, less environmental pollution, and full play to the advantages of human resources."[2] The 17th CPC National Congress stated that "we will keep to the new path of industrialization with Chinese characteristics and promote integration of informatization with industrialization."[3] Besides, the 18th CPC National Congress raised that "we should keep to the Chinese-style path of carrying out industrialization in a new way and advancing informatization, urbanization and agricultural modernization. We should promote integration of informatization and industrialization, interaction between industrialization and urbanization, and coordination between urbanization and agricultural modernization, thus promoting harmonized development of industrialization, informatization, urbanization and agricultural modernization."[4] The 19th CPC National Congress proposed that "China must see that the market plays the decisive role

---

[1] *Selected Works of Important Documents Since the 15th National Congress of the Communist Party of China* (Vol. II), Beijing: Central Party Literature Press, 2001, p. 489.

[2] *Selected Works of Important Documents Since the 16th National Congress of the Communist Party of China* (Vol. I), Beijing: Central Party Literature Press, 2004, p. 16.

[3] *Selected Works of Important Documents Since the 17th National Congress of the Communist Party of China* (Vol. I), Beijing: Central Party Literature Press, 2009, pp. 17-18.

[4] *Selected Works of Important Documents Since the 18th National Congress of the Communist Party of China* (Vol. I), Beijing: Central Party Literature Press, 2014, p. 16.

in resource allocation, the government plays its role better, and new industrialization, informatization, urbanization, and agricultural modernization go hand in hand."[1]

In the construction of socialist modernization, China insists on promoting the deepening of industrial division of labor, the adjustment of economic structure and the upgrading of the industry chain through information technology, so as to create new competitive advantages. First of all, China transforms and upgrades the traditional industries through information technology. It proposes to boost the adjustment and upgrading of traditional industries through information technology, promote the dissemination and application of information technology in traditional industries such as energy, transportation, metallurgy, machinery and chemical industries, and accelerate the upgrading and transformation of industries with high energy consumption, high resource consumption and high pollution. In addition, China also rapidly improves the in-depth integration of information technology in the whole industry chain of enterprises, and realizes the informatization, smartness and networking of the whole lifecycle of products such as R&D, production process, and marketing management. China launches manufacturing upgrading projects, formulates the action plan of Made in China 2025, accelerates the application of new-generation information technologies such as big data, cloud computing and the IoT, vigorously develops smart manufacturing, and drives the transformation and upgrading of traditional industries through various ways of promoting the national intelligent manufacturing demonstration zone, building manufacturing innovation center, and improving the policy system for building a manufacturing power. Secondly, China cultivates and expands strategic emerging industries based on information technology. It continuously reforms its policy system and promotes independent innovation of core and key technologies. Moreover, it formulates and implements development plans of strategic emerging industry, develops information industries based on artificial intelligence, integrated circuits and fifth-generation mobile communication technologies, so as to enhance the market competitiveness of emerging industries.

In the integrated development of information technology and agricultural modernization, the CPC and Chinese government insist on taking information technology as the commanding heights of agricultural modernization, promote the information technology and smart equipment in agricultural production and management, foster

---

[1] Xi Jinping, *Secure a Decisive Victory in Building a Moderately Prosperous Society in All Respects and Strive for the Great Success of Socialism with Chinese Characteristics for a New Era*, Beijing: People's Publishing House, 2017, pp. 21-22.

internet + agriculture, and establish and improve intelligent and networked agricultural system, thus boosting the process of agricultural industrialization. China has actively promoted the construction of information infrastructure for issues related to agriculture, rural areas and rural people, integrated agricultural information resources, and established a public information service platform for the agriculture-related issues, so as to realize the coordinated development of informatization and agricultural modernization. China has also vigorously implemented the "internet +" strategy in rural areas, developed "internet + modern agriculture", and improved agricultural production, operation, management and service through the internet.

8.1.5　The national information security in information technology application

Without ensuring cybersecurity, we cannot safeguard national security; without promoting information technology, we cannot realize modernization. Cybersecurity and information technology are as important to China as wings are to a bird, and are the key strategic issues related to the development of the country and the work and life of the people. President Xi Jinping pointed out, "to promote cyber security and information technology, we should balance security and development, and ensure that the two proceed in tandem and stimulate each other to secure long-term development."[1] In practice, China places equal emphasis on information technology and national information security, constantly increases the levels of security protection on basic information network and major information system, and stresses respecting the sovereignty of the network in international cooperation, so as to provide a favorable environment for national economy and information technology through society to build China an internet power. China has mainly accumulated some experience in information security.

Firstly, China has formulated and implemented national information security strategy, established leading group of cybersecurity and information technology, and set up a management system and working mechanism for information security. China has established a leading group of cybersecurity and information technology to formulate relevant development strategies and deal with major issues in various fields such as economy, politics, culture, society, and military. The National Cyberspace Security Strategy, released by the Cyberspace Administration of China in 2016, specified nine major strategic tasks for strengthening cybersecurity, including

---

[1] "The Establishment of the Central Cyberspace Leading Group", *Beijing News*, Feb. 28, 2014.

guaranteeing cyberspace sovereignty, safeguarding national security, protecting key information infrastructure, strengthening cyberculture construction, cracking down on cyber terror and crimes, improving cyber management system, consolidating the foundation of cybersecurity, promoting cyberspace defense capability, and boosting the international cooperation on cyberspace.[1]

Secondly, China has established a national system for cybersecurity in critical information infrastructure and implemented a cyber security review system to ensure the security of critical information infrastructure. China has set up the classified protection system of information security, so as to guarantee the safety of national major information infrastructure and ensure the safe operation of basic information system that offers such the services as public communications and broadcast television transmission, as well as the major information systems of government agencies and in the fields of energy, finance, transportation, education, scientific research, hydraulic engineering, commercial manufacture, healthcare, social security and public service. Leading group for special remediation of internet financial risks has been built to regulate and safeguard the safe operation of internet finance, and the cybersecurity review system has been set up to conduct safety review on major IT products and services used in key information infrastructure. Moreover, the country has also built information security monitoring system and enacted Emergency Plan for Public Internet Network Security, and gradually improved the monitoring and early warning of cybersecurity, public internet emergency warning system, and emergency response mechanism for major cybersecurity incidents.

Thirdly, China has strengthened efforts to develop and manage internet culture, and enhanced the awareness of cybersecurity and protective skills in the whole society. In the information age, the internet has been a vital means for the dissemination of culture and thoughts. China attaches great importance to the internet culture, actively implements network content construction projects, strengthens the construction of online ideological and cultural front, develops a positive internet culture with Chinese characteristics, advocates civilized behaviors in cyberspace, strengthens ethical standards, and establishes a sound and safe cultural cyberspace. In the meantime, China vigorously advocates education on cybersecurity across the country, incorporates cybersecurity education into the curriculum, enhances netizens' abilities to identify and resist illegal and criminal activities such as illegal and harmful information and cyberfraud, and

---

[1] Cyberspace Administration of China, National Cyberspace Security Strategy, Website of Cyberspace Administration of China, Dec. 27, 2016, http://www.cac.gov.cn/2016-12/27/c_1120195926.htm.

actively guides them to participate in the internet cultural creative practice and to resist to the inappropriate content.

In addition, China has actively promoted independent innovation plans for key information technologies to ensure the independent and controllable core technologies and boosted the building of standardization in the national information security, so as to entail its infrastructural and prescriptive role in information safety protection system construction.

8.1.6   Reinforcing the effective institutions, mechanisms and rule of law in development of informatization

During the process of informatization, information is the core, network is the basis, and system is the safeguard. To ensure the success in informatization, the CPC Central Committee and the State Council strive for institutional improvement, actively drive rule of law and standardization, and underline the protection of intellectual property, fostering a sound institutional environment.

For the coordination and sustainability of China's advancement in development of informatization, it has given full play to the advantages of the socialist system and continuously deepened and improved institutional reforms in this field. First, China has regulated corporate governance structure and perfected market access and exit mechanism. Second, China has set up a standardized regulatory system to meet the needs of network integration and information technology. Third, it has formulated investment and financing policies in the information area and positively guided non-state capital to participate in the developing information technology and social financing mechanisms. Fourth, it has introduced fiscal levy and banking policies for information industry and SMEs. Fifth, it has strengthened standardized construction and management and constantly accelerated the development of standards that apply to the industry policy. China has promoted technological innovation through institutional reform, strengthened the primary position of enterprises in the market, improved the enthusiasm of SMEs in informatization, and achieved a reasonable allocation of resources.

In rule of law, the CPC and Chinese government have accelerated the construction of legal system in informatization, focusing on formulating and improving laws and regulations on information infrastructure, government information publicity, e-government, e-commerce, information security, and individual information protection. Besides, it has continuously improved the framework of laws and administrative regulations covering network infrastructure, network service providers, network users, network information, etc., and advanced the process of informatization legislation in a reasonable and orderly manner. China takes legal construction of information network security as a priority. At the 24th Meeting of the Standing Committee of the 12th National People's Congress on November 7, 2016, the Cybersecurity Law of the People's Republic of China was issued and implemented on June 1, 2017, mainly covering network operation security, especially the key information infrastructure, network information security, monitoring and early warning and emergency disposal. Furthermore, the laws and regulations system related to network information security have been gradually improved, such as Decision of the Standing Committee of the National People's Congress on Preserving Computer Network Security, Regulations of the People's Republic of China on Protecting the Safety of Computer Information Systems, Administrative Measures for the Security Protection of Computer Information Networks Linked to the Internet, and Computer Virus Prevention Provisions. Meanwhile, Law of the People's Republic of China on Promoting the Transformation of Scientific and Technological Achievements effectively protects the fruits of scientific and technical innovation, boosts the course of transformation of high new technology into productivity, and urges sustainable process of the informatization in China.

8.1.7   Training more information technology personnel

Highly skilled (IT) personnel are the key to the success of informatization. During construction of informatization, China has continuously improved the personnel training system and fostered more qualified personnel. Since the reform and opening up, various national policies on informatization have emphasized the improvement of talent training system and IT talent teams. The Guiding Opinions of the State Council on Vigorously Advancing the "Internet +" Action, and Notice of the State Council on Issuing the "Broadband China" Strategy and Its Implementation Plan proposed to strengthen internet skills training for personnel in manufacturing, agriculture and other fields, and reinforce the introduction and training of high-level and inter-disciplinary professionals. The 2006-2020 National Informatization Development Strategy regarded national information skills education and training program as major strategic actions, laying a foundation for the advancement of informatization in China.

The personnel training and improvement of personel's overall quality in informatization in China are mainly carried out in the following aspects. First, China should vigorously develop IT education and basic IT curriculum system, and build "an IT personnel training system that is based on schooling, focuses on-the-job training, integrates elementary education and vocational education, and advocates complementarity between public and commercial training"[1], thus fostering basic skilled IT personnel. Second, it should increase government funding support, vigorously cultivate management personnel in IT application, and improve the IT skills and information management capabilities of officials and civil servants. Third, the government should strengthen the policy preference and financial investment in rural areas, develop rural IT education, and nurture the IT professional team to gain coordinated development in rural areas and remote areas. Fourth, it should take the market as the guide to play the decisive role of the market mechanism in the allocation of resources for IT professionals, and constantly cultivates the composite informatization talents that meet the market demand. Fifth, it should reinforce international exchanges and cooperation of IT talents, adhere to the two-way approaches of "bringing in" and "going global", encourage domestic IT practitioners to receive overseas trainings, and appeal to overseas IT elites to participate in Chinese IT industry with preferential policies. Sixth, it should strengthen the training of professional through IT projects and promote the quality and capabilities of IT staff in practice.

8.2   Development strategy of informatization with Chinese characteristics

Since the founding of the People's Republic of China in 1949, China's information industry has been moving forward in exploration and has made great achievements. The success of informatization with Chinese characteristics is attributable to the CPC's leadership and to the principal national strategies specified for China's economic and social development. Strategies, including the strategy of independent innovation development, the strategy of opening up, the strategy of building up the strength of the country with talented people, the strategy of coordinated development, the strategy of the sharing development and the strategy of the sustainable development, are the guidelines to the stable development of China's informatization, driving the socialist modernization with Chinese characteristics to a new era.

8.2.1   The strategy of independent innovation

China's informatization is always committed to innovation-driven development,

---

[1] China Informatization Almanac Compilation Committee, *China Informatization Almanac 2015*, Beijing: Publishing House of Electronics Industry, 2016, p. 385.

strengthens innovation's leading role, and enhances the national information technology level and international competitiveness with innovation-driven development. As early as the founding of the People's Republic of China in 1949, the CPC Central Committee and the State Council put forward the policy of "self-reliance, supplemented by foreign aid" to take the path of independent development of information technology and explore a road of socialist modernization and development with Chinese characteristics. In addition, China gave the priority to innovation among the five concepts for development (innovation, coordination, green development, opening up and sharing) to guide its socialist modernization. For instance, the 18th CPC National Congress proposed to implement innovation-driven development and follow the path of independent innovation with Chinese characteristics, and the 19th CPC National Congress set out that innovation is the primary driving force for development.

In order to promote China's scientific and technological innovation, the CPC Central Committee and the State Council have increased the efforts to strengthen the top-level design of innovation-driven development and formulated the Outline of National Innovation-Driven Development Strategy of China, providing guidelines for national development based on innovation. To build an innovative country driven by talent pool, China must promote the coordinated development of scientific and technological innovation and institutional innovation, and drive all-around social innovation with scientific and technological innovation.

Information technology is the key element to informatization. Since the founding of the People's Republic of China in 1949, China has attached great importance to investment in scientific and technological research and development, the implementation of major science and technology projects, and the promotion of technological innovation. The national strategy of informatization clearly specified to implement the independent innovation plan of key information technology, increases investments in R&D, and makes breakthrough on key generic technologies. Moreover, China has actively constructed innovation platforms of the new generation of artificial intelligence for opening up, industrial technology research base construction project and intelligent manufacturing innovation project, and strengthened the R&D of key core technologies to improve the national independent innovation capabilities. As shown in 2006-2020 National Informatization Development Strategy, China takes the independent innovation plan of key information technologies as a strategic action for the development of information and technology, giving priority to launching standards with independent intellectual property rights, and grasping the initiative of industrial development through independent innovation of key core technologies.

China has made great efforts to reinforce innovation system. It fully plays the enterprises' dominant role in market-oriented mechanism, establishes innovative mechanism and system with in-depth collaboration between industries, universities, research institutes, governments, and users, and guides and supports the concentration of factors of innovation in enterprises. Therefore, enterprises are becoming increasingly prominent in the innovation of industrial technology. During the industrial informatization, China sets up manufacturing innovative network with manufacturing innovation center as a core carrier, facilitates cooperative sharing between the government and the society, motivates innovative enthusiasm across the country, consolidates the system of industrial application of scientific and technological achievements, improves their productivity transformation, and strengthens legislation and intellectual property protection to foster a sound environment for technical innovation.

China has constantly strengthened the construction and improvement of innovative talents cultivation system. It establishes and improves personnel training system based on the whole industrial chain of enterprises, focuses on nurturing creative talents, carries out cultivation projects of excellent engineers, improves all kinds of talent information bases and the mechanism for the flow of talents.

With the improvement of the national innovation projects, innovation system, and the innovative talent training system, Chinese's capability of independent innovation of industrial technology has remarkably strengthened. At present, China has made breakthroughs in a wide range of major technological and equipment fields, including quantum communication, aerospace, manned deep-sea exploration, large aircraft, BeiDou Navigation Satellite, supercomputers, high-speed rail equipment, megawatt-level power generation equipment, power-generating units generating one million kilowatt-hours (kWh) of electricity and deep-sea oil drilling equipment. By doing so, China has formed internationally competitive enterprises and laid the foundation to build China into an industrial power.

8.2.2   The development strategy of opening up

In the course of informatization, China unswervingly adheres to international exchanges, opening up and cooperation, increases the national information capacity with an open environment, and vigorously calls for establishing a community with a shared future in cyberspace. In July, 2014, Chinese President Xi Jinping addressed at Brazilian National Congress: "The international community as a whole should work together to build a peaceful, secure, open and cooperative cyberspace on the basis of the principles of mutual respect and mutual trust. We will give impetus to the establishment of multilateral, democratic, and transparent international internet governance systems."[1] Due to the economic globalization and openness of the network, it is of vital importance for China to drive international exchanges and cooperation in informatization and cybersecurity protection. China adheres to open operation with a global vision in informatization, and takes full use of domestic and overseas resources to coordinate standards for "bringing in" and "going global".

With the development of information technology, China insists on integration of introducing advanced technology and strengthening the capacity of independent innovation, and gradually enhances the independent IT equipment manufacturing capacity. China is a latecomer in informatization. In the early stage, with less independent intellectual property rights of information technology, the CPC Central Committee and the State Council adhered to the principle of opening up and cooperation, made full use of domestic and foreign resources, introduced international advanced information technology, sticked to the guideline of "introduction, digestion, absorption, and innovation", and integrated the introduction and independent innovation, thus gradually enhancing the capacity of independent innovation. At the same time, it consolidated enterprises' dominant position of innovation and encouraged them to take active part in technical innovation according to the needs of market through enacting a series of preferential policies. Currently, China's information technology with independent intellectual property rights has gained great achievements. In Wuxi International Supercomputer Center in China, the supercomputer "Sunway TaihuLight" powered by a home-made chip held the current world record; the BeiDou Navigation Satellite has been independently constructed and operated by China has become an integral part of the global radio navigation system and has entered the stage of industrial application and international promotion. Chinese scientists have realized the world's longest quantum secure direct communication (QSDC) of 100 kilometers, taking the lead in launching the "Mozi" quantum satellite into Space. The core devices of communication network equipment have reached the international leading level in many technologies.

In terms of standards of information technology, China actively participates in the international standardization and drives bidirectional conversion of national standard and international standard. At present, China has set up cooperation

---

[1] "Xi Jinping Proposes Fundamental Principles for Building an International Internet Governance System", *China News*, Nov. 16, 2016, http://www.chinanews.com/gn/2016/11-16/8065105.shtml.

mechanisms in IT standardization with the European Union, Germany and the UK, with the international exchange and cooperation in key areas of IT standardization continuously progressing. Since 2014, China has actively advocated holding the World Internet Conference, establishing the international platforms for interconnection between China and the rest of the world and building a platform for global internet to be shared and governed by all. In terms of cybersecurity, China calls for putting in place a multilateral, democratic and transparent global internet governance system.

All the countries could jointly build and share the information infrastructure with international exchanges and collaboration. While advancing the global information technology, China's capability of informatization has been tremendously strengthened. Through the decades of development, China has made enormous progress in the capabilities of independent innovation in IT industry, IT application, information transmission and information security, and competitive edges and capabilities of China's informatization have been remarkably improved.

8.2.3   The strategy on developing a quality workforce

The improvement of workforce's quality is the decisive force of technological progress, and talented people are the key to innovation and development and an important strategic resource to keep a firm hold on the initiative of international competition. China deems it a major strategy to cultivate IT professionals in IT application, follows the principle of the Party exercising leadership over personnel, actively cultivates cultivate a large number of world-class scientists and technologists in strategically important fields, scientific and technological leaders, and young scientists and engineers, as well as high-performing innovation teams, and focuses on training innovation-oriented and inter-disciplinary talents.

In the cultivation of talented personal, China proposes the strategy of developing China through science and education and playing the full role of talents, implements national key talents programs, and gradually promote the development of the system talents pool. The CPC and Chinese government vigorously establishes IT talents training system with the combination of primary and vocational education and mutually complementary nonprofit and commercial training, unremittingly improves the cultivation, selection, application, appraisal and motivation of talents mechanism, strengthens the collaboration strengthen collaboration between industries, universities, research institutes, and users, and deepens order-based talent training to improve the ability of talent mapping.

Opinions of the CPC Central Committee on Deepening the Reform of the System Mechanism for Talent Development proposed to carry out the institutional mechanism reform for talent development and establish a personnel system that are internationally competitive. China constantly improves multi-levelled talents cultivation system with an integrated process of R&D design, production and management and service. Talents of IT application include both IT talents and IT management talents. The IT researchers, enterprise managers, IT users and government administrators are the important driving forces for information application advancement. Focusing on key talents projects, China increases its support for leading personnel in the information industry, and fosters world-class scientists, leading talents in network science and technology, outstanding engineers, high-level innovation teams and information managers. What's more, China formulated Grass-Roots Growth Plan for College Graduates, covering graduates from colleges and universities with policies support to vigorously cultivate them and improve talents cultivation mechanism. The CPC Central Committee and the State Council are committed to policy guidance and implement the projects of Doctorial Professional Service Group and Western Light Talent Culture to distribute talents, providing intellectual support for the economic advancement in the central and western regions.

In terms of building talents system, China cultivates inter-disciplinary talents in information industry, actively plays the role of the market mechanism in staffing, expands the opening up, and improves the policy of attracting talents from overseas, so as to attract and support high-level overseas talents to return to China for innovation and entrepreneurship. With the implementation of the strategy of making a strong country through talented personal, China has achieved great success in informatization. With the improvement of the high-tech talent pool, China will unleash its huge potential in IT application and greatly accelerate the process of socialist modernization.

8.2.4 The strategy of coordinated development

China always follows the coordinated development strategy in information industry, promotes the balanced development of upstream and downstream of industrial chain, eastern, central and western regions, urban and rural areas, and information technology and information security, endeavors to narrow and even eliminate digital divide, and achieves the comprehensive, harmonious, sound and sustainable development.

China follows the principle of energetically driving the coordinated development of the entire industrial chain and optimizing the whole production chain during the information technology development. During the industrial information, China positively strives for information throughout the whole life of products, thus forging the all-round information in R&D and design, production, management and operation, and aftersales. In agriculture, China takes information in the whole process as a goal to constructively boost joint informatization development in production, operation, management and services, and to drive the coordinated development throughout the entire industry chain.

Facing with the urban-rural dual structure in socio-economic development, China implements a policy to narrow the digital divide in the development of information technology, so as to narrow the gap in the access to use information resources and the level of IT application between different regions, urban and rural areas, and different social groups for a coordinated development. During the implementation of "Broadband China" Strategy, it gives a priority to advancing coordinated development of regional broadband networks and makes great efforts to the harmonious improvement of eastern, central and western regions and rural areas. First of all, China should support the network upgrade and innovative applications in the eastern region and take advantage of the eastern region to improve the level of information technology and narrow the gap with the world's advanced level. Secondly, China should give appropriate policy preference to the central and western regions, create a favorable policy environment for the development of information technology in the backward regions, and actively guide the R&D centers and innovation platforms to settle in the central and western regions. Like this, due to these preferential policies to incline to the central and western regions, China progressively forges information infrastructure and increases the nurture of IT talents to bring about an equal development to the society and eliminate regional differences during the informatization. During his research trip in the western region in 2014, Li Keqiang emphasized the need to accelerate the development of information infrastructure in the western region and promote the transfer of industries from the eastern region to the central and western regions, offering opportunities for the development of the central and western regions.

Moreover, China constantly strengthens the coordinated development of information technology in urban and rural areas. While insisting on the steady development of industrial information technology, it focuses on supporting the information technology in agriculture, rural areas and rural people. Since agriculture is the foundation of the national economy, China, as a large agricultural country, regards agriculture as the focus of national development of information technology, promotes the information technology in targeted poverty alleviation, and concurrently forges the construction of information infrastructure and poverty alleviation in rural areas. The CPC and Chinese government increase the support to the rural areas through diverse measures, including consolidating the construction of information infrastructure through internet access at low price or free, enhancing the access of information services to the public through public service platforms, strengthening farmers' information application level by education and training, improving their capabilities to have access to network information and making great efforts to eliminate the digital divide. The 19th CPC National Congress in 2017 proposed to implement the rural revitalization strategy, making the issues related to agriculture, rural areas and rural people the top priority of the Party's work. The development of the information technology for agriculture, rural areas and rural people is the key to rural revitalization, and informatization is indispensable for cultivating new agricultural business entities, building modern agricultural industrial system and realizing the integrated development of three major industries in rural areas.

In the development of information technology, China has always taken the safeguard of cybersecurity as a major task, and endeavored to deal with the relationship between cybersecurity and the development of information technology, promoting their coordinated development and progress. The government continually strengthens the function of national security supervision, actively establishes cybersecurity laws, enhances network culture building, cracks down cybercrimes, and purifies network ecology, thus creating a safe and sound environment for the development of information technology. Since the 18th CPC National Congress, the national leadership has attached great importance to the issue of cybersecurity. In 2014, the central government established the Central Leading Group for Cyberspace Affairs, with Xi Jinping as its leader, to plan and coordinate major issues of cybersecurity and informatization in various fields, including economy, politics, culture, society and military.

8.2.5 The strategy of development shared by all

China's development of information technology puts people first and implements the strategy of development shared by all, so as to make all Chinese people stronger sense of benefit in information technology. The CPC represents the development trend of China's advanced productive forces, the orientation of China's advanced culture, and the fundamental interests of the overwhelming majority of the Chinese people, with its fundamental purpose of serving the people wholeheartedly. The Party and State leaders put forward a people-centered development approach, focus on safeguarding and improving people's livelihood, and insist on making the fruits of reform and development benefit shared by all people in a greater and fairer way. On the way to lead all Chinese people to develop information technology and build a modern socialist country, the CPC has always put people first, making the fruits of development of information technology shared by all people and steadily moving the nation towards the goal of common prosperity.

When formulating the strategy of informatization, China proposed to put people first, deliver welfare and benefits to all the people, and foster an information environment available and affordable to the people. In the course of information infrastructure building, it set up public networks in remote rural areas at low price or free of charge, carried out the project of network's coverage to all villages, increased the internet usage in rural areas, and actively played the role of the internet in poverty alleviation. The implementation of the "Broadband China" Strategy and the "internet +" strategy has effectively reduced network fees, improved the universal service compensation mechanism for telecommunications, provided support for broadband construction, operation and maintenance in rural and remote areas, and made the internet accessible to an infrastructure that can be used by all industries, fields and regions, and interconnect people, machines and things ubiquitously. The country makes full use of the sharing nature of internet to provide a favorable public information service platform for all industries, sectors and social levels, and promotes the internet application in medical, health, transportation and other livelihood projects. In improving the protective measures for IT application, we shall channel great energy into developing inclusive finance, implementing preferential fiscal and taxation policies, and creating an environment for the development of information technology that benefits all people.

When implementing the IT application, China has built "12316" comprehensive information service platforms to provide services for farmers, agricultural technology, agricultural materials, agricultural loans, agricultural insurance, storage, logistics, and e-commerce, improving farmers' capabilities of scientific production and management. It has also implemented e-commerce poverty alleviation projects by establishing inclusive e-commerce platforms, e-commerce incubation centers and precise databases, making the fruits of modern information technology development available to every region and every citizen. The CPC and Chinese government pay great attention to the expectations and needs of the people, promote the equalization of basic public services by its application, develop the "internet + public services", and accelerate the development of emerging services based on the internet, such as medical care, health, elderly care, education, tourism and social security.

8.2.6 The strategy of sustainable development

The path of development of information technology with Chinese characteristics is a path of innovation, opening up, and coordinated, shared and sustainable development.

China adheres to the independent innovation, constantly increases investment in R&D, and improves the capability of independent innovation, forging a path of the innovative development of information technology, which is a road of sustainable development. In the process of new types of industrialization, agricultural modernization and informatization of service industry, only with independent intellectual property rights and mastery of key core technologies can China improve the capability to share profits in international cooperation and accumulate experiences for the national sustainable development.

What's more, China always adheres to the opening up, actively participates in economic globalization, integrates into the international division of labor system, and promotes the informatization in international exchanges and cooperation. There are differences in resource natural endowments and comparative edges of countries around the world, and only by laying out the industrial chain globally can we achieve optimal allocation of resources, reduce costs, and improve efficiency, so as to keep its competitive edge in international competition. Besides, it is propelling international cooperation in safeguarding cybersecurity to create a healthy and favorable international environment for the development of information technology. Therefore, the road of opening up and cooperation in informatization is also a road of the sustainable development.

China has consistently upheld the coordinated development of the eastern, central and western regions and of urban and rural areas. On the one hand, China is the largest developing country in the world with a vast geographical territory, and the problem of unbalanced development between regions has remained unresolved for a long time due to the factors such as resources, environment and history. As a result, the CPC Central Committee and the State Council have innovatively put forward the new industrialization driven by informatization, improved information infrastructure of the central and western regions, applied preferential policies to the central and western regions, and arranged more talented personal to serve the backward regions to provide permanent impetus for sustainable economic and social development. On the other hand, China, as a large agricultural country, has synergistically boosted agricultural modernization and informatization, driving the modernization of agriculture, rural areas and farmers by information technology, and implemented the rural revitalization strategy to promote the coordinated development of urban and rural areas. It has combined targeted poverty alleviation and informatization in agriculture, provided poor households with opportunities for development through information technology, information networks and information resources, and enhanced farmers' capacity to acquire, master and apply information technology, thus offering endogenous motivation for complete poverty alleviation. Therefore, the road of coordinated development of China's information technology is also a road of sustainable development.

China always puts people first and implements the strategy of development shared by all, so as to make all Chinese people stronger sense of benefit in information technology. By making good use of information technology, the CPC Central Committee and the State Council lead the people to common prosperity. The improvement of people's living standard will, in turn, create more and higher level of consumer demands and push the national economy to shift gear from high speed growth to quality growth, thus further promoting the development of information technology. Informatization has driven a virtuous circle and sustainable development. As a result, the road of shared development of information technology in China is also a path of sustainable development.

8.3   Challenges to informatization in China

The CPC Central Committee and the State Council attach great importance to the development of information technology, take it as a national strategy for development, actively make various policies, and constantly improve the supporting measures to accelerate the informatization. Although China has made great progress in informatization, there are also some problems demanding prompt solution, such as insufficient capacity for independent innovation in information technology, core technology and equipment controlled by others, insufficient development and utilization of information resources, low-level of application of information technology, unbalanced development of information technology, and cybersecurity issues.

8.3.1   Insufficient capacity for independent innovation in information technology

Although the size of China's internet users and the scale of the information industry have leaped to the forefront of the world, the development of China's core information technology is still sluggish. In particular, high-end chips, core software, key components, instruments and other areas of independent intellectual property rights are not competitive enough, and the external dependence on core technologies is high. At present, China's independent innovation capacity is insufficient, including inductors, high-precision sensors required for the development of the IoT, integrated circuits, key equipment of the flat-panel displays, automatic assembly machines, and parts of technologies and equipment rely on import for a long time. New-type display devices, covering high-performance integrated circuits, smart TVs, 5G technology R&D and high-speed broadband, smart hardware, and OLED, have become the hot spots for the development of a new generation of information technology. However, the innovation level of China's new generation of information technology R&D is not so high, China's electronic information industry in the international division of labor engages mainly in processing and manufacturing links, occupying the lower end of the global value chain with the low value-added of products. The lack of independent innovative capability of the key core technologies in China poses a serious challenge to the security in national defense, military and other fields.

China's independent innovation capacity of information technology is not strong, for the main position of technological innovation of enterprises has not been given full play. The lack of comprehensive, inter-disciplined and professional IT personnel is also an important factor leading to the insufficient independent innovation capability in China. The imperfection of training systems have hindered the qualified IT personnel development. The disconnection between the theoretical training of and the practical IT application leads to a low conversion rate of scientific research achievements, which further affects the development of information technology in China.

8.3.2 Improving the utilization of information resources

After a long period of development, China has established more comprehensive databases for population basic information, corporation basic information, natural resources and space-geographic basic information, macro-economy, and cultural information resources, etc., which has accumulated abundant information resources for the development of information technology. However, because of the low level of information resource utilization in China, the IT industry failed to give full play its role in the improvement of economy and society.

At present, the development of information technology in China has entered a stage of promoting in various fields and at different levels in an all-round way, with the increasing demand for information technology. However, the potential of information technology has not yet been fully realized, and the IT lags behind the actual demand, especially in the regions with more backward economic level and the vast rural areas. In addition, there is the problem of insufficient productivity transformation of research results. Constrained by the unsound scientific and technological innovation service system and the imperfect development of science and technology intermediaries such as science and technology incubation centers, a disconnection exists between scientific and technological achievements and practical applications.

8.3.3   Unbalanced development in IT application

Influenced by the dual economic structure, urban-rural dual structure of China's development of information technology is also prominent. There is a large gap between different regions, different fields and different social groups in terms of the level of IT application, network penetration and overall level of informatization, and the digital divide between urban and rural areas, regions and industries is still evident. In the fields of integration of informatization and industrialization, the gap between the eastern, central and western regions is increasingly expanding. Data from China Center for Information Industry Development show that the average index of the integration of informatization and industrialization in 2015 was 86.06 in the eastern region, 73.40 in the central region, and 59.93 in the western region. In recent years, although the state has increased its policy support for the informatization in agriculture, rural areas and rural people, the information gap between rural and urban areas is still prominent and the digital divide still remains due to the lagging development of rural network and information infrastructure and the low level of information technology mastered by farmers.

8.3.4   The rampant problem of cybersecurity

The national information security management system continues to be improved, but the problem of China's cybersecurity is rampant, where the proliferation of network viruses, hacking patterns, a large number of network security vulnerabilities, a variety of network attacks, network theft, cyberterrorism and cybercrime are still serious. China's information network security legislation is lagging behind, with fewer and lower levels of internet-related legislation. As China's cybersecurity management institutions have scattered resources, limited full-time management personnel, and scarce high-end technical personnel, capabilities of information security monitoring and emergency command need to be improved.

There is no national security without cybersecurity. China has not yet established a complete national information security protection system, management system and supervision system. Moreover, internet users have weak awareness of security and lack of independent judgment of complex network information and a high alertness to cybercrime. As a result, cybersecurity is still a key problem to be solved in China's informatization.

8.4 Outlook on informatization with Chinese characteristics

Today, the development of information technology is a major trend in the world's socio-economic development, and is an inevitable choice for China to accelerate modernization and industrialization. After more than 40 years of the reform and opening up, China has gradually improved its level of information technology, accelerated the integration of information technology with agriculture, industry and services, and the continuously optimized traditional industrial structure. Accordingly, the information industry has become a new growth area in economy, and the digital economy has entered the fast lane of development. At present, China has entered a new era of socialism with Chinese characteristics and is in the critical development stage of building a moderately prosperous society and achieving the great rejuvenation of the Chinese nation. The principal challenge facing Chinese society has evolved into the gap between imbalanced and insufficient development and the people's growing expectations for a better life. Therefore, in the new era, China must be committed to pursuing the path of socialist modernization under the leadership of the CPC, and the path of development of information technology with Chinese characteristics, driving modernization with information technology, continuously enhancing the country's capacity of informatization, and making information technology better benefit the society and the whole people.

8.4.1 Improving information infrastructure by building a three-dimensional ubiquitous network

Information infrastructure, especially network basic infrastructure, is the basis for the development of information technology, an extremely important information resource, and a crux deciding success or failure of informatization. The CPC and Chinese government have made it a strategic priority for the national development of information technology to improve the comprehensive information infrastructure and build a ubiquitous network with three-dimensional coverage of land, ocean, air and aerospace.

Since ubiquitous and sophisticated infrastructure is the cornerstone of information development, China is accelerating the implementation of strategies such as "Broadband China" strategy and "internet +" to consolidate the network foundation and actively build the infrastructure for the ubiquitous interconnection of people, machines and things. First, it organizes and implements a new generation of information infrastructure construction project, promotes the integration of the three networks from the aspects of business, network and terminal, implements the optical transformation of broadband network, and greatly increases the network access rate. Second, it accelerates the application of photoelectric sensor, RFID and others to expand network functions, realizes the transformation to the next-generation network, and facilitates the business application of the next-generation internet. Third, it actively boosts the full coverage of network in rural areas step by step, and covers remote areas, forest-pastoral areas, islands and other areas with mobile cellular and satellite communications, so as to achieve coordinated development between urban and rural regions, and accomplish full coverage of broadband networks, 3G and 4G networks. Fourth, it speeds up the independent R&D of new technologies in key areas such as broadband wireless communications, next-generation broadcast and television networks, next-generation internet, cloud computing, and the IoT, actively participates in the formulation of international standards, and enhances the capacity for independent development. Fifth, it coordinates the construction and application of the BeiDou Satellite Navigation System, improves the global service capability of the BeiDou satellites, and builds an information network that integrates the space and the earth and interconnects with each other.

The common development and shared growth of network information infrastructure are the future development trends. Therefore, the CPC and Chinese government should energetically introduce civil society resources into the construction of information infrastructure to improve market vitality, actively optimize the layout of international networks, carry out joint R&D of technologies, strengthen international cooperation in network infrastructure resources, promote the favorable medium for development of the international internet, and provide a good international environment as well as high-quality information infrastructure for the development of information technology.

8.4.2   Comprehensively reforming the application of IoT and other new generation of information technology

The IoT is an intensive integration and comprehensive application of the next-generation information technology, and the strategic focus of China's information technology development lies in building an internationally competitive IoT industry system and creating an economic society with smartness, refinement, and networking. At present, China already has a certain foundation in the development of the IoT with a high level in technology research and development, industrial cultivation, and industry applications, so the typical feature of the future development of information technology in China are the new generation of information technology innovation and development represented by the IoT and its application in the economic and social fields.

In order to promote the orderly and healthy development of the IoT, China needs to make overall plans, take enterprises as the principal part and application demand as the orientation, and create an internationally competitive IoT industry system, IoT data network and integrated management system through innovative development. First, the state plans to build about 20 IT innovation centers and improve the new generation of information technology innovation platform during the 13th Five-year Plan. Supported by the IoT technology R&D laboratories, engineering centers and enterprise technology centers and other innovation platforms, significant breakthroughs have been made in basic common technologies, including the core IoT chip, software, instrumentation, and in key technologies, covering sensor networks, smart terminals, big data processing, intelligent analysis, service integration, providing the technical basis for the industrial application of the IoT. Second, China continuously innovates the policy system conducive to the development of the IoT, improves the service support system for its developments, establishes special funds for its development, and strengthens fiscal levy policy support, fostering a benign environment for the healthy development of the IoT. Third, with the innovative development of IoT technology and the improvement of the IoT support and protection system, China gradually improves the level of application of the IoT, accelerates the transformation and upgrading of traditional industries, promotes energy conservation and emission reduction, and ensures safe production. The integration and sharing nature of the IoT will promote its comprehensive application in economic fields such as industry, agriculture and trade circulation, as well as public services such as social security, healthcare and livelihood services. On November 21, 2017, China successfully launched Jilin-1 Video 04, 05 and 06 satellites, and the observation capacity of the constellation has been significantly improved, which will promote the development of China's remote sensing industry as well as the application of the IoT. The IoT connects sensors, controllers, machines and workers together, enabling remote management as well as intelligent production and promoting further productivity improvements.

8.4.3   Deepening the integration of informatization and industrialization and promoting intelligent and green manufacturing

Innovation and integration are key factors in the development of information technology, so China constantly strengthens the integration of informatization and industrialization strategy based on innovation development. Since the reform and opening up, it has always taken the integration of informatization and industrialization strategy as the central task. The 16th CPC National Congress proposed to adhere to the new industrialization road of driving industrialization by informatization and promoting informatization with industrialization; the 17th CPC National Congress put forward to vigorously facilitate the integrated development of informatization and industrialization, and build an industrial power; the Fifth Plenary Session of the 17th CPC Central Committee and the 18th CPC National Congress further proposed to forge the deep integration of informatization and industrialization; the 19th CPC National Congress required to drive the integrated development of new industrialization, informatization, urbanization and agricultural modernization. Since then, China has adhered to the new path of industrialization with Chinese characteristics, further implemented the integration of informatization and industrialization strategy, gradually upgraded and optimized the industrial structure through informatization, and achieved intelligent manufacturing, green manufacturing and service-oriented manufacturing.

Under the leadership of the National Leading Group for the Construction of a Manufacturing Power and the overall planning and policy coordination of relevant government departments, the major projects and key projects of the integration of informatization and industrialization strategy have been gradually facilitated and implemented, and the pace of transformation and upgrading of traditional industries has been accelerated. Guided by the strategy of Made in China 2025, China will keep up accelerating its progress towards the ranks of manufacturing powerhouses led by innovation. Mobile internet, big data, cloud computing, IoT and other new generation of information technology will accelerate innovation and spread application in the manufacturing sector, promoting the transformation of "Made in China" to "Intelligent Manufacturing in China". China sticks to the strategic approach of making full use of the selected units to promote work in the entire area, unremittingly implements intelligent manufacturing demonstration project, and actively carries out intelligent manufacturing demonstration city pilot, key industry demonstration of intelligent manufacturing in batches by stages, gradually spreading the successful experience, and progressively achieving the intelligent transformation in enterprise workshops, departments, and factories. Therefore, it should take advantage of enterprises' dominant role, increase investment in R&D, strengthen the integration between industries, universities and research institutes, improve enterprises' capability of independent innovation, and promote the automation of the production process and the level of information technology.

The comprehensive improvement of green manufacturing based on information technology is the strategic task and focus of building China a strong manufacturing country. The integration and development of information technology and traditional manufacturing will further promote energy conservation and emission reduction, reduce environmental pollution, and truly realize green manufacturing. The country should build a low-carbon, recycling, intensive green manufacturing system by increasing the R&D of advanced energy-saving and environmental protection technologies, accelerate the green upgrading and transformation of manufacturing industries, and promote the efficient recycling of resources. Under the national integrated planning and deployment, it should promote technologies to enable products that are lightweight, low power, and recyclable, gradually eliminate backward technology, and comprehensively impel the green transformation of traditional manufacturing industries such as iron and steel, non-ferrous, chemical, building materials, light industry, printing and dyeing. Besides, it should also actively build a green supply chain, accelerate the establishment of low-carbon, environmentally friendly, energy-saving systems for procurement, production, marketing, logistics and recycling, and achieve green development of the entire industry chain.

In the process of industrialization driven by informatization, the internet has played an increasingly important role in the transformation and upgrading of traditional industrial projects, and the information technology in the industrial production system will give rise to diversified new manufacturing services, including industrial R&D and design services, industrial software, information services and modern logistics, etc. With the overall information technology in the manufacturing field, the development of the productive service industry for the integration of informatization and industrialization will be accelerated to promote the production of manufacturing to the high-end extension of the value chain. China should promote the synergistic development of production and services, facilitate the transformation of low-end production-based manufacturing to service-based manufacturing, and continuously develop new forms of online support services, personalized customization services, and network precision marketing.

8.4.4   Further promoting the informatization in agriculture

Promoting agricultural development with modern information technology has become a momentous strategic deployment for the transformation of traditional agriculture to a modern one in China. Since the release of the No.1 Central Document for 2014. Entitled Several Opinions on Comprehensively Deepening Agricultural Reform to Promote Agricultural Modernization proposed to build the technology system of informatization and mechanization in the entire process of agricultural production, the IT application is the key to China's agricultural modernization. The full integration of the modern information technology, such as agricultural IoT, precision equipment, big data and cloud computing, and the whole agricultural process, covering production, operation, management and service, is beneficial to the intelligent agriculture, precision agriculture, and digital agriculture, which improves the agricultural productivity and efficiency. With the application of cloud computing in the whole agricultural industrial chain, the application systems gradually get improved, such as agricultural information resource storage, monitoring and management of agri-ecological environment, intelligent monitoring and control of agricultural production process, tracing to the source of quality and safety of agricultural products and follow-up management of agricultural products logistics, which advance agricultural scientific decision-making, automatic monitoring capability and agricultural warehousing and logistics efficiency.

With the implementation of the pilot project of applying agricultural technology in villages, rural broadband pilot project, project of full coverage of communications for every village, and direct broadcast satellite communication project, information services are gradually popularized, and the information infrastructure in rural areas is accelerated and improved. A favorable basic environment will speed up the comprehensive and deep integration of informatization and agricultural modernization.

With the continuous improvement of rural information infrastructure, internet-based rural e-commerce will become an important driving force for future development of information technology in agriculture. With the support of national policies, the Ministry of Agriculture and the Ministry of Commerce continue to promote the construction of public service platforms for agricultural business information and comprehensive demonstration of rural e-commerce, continuously developing the e-commerce for agricultural products and for agricultural production materials, thus driving the development of the county-level economy.

With a review of the experience gained from the first phase of the E-Agriculture Project, China is actively planning the second phase. The implementation of the second phase will further improve the national agricultural monitoring and management information system, national agricultural e-government system, service support system and information resource system and promote the quality and level of agricultural information services, thus providing a high-quality, high-level comprehensive information service system for the rapid development of agricultural modernization.

8.4.5   Boosting IT application in enterprises with the integrated e-commerce

In the era of internet economy, e-commerce has become the new area of growth in China's economy. China has seized the global trend of the development of information technology, implemented the "internet +" strategy to continuously improve the development environment of e-commerce, innovate the policy system, and carry out e-commerce demonstration projects, and has actively cultivated new areas and new business models of e-commerce. The full integration of the overall e-commerce between e-commerce and enterprise supply chain will become the main form of e-commerce development in China.

The integrated e-commerce based on global supply chain will create a new business management concept and become an important means of enterprise information development. With the continuous improvement of the IT application in enterprises, the internal operation and management, the business activities of each link in the upstream and downstream of the enterprise supply chain and the business activities of enterprises, such as the whole business activities of production and operation, will be networked, digitalized and electronized. Based on global supply chain network management, the integrated e-commerce can build a collaboration platform of global supply chain for enterprises, integrate enterprise management, information technology and business activities, and continuously improve the quality of business management and expand business scope. Therefore, enterprises should have a global vision and actively build an overall e-commerce platform to realize the IT application and networking of internal business management, e-commerce transactions and partnership management through an integrated e-commerce portal, business collaboration platform and enterprise management system, so as to boost the high-speed development of enterprises.[1]

As early as 2006, Beijing Netcom Online Network Technology Co., Ltd. publicly proposed to build an integrated e-commerce platform, and then Chongqing Golden Abacus Software Co., Ltd. released the first integrated e-commerce platform of ERP software and e-commerce applications for SMEs in China.[2] Due to the innovative development of information technology and the improvement of IT application in enterprises, the integrated e-commerce that integrates enterprises, suppliers, distributors and customers in one platform will become the inevitable trend of future e-commerce development. Thanks to the openness of the platform and the full range of services, enterprises are able to obtain integrated services in business management, thus obtaining unlimited business opportunities with higher efficiency. With the economic globalization and the development of cross-border e-commerce, the integrated e-commerce based on information technology and the internet will increasingly become a choice of a number of enterprises.

8.4.6 Moving from a large network country to a strong cyberpower

China continues to implement the strategy of strengthening China through internet technology and accelerate the transformation of its economy and society. Since the 18th CPC National Congress, the CPC Central Committee with Xi Jinping as its core, has accelerated the deployment to comprehensively implement the strategy of building China a cyberpower. In 2014, Xi Jinping first proposed a vision for building a strong cyberpower at the first meeting of the Central Leading Group for Cyberspace Affairs: "We should, based on both the international and domestic situations, make overall plans, coordinate all related parties, promote innovative development, and work hard to build China into a cyberpower."[3] The Proposals of the CPC Central Committee of Formulating the 13th Five-Year Plan for National Economic and Social Development issued at the Fifth Plenary Sessions of the 18th CPC Central Committee in 2015 proposed to implement the strategy of building China a cyberpower.

To achieve China's progress from a large network country to a strong cyberpower, joint efforts must be made in the following areas: first, strengthening the leading role of

---

[1] Mao Huayang, Wei Ran, "Discussion on the Development and Framework Model of Whole-Course E-commerce", *China Management Informatization*, 2008(17), pp. 95-97.

[2] Wu Cheng, *Integrated Strategic Research on Informatization: Review, Status Quo and Foresight of China's Information*, Beijing: Science Press, 2013, p. 236.

[3] Zhang Yang, "Pressing Ahead for a Cyberpower: An Overview on Promotion of Cybersecurity and Informatization", *People's Daily*, Nov. 27, 2017.

innovation and accelerating the research and development of key core technologies with independent intellectual property rights; second, building and improving comprehensive information infrastructure to provide hardware support for IT application; third, establishing a rich and comprehensive information service platform to offer an all-weather, omnidirectional services for IT application; fourth, cultivating innovative and complex information technology and cybersecurity talents to provide talent support for IT application; fifth, speeding up the legislative process and improving the laws and regulations and policy supervision system for internet information content management and critical information infrastructure protection; sixth, proceeding with the implementation of institutional reforms as well as preferential fiscal policies to combine institutional innovation and technological innovation and encourage enterprises to become the entities of technological innovation and IT application; seventh, carrying out cyberspace governance and building a good network ecology; eighth, actively conducting international exchanges and cooperation, following principle of consultation and cooperation for shared benefits, and allowing people to share the fruits of internet development.

Guided by the vision of innovative, coordinated, green, open and shared development, the CPC has led the people of all ethnic groups in China to struggle for the historical achievements of reform and opening up and socialist modernization, developing a path of information development in line with the reality of the primary stage of development of socialism with Chinese characteristics. The information development path with Chinese characteristics has been explored in practice, and is a choice of history and the people. With the advancement of socialist modernization, China's road of IT application will also continue to advance with reforms. In the new era of building socialism with Chinese characteristics, the CPC will continue to implement the people-centered development concept, persist in deepening reforms, innovating management systems and improving various safeguards, boost the integrated development of new industrialization, informatization, urbanization, and agricultural modernization, and promote the development of national information technology to a higher level, so as to build China a strong modern country in the world and realize the great rejuvenation of the Chinese nation.

Bibliography

[1] Bai Chenxing, "The Problems of Logistics Informationization in China and Its Solutions", *Reformation & Strategy*, 2010(6).

[2] Bao Lin, Zhu Sen, "The Popularization of Internet in China and Its Countermeasures for Development", *Practical Electronics*, 2013(5).

[3] Bart van Ark，Robert Inklaar and Robert H. McGuckin, "ICT and Productivity in Europe and United States. Where Do the Differences Come From?", *CESifo Economic Studies*, 2003, 3(49), pp. 295-318.

[4] Bi Hongwen, Li Jinxia and Song Lijuan, "Status and Trends of Agricultural and Internet of Things Research in China Based on Bibliometrics", *Northern* Horticulture, 2015(24).

[5] Bu Xuan, "The Growth Rate of China's Internet Business Revenue Steadily Increased in the First Half of the Year", *China Electronics News*, Aug. 8, 2017.

[6] Charles K. Wilber, *The Political Economy of Development and Underdevelopment*, Chinese Edition, translated by Gao Zuan et al., Beijing:The Commercial Press, 2015.

[7] Chen Fei, Kang Song, "Considerations on Promotion of Agriculture Informatization in China", *Research of Agricultural Modernization*, 2006(2).

[8] Chen Guipeng, He Junhai and Su Xiaobo et al., "Design and Implementation of Tea Garden Environment Monitoring System Based on Wireless Sensor Network", *Guangdong Agricultural Sciences*, 2014(14).

[9] Chen Jiaxi, "A Chinese Solution to Internet Development and Governance: a Study of Xi Jinping's Thought on Network Governance", *Theoretical Horizon*, 2017(7).

[10] Chen Jiayi, Xu Ling, "Analysis of the Present Situation and Development Prospect of Logistics Informatization in China", *Logistics Sci-Tech*, 2016(6).

[11] Chen Jiushan, "Jiangxi Yudu: Practice and Exploration of E-Commerce and Poverty Alleviation", *China State Finance*, 2016(2).

[12] Chen Lidan, Wang Min, "Study on the Current Situation of Internet Development in China: Interpretation of ITU 2014 Measuring the Information Society Report", *Journalism Lover*, 2016(1).

[13] Chen Xiaohua, *Introduction to Agricultural Informatization*, Beijing: China Agriculture Press, 2012.

[14] Chen Xiaoqin, Wang Zhao, "Discussion on the Implementation Path of Rural E-Commerce Poverty Alleviation under the Background of Internet +", *Journal of Socialist Theory Guide*, 2017(5).

[15] Chen Yuan, "Model Studies Based on Consumer Demand C2B E-commerce", *Pioneering with Science & Technology Monthly*, 2013(6).

[16] Chen Yundi, "The Development Process of China's Informatization", *Digital Space*, 2003(2).

[17] Cheng Dening, Wang Hao and Huang Yang, "Transformation and Upgrading of China's Agricultural Industry Chain Under the Background of 'Internet + Agriculture'", *Rural Economy*, 2017(5).

[18] Chinainfo100, China Information Economy Development Report China Info 100 Website, Jan. 14, 2017.

[19] Chu Chengxiang, Mao Huiqin, "Create a New Model of Agricultural Information Service", *China Telecommunications Trade*, 2012(6).

[20] Committee for Cadre Training Series Knowledge on Deep Fusion of Information and Industrialization, *Book of Manufacturing Transformation for Cadres*, Beijing: Publishing House of Electronics Industry, 2012.

[21] Committee for Cadre Training Series Knowledge on Deep Fusion of Information and Industrialization, *Book of Innovative Development of Producer Service Industry for Cadres*, Beijing: Publishing House of Electronics Industry, 2012.

[22] Cui Wenshun, "The Application and Development Prospects of Cloud Computing in Agricultural Informatization", *Agricultural Engineering*, 2012(1).

[23] Ding Liang, Fan Zhimin, "Scientific Connotation and Historical Position of Rural informatization", *Journal of Xi'an University of Finance and Economics*, 2015(2).

[24] Ding Riqing, "Is China's Government Heading in the Right Direction for Cloud Computing?", *Internet Weekly*, 2012(10).

[25] Donald J. Bowersox, David J. Closs and M. Bixby Cooper et al., *Supply Chain Logistics Management*, Chinese Edition, translated by Ma Shihua, Zhang Huiyu, Beijing: China Machine Press, 2014.

[26] Dong Liren, "Intelligent Governance: A Study of Government Governance

Innovation in the 'Internet +' Era", *Administration Reform*, 2016(12).

[27] Fang Binxing, Du Aning and Zhang Xi et al., "Research on the International Strategy for National Cyberspace Security", *Strategic Study of CAE*, 2016(6).

[28] Fang Xia, "Analysis on the Status and Development Factors of Internet of Things in China", *Application of Electronic Technique*, 2010(6).

[29] Feng Xing, Wei Shuai, "Research on the Development Status and Problems of Internet Finance in China", *Business*, 2016(18).

[30] Fritz Machlup, *The Production and Distribution of Knowledge in the United States*, Princeton: Princeton University Press, 1962.

[31] Fujian Information Association, "Scientific Development Report of E-Government in Fujian Province", *Channel Science*, 2011(1).

[32] Gao Puo et al., "The Development Prospect of and Suggestion on Rural E-Commerce in China", *Modern Agricultural Sciences and Technology*, 2016(3).

[33] Gao Xinmin, "Understanding of National Informatization Development Strategy and Current Main Tasks", *The Chinese Journal of ICT in Education*, 2014(11).

[34] Guo Chengzhong, "China's Information Construction Has a Long Way to Go", *China Electronics News*, Dec. 14, 2004.

[35] Guo Chengzhong, "Information Story One: Review on China's Informatization", *China Information Times*, 2004(18).

[36] Guo Chengzhong, "Information Story Two: Review on China's Informatization", *China Information Times*, 2004(19).

[37] Guo Leifeng, Qian Xueliang and Chen Guipeng et al., "Application Status and Prospect of IoT in Agriculture: A Case Study of Application of Agricultural Production Environment Supervising", *Agricultural Outlook*, 2015(9).

[38] Guo Li, "Analysis of the Current Situation of the Integration of Informatization and Industrialization in China", *Informatization Construction*, 2012(2).

[39] Guo Shaohua, "Investigation and Reflection on the Development of Agricultural Informatization in China", *Agricultural Archaeology*, 2011(6).

[40] Han Yu, "On Security of Electronic Information Industry in China: Problems and Countermeasures", *Tianjin Science & Technology*, 2015(12).

[41] He Jinsong, "The First Meeting of the National Informatization Leading Group Held in Beijing", *Engineering Geology Computer Application*, 2002(25).

[42] He Xinzhou, "Development Trend of Mobile Internet and its Impact on the China's Economy", *China Computer & Communication*, 2015(18).

[43] He Ying, "Ideas for the Construction of China's Manufacturing Innovation

Index System", *China Industry Review*, 2015(9).

[44] He Yong, Nie Pengcheng and Liu Fei, "Advancement and Trend of Internet of Things in Agriculture and Sensing Instrument", *Transactions of the Chinese Society of Agricultural Machinery*, 2013(10).

[45] He Zizhen, "Research on the Development and Existing Problems of Internet Finance in China", *Managers' Journal*, 2015(8).

[46] Hong Yi, Du Ping, *Annual Report on China's E-Government Development (2012)*, Beijing: Social Sciences Academic Press, 2013.

[47] Hou Qianru, Lin Yang and Guo Pengfei, "Study on the Present Situation and Countermeasures of Agricultural Informatization in China", *China Agricultural Information*, 2011(3).

[48] Hu Angang, "China's Featured Independent Innovative (1949-2012)", *Bulletin of Chinese Academy of Sciences*, 2014(2).

[49] Hu Jintao, "Firmly March on the Path of Socialism with Chinese Characteristics and Strive to Complete the Building of a Moderately Prosperous Society in All Respect", *People's Daily*, Nov. 9, 2012.

[50] Hu Jintao, "Hold High the Great Banner of Socialism with Chinese Characteristics and Strive for New Victories in Building a Moderately Prosperous Society in All Respects", *People's Daily*, Oct. 25, 2007.

[51] Hu Junrong, "New Development Trend and Scientific Development Law of Electronic Information industry", *Electronics World*, 2012(11).

[52] Huang Hao, "Issues and Policy Recommendations for the Construction of E-Commerce Demonstration Bases in China", *E-Business Journal*, 2013(8).

[53] Hui Fang, Xu Heng and Liu Jing, "A Leap Forward of the Overall Strength of Industrialization and Informatization in 12th Five-Year Period", *China Electronics News*, Dec. 25, 2015.

[54] I. A. Essa, "Ubiquitous Sensing for Smart and Aware Environments. Technologies Towards the Building of an Aware Home", *IEEE Personal Communications*, 2000, 5(7), pp. 47-49.

[55] Immanuel Maurice Wallerstein, *The Modern World-System*, Chinese Edition, translated by Guo Fang et al., Beijing: Social Sciences Academic Press, 2013.

[56] "Implementation Opinions of Jilin Province Leading Group on Taking the Lead in Realizing Agricultural Modernization in 2016", *Jilin Agriculture*, 2016 (10).

[57] "Interpretation of the 12th Five-Year National Government Informatization Project Construction", *Cc News*, 2017(9).

[58] Jia Wenyi, "Overview of the Development of O2O E-Commerce Model in China: An Analysis of the Current Situation, Problems and Countermeasures", *Journal of Commercial Economics*, 2016(24).

[59] Jiang Hongbo, *Introduction to Electronic Commerce*, Beijing: Tsinghua University Press, 2009.

[60] Jiang Yongsheng, Peng Junjie and Zhang Wu, "Cloud Computing and Standardization of Cloud Computing Implementation: Review and Exploration", *Journal of Shanghai University (Natural Science Edition)*, 2013(1).

[61] Jiang Zemin, "New Characteristics in the Development in Worldwide Electronic & Information Industry and Strategic Considerations of the Development in Electronic & Information Industry in China", *Journal of Shanghai Jiaotong University*, 1989(6).

[62] Jiang Zemin, "New Characteristics in the Development in Worldwide Electronic & Information Industry and the Development Strategic Issues of China", *Forum on Science and Technology in China*, 1991(1).

[63] Jin Jiangjun, Shen Tiyan, *Integration of Informatization and Industrialization: Approaches and Practice*, Beijing: China Renmin University Press, 2012.

[64] Jorge Verissimo Pereira, "The New Supply Chain's Frontier: Information Management", *International Journal of Information Management*, 2009, 5(29), pp. 372-379.

[65] Karl Marx, *Das Kapital*, Vol.1, Beijing: People's Publishing House, 2004.

[66] Kong Fantao, Zhang Jianhua and Wu Jianzhai et al., *Research on the Development of Agriculture Whole Process Informatization*, Beijing: Science Press, 2015.

[67] Lang Xianping, *Saving China's Manufacturing Industry*, Beijing: The Oriental Press, 2015.

[68] Li Bing, Wang Yang, "Leapfrogging into the Information Society: Rapidly Overcoming the 'High Altitude Reaction'", *Information China*, 2010(12).

[69] Li Boqun, "The Development Status and Prospect of E- Commerce in China", *The World of Survey and Research*, 2015(1).

[70] Li Daoliang, *Rural Informatization and Digital Agriculture*, Beijing: China Architecture and Building Press, 2010.

[71] Li Fengchun, Tang Duan, "Probing the Way for Targeted Poverty Alleviation Through Agricultural Products E-Commerce", *Governance*, 2015(33).

[72] Li Guan, *Modern Enterprise Information and Management*, Beijing: Tsinghua University Press, 2014.

[73] Li Guangqin, "Industrialization Driving Informationization or Informationization Driving Industrialization: an Empirical Analysis Based on the Revised Fider Model", *Statistics & Information Forum*, 2014(5).

[74] Li Jian, Wang Jing and Kang Ping et al., "Research on the Application Status and Development Countermeasures of Agricultural Internet of Things Technology in China", *Internal Combustion Engine & Parts*, 2017(9).

[75] Li Shenglong, Zhang Yibao, "The Research of Electricity Suppliers Poverty Alleviation in Remote Areas: An Example of Tongren, Guizhou", *Journal of Guizhou University of Engineering Science*, 2016(6).

[76] Li Wanshan, "Exploration on Present Situation and Trend of Development of the Mobile Internet in China", *Wireless Internet Technology*, 2015(19).

[77] Li Xingshan, *Theory and Practice of the Socialist Market Economy*, Beijing: Central Party School Press, 2004.

[78] Li Yizhong, "Present Situation and Prospect of Industry and Informatization Development in China", *Electric Age*, 2010(1).

[79] Li Yong, Zhang Jiang and Guo Bin, "Analysis of the Development Trend and Current Development Status of the Electronic Information Industry", *Practical Electronics*, 2015(24).

[80] Li Zhongmin, "Development Status and Strategies for Internet of Things in China", *Computer Era*, 2011(3).

[81] Lin Zhenqiang, "Development of E-Commerce and Construction of a Logistic System", *Logistics & Material Handling*, 2012(9).

[82] Liu Benzhi, "Promote Agricultural Industrialization with Information Agriculture", *China Information Times*, 2004(11).

[83] Liu Guoguang, "Party and Government's Effort to Promote China's Informatization", *Information China*, 2004(21).

[84] Liu Haikun, "Analysis of Computer Network Security Under the Background of 'Cloud Computing'", *Minying Keji*, 2016(12).

[85] Liu Jifang, Kong Fantao and Wu Jianzhai et al., "Discussion on Development of 'Internet +' Modern Agriculture", *Guizhou Agricultural Sciences*, 2017(3).

[86] Liu Jin, Gu Jiaqiang, "The Status Quo and Development Strategy of Internet of Things in China", *Enterprise Economy*, 2013(4).

[87] Liu Meirong, "Research on the Development Trend of Mobile Internet in China", *Knowledge Economy*, 2014(10).

[88] Liu Mingzhi, Lyu Bingbing, "Linqu County: Growing Peaches Through

Internet of Things", *Farmers's Daily*, Aug. 17, 2017.

[89] Liu Shengqi, "A Comparative Study on the Three Competitive Force Models of Electronic Information Industry Chain", *Practical Electronics*, 2016(22).

[90] Liu Wanqiang, Wang Bo, "Research on Current Situation and Development of Logistics Informatization in China", *Logistics Sci-Tech*, 2006(8).

[91] Liu Xiaohui, *Logistics Information Management*, Beijing: China Logistics Publishing House, 2007.

[92] Liu Xinwei, "The Two 'Dark Horses' of E-Commerce and Express Delivery are Driving Hand in Hand", *China's Foreign Trade*, 2017(7).

[93] Liu Yan, "Weiku Guides Whole-Course E-Commerce", *Science and Technology Daily*, Apr. 7, 2010.

[94] Lu Lina, "The Main Problems and Solutions of Agricultural Informatization in China", *Guangming Daily*, Jul. 14, 2004.

[95] Lu Rong, Zhu Mei, "Accelerating the Construction of Rural Infrastructure to Strengthen the Cornerstone of a Well-Off Society in an All-round Way", *Guiyang Daily*, Jan. 30, 2016.

[96] Lu Shan, *The Blue Book on the Development of Informatization in China (2015-2016)*, Beijing: People's Publishing House, 2016.

[97] Lu Shan, *The Blue Book on the Integration of Informatization and Industrialization in China (2015)*, Beijing: People's Publishing House, 2016.

[98] Lu Xin, "The Status and Tendency of Information and Internet Security", *Information China*, 2008(10).

[99] Luo Junzhou, Jin Jiahui and Song Aibo et al., "Cloud Computing: Architecture and Key Technologies", *Journal on Communications*, 2011(7).

[100] Luo Yi, "Study on Agricultural E-commerce in China: A Research Based on Cases", *China Business and Market*, 2012(9).

[101] Lyu Xinkui, *Chinese Informatization*, Beijing: Publishing House of Electronics Industry, 2002.

[102] Lyu Liansheng, "Research on Primary Trend of Agriculture Internet of Things and Countermeasures of Anhui Province", *Sci-Tech innovation and Productivity*, 2013(2).

[103] M. Kashiha, C. Bahr and S. A. Haredasht et al., "The Automatic Monitoring of Pigs Water Use by Cameras", *Computers and Electronics in Agriculture*, 2013(90), pp. 164-169.

[104] Ma Yan, Xun Ye, "Development and Innovation of Logistics Informatization

in China's Logistics Enterprises", *Logistics Engineering and Management*, 2012(1).

[105] Mao Huayang, Wei Ran, "The Discussion about the Development and Construction Model of the Integrated (Entire Process) E-Commerce", *China Management Informationization*, 2008(17).

[106] Marign Janssen, Anton Joha, "Emerging Shared Service Organizations and the Service-oriented Enterprise: Critical Management Issues", *Strategic Outsourcing: An International Journal*, 2008, 1(1), pp. 35-48.

[107] Mark Weiser, "The Computer for the 21st Century", *Scientific American*, 1991, 3(1), pp. 66-75.

[108] Mei Fangquan, "Strategic Analysis of Agricultural Informatization in Driving Agricultural Modernization", *Chinese Rural Economy*, 2001(12).

[109] Meng Seren, "The Construction of Electronic Information Industry Development Mode", *Electronic Technology & Software Engineering*, 2017(1).

[110] Min Lu, "Brief Introduction to the Development Status and Trend of China's Mobile Internet", *China's Science and Technology Information*, 2015(1).

[111] National Manufacturing Strategy Advisory Committee, *China Manufacturing 2025 Bluebook (2016)*, Beijing: Publishing House of Electronics Industry, 2016.

[112] Nie Linhai, "Policy Interpretation of the Creation of National E-Commerce Model Cities", *China Venture Capital*, 2012(6).

[113] Ou Xiaohua, "Research on the Status Quo and Countermeasures of Internet of Things in China", *China Business*, Trade, 2013(3).

[114] Pan Yamei, "Analysis on the Operational Pattern and Development Prospect of Fourth Party Logistics", *Journal of Commercial Economics*, 2016(12).

[115] Paul Alexander Baran, *The Political Economy of Growth*, Chinese Edition, translated by Cai Zhongxing et al., Beijing: The Commercial Press, 2014.

[116] "Promoting 'Internet + Government Services' for the Benefit of the People", *Information on China Construction*, 2017(7).

[117] Qian Shufa, *Labor Division Evolution, Organizational Innovation and Economic Progress: Research on Marx's Theory of Society Labor Division System*, Beijing: Economic Science Press, 2013.

[118] Qin Hai, "How to Understand and Implement the National Information Development Strategy", *China Information Times*, 2007(1).

[119] Qin Huaibin, Li Daoliang and Guo Li, "Recent Advances in Development and Key Technologies of Internet of Things in Agriculture", *Journal of Agricultural Mechanization Research*, 2014(4).

[120] Qin Wei, "Ccid Forecasts the Development Trend of China's Electronic Information Industry in 2015", *China Equipment*, 2015(Z1).

[121] Qu Chao, Li Xiaojing, "A Study of Domestic and Foreign Information Industry Classification Criteria: Based on the Input-Output Analysis of ICT Industry in Liaoning Province", *Journal of Dalian Maritime University: Social Science Edition*, 2015(3).

[122] Qu Weizhi, *Exploration on the Road to Industrialization with Chinese Characteristics*, Beijing: Publishing House of Electronics Industry, 2008.

[123] Ran Zhilin, "C2B Model of Bidding Websites", *China Internet*, 2009(12).

[124] "Release of ITU's 'Measuring the Information Society Report' 2017", *Ren Min You Dian*, Nov. 22, 2017.

[125] Ren Yi, "Analysis of the Current Situation and Development Trend of B2C E-Commerce in China", *Journal of the Party School of CPC Chengdu*, 2010(4).

[126] Research Group of the Information Center of the Ministry of Agriculture, *Agricultural Informatization Research Report 2016*, Beijing: China Agriculture Press, 2017.

[127] Ruiwen, "ITU Releases 2016 'Measuring the Information Society Report'", *Ren Min You Dian*, Nov. 30, 2016.

[128] S. C. Bhargava, Arun Kumar and Mukherjee, "A Stochastic Cellular Automata Model of Innovation Diffusion", *Technological Forecasting and Social Change*, 1992(44), pp. 87-97.

[129] *Selected Works of Hu Jintao*, Vol. 3, Beijing: People's Publishing House, 2016.

[130] *Selected Works of Jiang Zemin*, Vol. 1, Beijing: People's Publishing House, 2006.

[131] *Selections of Marx and Engels*, Vol.1, Beijing: People's Publishing House, 2012.

[132] *Selections of Zhou Enlai*, Vol Ⅱ, Beijing: People's Publishing House, 1998.

[133] Shi Haibin, "Brief Analysis on Prospect of the Development of E-Commerce in China", *China Journal of Commerce*, 2010(28).

[134] Shi Hongrui, "On the New Thinking of Informationization Construction and Development in China", *Research on Library Science*, 2006(10).

[135] Shi Yuren, "The Whole Process of E-Commerce: New Stage or New Model", *Market Modernization*, 2007(6).

[136] Shi Zhongquan, "Mao Zedong and the eighth National Congress of the CPC(Ⅰ)", *Hunan Tides*, 2016(9).

[137] *Selected Works of Deng Xiaoping*, Vol. 2, Beijing: People's Publishing House, 2001.

[138] Song Ze, "On the Key Points of Advancing Chinese Logistics Industry in the 13th Five-Year Plan Period", *Finance & Trade Economics*, 2015(7).

[139] Successful Opening of the National Scientific and Technological Conference in Beijing, *Science & Technology Industry of China*, 1995(6).

[140] Sun Qibo, Liu Jie and Li Zang et al., "Internet of Things: Summarize on Concepts, Architecture and Key Technology Problem", *Journal of Beijing University of Posts and Telecommunications*, 2010(3).

[141] Sun Zhiwei, "Research on the Development of Modern Logistics Industry in China Based on Informatization", *Logistics Sci-Tech*, 2010(4).

[142] Tang Jing, "The Present Situation and Outstanding Problems of Independent Innovation Capacity Construction in Industry and Informatization in China", *Science & Technology Information*, 2011(15).

[143] Tao Libei, "Analysis on the Development Status of B2C E-Commerce in China", *China Management Informationization*, 2015(22).

[144] The 11th Five-Year Plan Summary and the 12th Five-Year Plan Launch Conference of National Village Access Project: An Important Speech of Xi Guohua, Vice Minister of Industry and Information Technology, *Digital Communication World*, 2011(5).

[145] "The Integration, Application-Based, and Solid Promotion of China's Government Informatization Construction: Interpretation of the 12th Five-Year National Government Informatization Project Construction Plan", *E-Government*, 2012(7).

[146] "The 'Longnan Model' of Poverty Alleviation-CCTV (CCTV News) Reports Behind the Rural Tourism in Longnan", *Longnan Daily*, Aug. 16, 2016.

[147] The Compilation Committee of China Informatization Almanac, *China Informatization Almanac 2015*, Beijing: Publishing House of Electronics Industry, 2016.

[148] "The Establishment of the National Central Network Security and Informatization Leading Group", *The Beijing News*, Feb. 28, 2014.

[149] "The Full Launch of Plans for a New Generation of Artificial Intelligence Development", *Economic Information Daily*, Nov. 16, 2017.

[150] "The Opening of Central Economic Work Conference in Beijing", *People's Daily*, Dec. 12, 2014.

[151] "The Outline of the 10th Five-Year Plan (2001-2005) for National

Economic and Social Development", *People's Daily*, Mar. 18, 2001.

[152] "The Proposal of the CPC Central Committee for the Formulation of the 10th Five-Year Plan for National Economic and Social Development", *People's Daily (Overseas)*, Oct. 19, 2000.

[153] "The Subject Group of Into the Information Society: China Information Society Development Report 2010, Approaching the Information Society: Theory and Methods", *E-Government*, 2010(8).

[154] *The Writings of Mao Tse-tung*, Vol.7, Beijing: People's Publishing House, 1993.

[155] Tu Jun, Huang Min and Bo Guihua, "A Review of Research on Fourth Party Logistics", *Systems Engineering*, 2013(12).

[156] W. G. Hoffmann, *The Growth of Industrial Economics*, Manchester: Manchester University Press,1958.

[157] W. T.Walker, "Emerging Trends in Supply Chain Architecture", *International Journal of Production Research*, 2005, 6(43), pp. 3517-3528.

[158] Wan Xuedao, Feng Zhongke, "The Status Quo and Prospect of Agricultural and Rural Informationization in China", *Compilation of Papers from the Conference on Innovation and Discipline Development of Agricultural Information Technology in China*, 2007(10).

[159] Wang Chuanlei, Guan Jingwen and Wang Tao, "The Perplexity of Global Information Society Development and Its Coping Strategies", *E-Government*, 2011(11).

[160] Wang Chunhui, "Interpreting the Security Strategy of National Cyberspace", *Communications World*, 2017(3).

[161] Wang Weijian, "China's Supercomputing Project Wins Another Top International Award", *People's Daily*, Nov. 18, 2017.

[162] Wang Jiawei, "Study on the Current Situation and Model Innovation of Poverty Alleviation with Electronic Commerce in Poor Areas During 13th Five-Year Plan Period", *Agriculture Network Information*, 2016(4).

[163] Wang Jinsong, *Policies and Regulations on Building a New Countryside*, Yinchuan: Ningxia People's Publishing House, 2011.

[164] Wang Liping, Zhang Chaohua, "Investigation on the Basic Agricultural Information Supply Situation and the Tendency of Farmers' Information Demand", *Special Zone Economy*, 2012(12).

[165] Wang Mingguo, "The Current Situation and Problems of the Development of Internet Finance in China", *The Chinese Banker*, 2015(5).

[166] Wang Quanchun, Zhou Lyu and Long Wei et al., "Review on the Research of E-Commerce Poverty Alleviation in Rural Areas of China", *E-Business Journal*, 2017(3).

[167] Wang Shun, "Analysis of the Current Situation and Countermeasures of the Development of China's Internet Finance", *Managers' Journal*, 2016(3).

[168] Wang Wensheng, "Investigation on the Agricultural and Rural Informatization Policy of China's No.1 Central Document", *China Rural Science & Technology*, 2012(7).

[169] Wang Xiangdong, Zhang Caiming, "New Ideas on Rural Poverty Alleviation of China in the Internet Era: Inspiration of Shaji Model", *Informatization Construction*, 2011(2).

[170] Wang Xiangdong, "Four Questions on E-Commerce Poverty Alleviation", *Gansu Agriculture*, 2015(7).

[171] Wang Xiangdong, "More Mature Conditions for Carrying out E-Commerce Poverty Alleviation", *Gansu Agriculture*, 2015(11).

[172] Wang Xiangdong, "The Progress, Present Situation and Development Trend of E-Government in China", *E-Government*, 2009(7).

[173] Wang Xiaoyan, Pan Kailing and Deng Xudong, "Research on the Development Status of B2C E-commerce in China", *Economic Research Guide*, 2011(29).

[174] Wang Xifu, Shen Xisheng, *Modern Logistics Informatization Technology*, Beijing: Beijing Jiaotong University Press, 2014.

[175] Wang Yujing, "Innovation and Integration: Double Driving Forces For Chinese Informationization Promotion", *Journal of Xi'an University of Finance and Economics*, 2015(5).

[176] Wang Zhengqi, "Challenges and Countermeasures of China's Information Network Security under the New Situation", *Future and Development*, 2016(10).

[177] Wang Zhiyin, Wang Mingyu, "Study on the E-commerce of Agriculture Products in China", *China Journal of Commerce*, 2015(7).

[178] Wei Liqun, "The Direction and Path of China's Economic Transformation and Upgrade in the Future", *Globalization*, 2016(12).

[179] Wen Jun, Zhang Sifeng and Li Taozhu, "Overview on Developing Status Quo and Trend of Mobile Internet Technology", *Communications Technology*, 2014(9).

[180] William J. Mantin, "The Information Society-Idea or Entity?", *Aslib Proceedings*, 1988(40), pp.11-12.

[181] Wu Cheng, "'Two Integrations' and 'Deep Integration': The Current Situation, Problems and Future Prospects of China's Industrial Informatization", *Automation &*

Information Engineering, 2011(3).

[182] Wu Cheng, *Integrated Strategic Research on Informatization and Industrialization: Review, Status Quo and Foresight of China's Informatization*, Beijing: Science Press, 2013.

[183] Wu Dan, "Analysis of the Role of Agricultural Environmental Monitoring", *Beijing Agriculture*, 2012(6).

[184] Wu Longting, Long Jie and Lin Yuan, "Construction Process of Agricultural Informatization and Rural Information Service System in China", *Information China*, 2004(15).

[185] Wu Shengwu, Shen Bin, *Integration of Informatization and Industrialization: from China Manufacturing to China Intelligent Manufacturing*, Hangzhou: Zhejiang University Press, 2010.

[186] Wu Yongyi, "C2B Presale: Subverting Traditional Production and Marketing Model", *Software Engineering*, 2013(4).

[187] "Xi Jinping Presided over the Central Political Bureau Group Study Session to Emphasize the six 'Acceleration' to Build a Cyberpower", *People's Daily* (*Overseas Edition*), Oct. 10, 2016.

[188] Xi Jinping, "Accelerating Independent Innovation in Network Information Technology and Making Unremitting Efforts Towards the Goal of Building a Cyberpower", *China Information Security*, 2016(10).

[189] Xi Jinping, *Secure a Decisive Victory in Building a Moderately Prosperous Society in All Respects and Strive for the Great Success of Socialism with Chinese Characteristics for a New Era*, Beijing: People's Publishing House, 2017.

[190] Xi Jinping, *The Governance of China*, Vol. 1, Beijing: Foreign Languages Press, 2014.

[191] Xi Jinping, *The Governance of China*, Vol. 2, Beijing: Foreign Languages Press, 2017.

[192] Xia Yanna, Zhao Sheng, *China Manufacturing 2025: Industrial Internet Opens New Industrial Revolution*, Beijing: China Machine Press, 2016.

[193] Xia Yu, Sun Zhongfu and Du Keming et al., "Design and Realization of IoT-based Diagnosis and Management System for Wheat Production", *Transactions of the Chinese Society of Agricultural Engineering*, Vol.5, 2013.

[194] Xie Meijuan, "E-Commerce Poverty Alleviation: New Exploration of Poverty Alleviation Mode in the 'Internet +' Era", *Journal of the Party School of CPC Changchun Municipal Committee*, 2016(2).

[195] Xinhua News Agency, Publicity Ministry of Qingdao Municipal Committee of CPC, *Decoding Made in Qingdao*, Qingdao: Qingdao Publishing House, 2017.

[196] Xu Erqing, "Study on the Development of Logistics Informatization in China", *Consume Guide*, 2009(21).

[197] Xu Shiwei, "Current Status of Agricultural IoT in China", *Bulletin of Chinese Academy of Science*, 2013(6).

[198] Yan Fang, Liu Jun and Yang Xi, "Study of Logistics Information Development Strategy in the Internet of Things Environment", *Commercial Times*, 2011(4).

[199] Yang Lin, "Research on Standards System Framework of Agricultural IoT", *Standard Science*, 2014(2).

[200] Yang Qinghong, Lu Dong and Cheng Zhichao, "Analysis on Status Quo of Mobile Internet in China and Its Industrial Opportunities of the Development", *Economic Affairs*, 2012(3).

[201] Yang Yafen, "Research on the Framework of E-Government Body of Knowledge", *Journal of Library Science in China*, 2015(216).

[202] Yao Cong, Meng Yutong, "Analysis of the Development Trend of Electronic Information Industry and the Development Situation in China", *Heilongjiang Science and Technology Information*, 2014(3).

[203] Ye Jiali, "On Development Situation of China E-commerce and Its Problem", *Business & Economy*, 2010(7).

[204] Ye Shanshan, "Analysis of the Concept of Crowd Innovation, Crowd Sourcing, Crowd Support, and Crowd Funding", *Shaanxi Development & Reform*, 2015(6).

[205] Ye Xiumin, "Summary of the Ten-Year Development Experience of 'Shaji Model': A Typical Rural E-Commerce Model", *China Internet*, 2017(2).

[206] Yin Yanhai, "Exploring the Prospects for the Development of the Fourth Party Logistics in China", *Logistics Management*, 2010(10).

[207] Yu Haixia, "On the Great Significance of Promoting Agricultural Informatization Construction Energetically", *China Agricultural Information*, 2013(11).

[208] Yu Juran, "The Research of the Status Quo, Problem and Strategy of Agricultural Information in China", *Agriculture Network Information*, 2008(2).

[209] Zeng Shiqi, "E-Commerce Helps Transformation and Upgrading of Chinese Agriculture", *Newsletter About Work in Rural Areas*, 2016(18).

[210] Zhang Chengfen, Li Juan, "Development Situation and Trends of the Integration of Informatization and Industrialization in China", *Journal of Xi'an University of Posts and Telecommunications*, 2011(3).

[211] Zhang Hong, Dai Yuhu and Zhang Quan, "The Evaluation Study on the Competitiveness of the Regional Electronic Information Industry", *Journal of Statistics and Information*, 2014(3).

[212] Zhang Jianguang, "Interpretation and Recommendations of the International Telecommunication Union: Measuring the Information Society Report 2014", *Information China*, 2014(12).

[213] Zhang Jianhua, Zhao Pu and Liu Jiajia et al., "Application Situation and Outlook of Internet of Things in Dairy Farming", *Agricultural Outlook*, 2014(10).

[214] Zhang Qianlan, "Suning and the Poverty Alleviation Office Cooperate on E-commerce Poverty Alleviation", *Beijing Daily*, Sep. 26, 2015.

[215] Zhang Xingwang, "Drawing New Impetus from the 'Internet +' Initiative in Our Work Related to Agriculture, Rural Areas and Rural People", *Newsletter About Work in Rural Areas*, 2017(4).

[216] Zhang Xinmin, "The Current Situation and Prospects of Agricultural Informatization Development in China", *Agricultural Economy*, 2011(8).

[217] Zhang Xuelin, "Analysis of the Current Situation of B2C E-commerce Model Development in China", *Legality Vision*, 2015(22).

[218] Zhang Yan, Wang Xiaozhi, "Research on the Mode and Countermeasures of E-Commerce Poverty Alleviation in Rural Areas", *Agricultural Economy*, 2016(10).

[219] Zhang Yang, "Pressing Ahead for a Cyberpower: An Overview on Promotion of Cybersecurity and Informatization", *People's Daily*, Nov. 27, 2017.

[220] Zhao Guanghua, "The Government System Design for Development of Fourth Party Logistics", *Comparative Economic & Social Systems*, 2012(4).

[221] Zhao Li, Xing Bin and Li Wenyong et al., "Agricultural Products Quality and Safety Traceability System Based on Two-dimension Barcode Recognition of Mobile Phones", *Transactions of the Chinese Society of Agricultural Machinery*, 2012(7).

[222] Zhao Lin, Li Jingjing, "The Legalization Status and Improvement of Information and Internet Security in China", *Netinfo Security*, 2003(10).

[223] Zhao Xiaofan, "Information Resources Development and Utilization: The Core Task of National Informatization", *China Information Times*, 2004(8).

[224] Zhao Yan, Li Xiapei, "Innovation of Service Modes of Agricultural Product Logistics Parks", *Logistics Technology*, 2017(8).

[225] Zheng Ruiqiang, Zhang Zhemeng and Zhang Zheming, "The Functional Theory, Key Issues and Policy Tendency of E-Commerce Poverty Alleviation", *Journal of Socialist Theory Guide*, 2017(10).

[226] Zhong Ying, "Present Development and Competition Pattern of Internet in China", *Journalism & Communication*, 2006(4).

[227] Zhou Hongren, *Analysis and Forecast of China's Informatization*, Beijing: Social Sciences Academic Press, 2010.

[228] Zhou Hongren, *On Informatization*, Beijing: People's Publishing House, 2008.

[229] Zhou Hongren, *Progress of China's Informatization*, Beijing: People's Publishing House, 2009.

[230] Zhou Tingting, "Review on the development status of agricultural informatization in China", *Journal of Guangxi University of Finance and Economics*, 2015(1).

[231] Zhou Xiaohu, Chen Fen, *Information Management Case: Chinese Enterprise Study*, Beijing: Economy & Management Publishing House, 2014.

[232] Zhou Yingping, "Thought on Speeding Up Agricultural Informatization Construction in the New Era", *Science and Technology Management Research*, 2011(7).

[233] Zhou Yulin, "Tongren, Guizhou: 'Mother E-Commerce' Will Create a New Model of Entrepreneurship for Poverty Alleviation", *China Women's News*, Dec. 18, 2015.

[234] Zhou Zhenwu, Wang Qiaoru, "Xi Jinping's View of Network Security", *Journal of Huainan Normal University*, 2016(6).

[235] Zhou Zixue, *The Integration of Informatization and Industrialization: Exploration a Road to Optimization of Industrial Structure*, Beijing: Publishing House of Electronics Industry, 2010.

[236] Zhu Changzheng, Qu Junsuo, "Analysis of Current Situation of Logistics Informatization in China", *Journal of Xi'an University of Posts and Telecommunications*, 2010(6).

[237] Zhu Jingruo, Dong Jianxun, "Why Must China Vigorously Develop Circular Economy?", *People's Daily*, Jan. 12, 2004.

[238] Zhu Junhong, "Research on the Countermeasures of E-Commerce under Precision Poverty Alleviation Strategy", *E-Business Journal*, 2017(6).

[239] Zhu Yan, "Research on the Performance Efficiency of C2B New E-Commerce Model and Influence on Social Benefit", *Journal of Commercial Economics*, 2015(28).

[240] Zou Chengjun, "Application of the IoT in the Green House", *Internet of Things Technologies*, 2013(8).

[241] Zou Sheng, *Ten Lectures on IT Application*, Beijing: Publishing House of

Electronics Industry, 2009.

[242] Zou Sheng, *Twenty-Year Exploration of Informatization*, Beijing: People's Publishing House, 2008.

[243] Zuo Lirong, Che Mingcheng, "Evaluation and Countermeasure Analysis of Electronic Information Industry Competitiveness in 26 Provinces of China", *Journal of Commercial Economics*, 2017(12).